HARBRACE
COLLEGE
WORKBOOK

FORM 11C

Writing for the
World of Work

INSTRUCTOR'S EDITION

HARBRACE
COLLEGE
WORKBOOK

FORM 11C

Writing for the World of Work

INSTRUCTOR'S EDITION

Melissa E. Barth
Appalachian State University

HARCOURT BRACE JOVANOVICH, PUBLISHERS
San Diego   New York   Chicago   Austin   Washington, D.C.
London   Sydney   Tokyo   Toronto

Acknowledgment   For "The Unknown Citizen" by W. H. Auden, copyright © 1940 and renewed 1968 by W. H. Auden. Reprinted from *W. H. Auden: Collected Poems*, edited by Edward Mendelson, by permission of Random House, Inc.

Student's Edition   Instructor's Edition
ISBN: 0-15-531868-3   ISBN: 0-15-531869-1

Printed in the United States of America

TO THE INSTRUCTOR

Welcome to Form 11C of the *Harbrace College Workbook*. Like Forms 11A and 10B, Form 11C is designed to be used either independently or in conjunction with the Eleventh Edition of the *Harbrace College Handbook*. Form 11C focuses on the world of work: all of the examples and exercises deal directly with the working world and illustrate the writing skills that students will need as they pursue their careers. For this edition, all of the explanations and exercises have been carefully re-examined and significantly revised. In addition, many of the explanations and the majority of the exercises have been replaced, expanded, and otherwise updated.

Arrangement   The materials in Form 11C are arranged in sections that parallel the sections of the *Harbrace College Handbook*, Eleventh Edition. The numbers and letters denoting subdivisions within the sections in Form 11C correspond to those of the Handbook, with three exceptions: section **5** on case, section **7** on verb forms, and section **12/13** on the comma. Because of the special emphasis on certain skills in this version of the Workbook, an organization somewhat different from the Handbook seemed necessary in these three sections. You will also note that the section numbering system of Form 11C jumps from section **33** to section **35**, omitting the Handbook's section **34** on the research paper, a subject beyond the scope of most courses in which the Workbook is used. However, although Form 11C omits the research paper, section **35b** incorporates many of the skills required of students who will be writing the traditional college research paper.

   Section **1** of Form 11C covers the main points of grammar and punctuation; it is, in other words, a practical minicourse in the grammar and punctuation of sentences. Some students may be able to move directly from section **1** to the later sections that treat word choice and sentence effectiveness (sections **20** through **30**) or even to the sections that go beyond the sentence to longer units of composition (sections **31** through **33**). Other students will need additional review of basic areas—such as agreement, tense, and the uses of the comma and apostrophe—that is supplied in the intervening sections (**2** through **19**). Of course, the needs of the class or the individual student will determine how much time is devoted to sections **2** through **19** and how many of the exercises in each section are assigned.

Exercises   The subject matter of the exercises is the world of work. The exercises cover such topics as the importance of work, the job market, writing and speaking on the job, and work-related issues such as leisure time and women in the working world. Form 11C provides many more exercises related to basic areas of grammar and punctuation than are found in the other forms of the Workbook; students should not run out of exercise material before they have mastered a specific skill. For example, fifteen exercises deal with the use of the comma (six in section **1**, six in section **12/13**, and three in section **17**); twelve exercises stress the use of sentence-combining techniques to achieve an effective style.

Writing   Form 11C includes not only sections on writing paragraphs and essays but also a section (**35**) on the special kinds of composition students will need to have mastered in order to succeed in the world of work—for example, letters of application, letters asking for adjustments, memorandums, and reports.

The Dictionary   Proper use of the dictionary is stressed throughout Form 11C: in the study of nouns, adjectives, adverbs, and verbs, and in the sections on capitalization, abbreviations, italics, and numbers. But unless each member of the class is familiar with the dictionary, the best place to begin teaching and learning dictionary skills is section **19**.

Spelling   Although most students receive little formal instruction in spelling after elementary school, correct spelling is important to success in college and in other work. Form 11C does not presume to be a complete spelling manual, but it does emphasize throughout use of the dictionary to avoid various kinds of misspellings, and it covers all major spelling rules. In addition, it presents a list of words that are frequently misspelled in professional writing. Perhaps even more important, the "Individual Spelling List" at the end of the Workbook offers a chart on which students can record the words they misspell in their writing assignments and the reasons for the misspellings.

Note: Each of the forms of the Harbrace College Workbook is available in an Instructor's Edition as well as a Student Edition. The Instructor's Edition is an exact replica of the Student Edition, with answers to all exercises overprinted in a second color.

Acknowledgments   When it comes time to thank people who have made it possible for me to do what I do, I have to say that I owe a lot to all those school teachers who encouraged me to learn. The learning hasn't stopped; the list of my teachers has continued to grow. There isn't time enough to list them all here; they know who they are. I would also like to thank J. William Byrd, Dean of the College of Arts and Sciences, and Loyd Hilton, Chair of the Department of English, at Appalachian State University for their assistance and support. In preparing this Eleventh Edition of the Workbook, I have also been greatly helped by the thorough critiques of Rocco C. Blasi, Wilbur Wright College;

Harry V. Moore, John C. Calhoun State Community College; and Ann S. Peets, Albany Junior College. Finally, I am grateful for the guidance I have received from my editors, Stuart Miller, Sarah Helyar Smith, and Lisa Werries, and to others at HBJ: Don Fujimoto, Mandy Van Dusen, and Ben Werthman.

Melissa E. Barth

TO THE STUDENT

You learn how to write chiefly by correcting your own errors. Corrections made for you are of comparatively little value. Therefore your instructor points out the errors but asks you to make the actual revisions for yourself. Your instructor usually indicates a necessary correction by a number (or a symbol) marked in the margin of your paper opposite the error. If a word is misspelled, the number **18** (or the symbol **sp**) will be used; if there is a sentence fragment, the number **2** (or the symbol **frag**); if there is a faulty reference of a pronoun, the number **28** (or the symbol **ref**). Consult the pertinent explanation (see the guides inside the front and back covers), master the principle underlying each correction, and make the necessary revisions. Draw one line through words to be deleted, but allow such words to remain legible in order that the instructor may compare the revised form with the original.

In certain cases your instructor may require that you pinpoint your errors by supplying the appropriate letter after the number written in the margin. For example, after the number **12** in the margin you should take special care to supply the appropriate letter (**a**, **b**, **c**, **d**, or **e**) from the explanatory sections on the comma to show why the comma is needed. Simply inserting a comma teaches little; understanding why it is required in a particular situation is a definite step toward mastery of the comma.

Specimen Paragraph from a Student Theme

Marked by the instructor with numbers:

3	Taking photographs for newspapers is hard work, it is not the
12	romantic carefree adventure glorified in motion pictures and novels. For
18	every great moment recorded by the stareing eye of the camera, there are
	twenty routine assignments that must be handled in the same efficient
28	manner. They must often overcome great hardships. The work continues
24	for long hours. It must meet deadlines. At times they are called on to
	risk their lives to obtain a picture. To the newspaper photographer, get-
2	ting a good picture being the most important task.

Marked by the instructor with symbols:

cs   Taking photographs for newspapers is hard work, it is not the

,/   romantic carefree adventure glorified in motion pictures and novels. For

sp   every great moment recorded by the stareing eye of the camera, there are

twenty routine assignments that must be handled in the same efficient

ref   manner. They must often overcome great hardships. The work continues

sub   for long hours. It must meet deadlines. At times they are called on to

risk their lives to obtain a picture. To the newspaper photographer, get-

frag   ting a good picture being the most important task.

Corrected by the student:

3   Taking photographs for newspapers is hard work; it is not the

12 C   romantic, carefree adventure glorified in motion pictures and novels. For

18   every great moment recorded by the ~~stareing~~ *staring* eye of the camera, there are

twenty routine assignments that must be handled in the same efficient

28   manner. ~~They must often overcome great hardships. The work continues~~ *newspaper photographers must often*

24   ~~for long hours. It must meet deadlines.~~ *overcome great hardships and work long hours to meet deadlines.* At times they are called on to

risk their lives to obtain a picture. To the newspaper photographer, get-

2   ting a good picture ~~being~~ *is* the most important task.

CONTENTS

MECHANICS

PUNCTUATION

SPELLING AND DICTION

EFFECTIVE WRITING

SENTENCE SENSE

1

Develop your sentence sense.

Most people have a more sophisticated sense of what makes up a sentence than they realize. To demonstrate your own sentence sense, read the following paragraph through several times.

> a person has more than thirty-five thousand different kinds of careers to choose from most people try to choose their careers carefully because they know they will be working for most of their lives they want their careers to be meaningful to themselves and to others each person wants to choose a career that makes the best use of his or her interests and talents clearly the choice of a career is one of the most important and most difficult decisions one makes in life

For this paragraph to have meaning, you must use your sentence sense to group words into separate units of thought. You may have to read the paragraph several times to understand the meaning because the writer did not use the periods and capital letters that show where one sentence ends and another begins. Therefore you, the reader, must supply the markers that the writer neglected to provide. Consider the following revised version of the previous paragraph:

> A person has more than thirty-five thousand different kinds of careers to choose from. Most people try to choose their careers carefully. Because they know they will be working for most of their lives, they want their careers to be meaningful to themselves and to others. Each person wants to choose a career that makes the best use of his or her interests and talents. Clearly, the choice of a career is one of the most important and most difficult decisions one makes in life.

In writing *about* careers, only confusion will result from the writer's failure to follow a standard and accepted form that the reader clearly understands. But what about writing *for* a career? Imagine the harm that would be done if someone wrote this kind of label for a painkilling product:

> Take two tablets every four hours for relief of pain from muscular aches headache and toothache for no more than ten days do not exceed recommended dosage unless advised by a physician keep out of the reach of small children if pain persists consult a physician.

In this case the reader's possible misunderstanding of where sentences begin and end could have serious results for both the producer and the buyer of the product. Whatever the career, the first duty of the writer is to follow a form that will be clear to those who read the writer's message.

Your plan for learning to write for the world of work begins with developing a strong sentence sense. Almost all sentences are made up of a subject and a predicate. The subject tells who or what the sentence is about, and the predicate says something about the subject.

SUBJECT	+	PREDICATE
People	+	once had few choices in careers.

The subject is often a noun or pronoun—a word such as *people* or *they*. The predicate can be subdivided into two parts: the verb and the complement. The verb expresses an action, an occurrence, or a state of being. The complement receives or completes the action of the verb or says something about the subject. In the following examples, the subject is underlined once; the verb, twice; and the complement, three times. (You will be asked to follow this same pattern as you work the exercises in this section of the *Workbook.*)

SUBJECT	+	VERB	+	COMPLEMENT
People	+	once had	+	few choices in careers.

[*Had* is the verb; it expresses an occurrence. The complement completes the action of the verb.]

SUBJECT	+	VERB	+	COMPLEMENT
Choosing a career	+	is	+	an important decision.

[The complement says something about the subject.]

Order of Sentence Parts   The normal order for the three main sentence parts is subject, verb, complement (S—V—C).

NORMAL ORDER

S—V—C   Today's world offers many careers.

Some sentences have only a subject and a verb.

S—V   Prospective employers advertise in many places.

Although most sentences follow the S—V—C or S—V patterns, writers will sometimes vary the usual order for variety or emphasis.

NORMAL ORDER

S—V—C   The possibilities are many.

EMPHATIC ORDER

C—V—S   Many are the possibilities.   [The subject comes last.]

The writer also varies the normal order when asking most questions.

V—S—V—C Have you investigated various career opportunities? [A part of the verb precedes the subject.]

C—V—S—V How many career opportunities have you investigated? [The complement and part of the verb precede the subject.]

And the normal word order varies when a sentence begins with *there* or *it*.

V—S There are books about careers in the library. [The verb precedes the subject.]

V—S It is likely that you will find helpful information in the library.

The order of the main sentence parts is very important in a language such as English because the function of a word often depends on its position in the sentence. In the following examples, *employer* is a subject in the first sentence and a part of the predicate in the second; on the other hand, *employees* is a part of the predicate in the first sentence and a subject in the second. Only the *position* of these two words tells you what part they play in the sentence.

The employer praised the employees.

The employees praised their employer.

Both the subject and the verb will be explored in depth in the following pages of section **1**.

Deduct 5 for each incorrect answer.

Main Sentence Parts   Exercise 1–1

NAME _____ SCORE _____

DIRECTIONS   In the following sentences, the subject is underlined once, the verb is underlined twice, and the complement (when there is one) is underlined three times. If the main parts of the sentence are in the usual word order (S—V—C), write *usual* in the blank; if they vary from the usual order, write *varied* in the blank. When you finish the exercise, answer the questions and complete the revisions called for on the next page.

EXAMPLE

What would you have done to make a living during the 1700s?   *varied*

1. Your career in colonial America would probably have been

   farming.   *usual*

2. In the early days of colonial America, most families worked a

   farm for a living.   *usual*

3. Every person in these farm families had his or her work on

   the family farm.   *usual*

4. There were many chores to be done each day.   *varied*

5. Of necessity, families were very large.   *usual*

6. Some of the people in a farm-centered community made their

   living running the general store.   *usual*

7. Have you seen record books from a colonial store?   *varied*

8. An account book from the Cades Cove Community in Tennes-

   see lists the purchases families in the area made.   *usual*

9. What types of things would most families purchase?   *varied*

10. Things like tobacco, coal oil, coffee, and shoes were typical

    purchases.   *usual*

5

11. Most families <u>paid for</u> their <u>purchases</u> with products from their farms.　　　*usual*

12. During the 1800s, the <u>Agricultural Revolution</u> <u>began</u> to affect farm life in North America.　　　*usual*

13. Because of improved farming methods, fewer <u>people</u> <u>were</u> <u>needed</u> to work a farm.　　　*usual*

14. <u>Being built</u> everywhere were <u>factories</u>.　　　*varied*

15. Many <u>people</u> who had been farmers now <u>found</u> many <u>types</u> of jobs in the factories.　　　*usual*

QUESTIONS

1. Which sentence varies from the usual S—V—C word order for the sake of emphasis?　　　*14*

Rewrite the following sentences in the usual S—V—C word order:

4. *Many chores were to be done each day.*

7. *You have seen record books from a colonial store.*

9. *Most families would purchase types of things.*

14. *Factories were being built everywhere.*

1a Learn to recognize verbs.

Every sentence has a verb, even one-word sentences that trainers use to communicate with their dogs: *Stay. Fetch. Sit.* Even though the verb is usually the second main part of a sentence, when you look for sentence parts, find the verb first since no sentence can be a sentence without one.

Function   Like the words spoken by a dog trainer, most verbs express action. But other kinds of verbs express occurrences or states of being.

> ACTION   Most people now *work* eight hours a day.
>
> OCCURRENCE   Many people *choose* their careers during their teenage years.
>
> STATE OF BEING   Sometimes people *become* unhappy with their careers.

Note: The verb may appear as part of a contraction: I'*m* (I *am*), we'*re* (we *are*), he'*d* (he *had* or he *would*).

Sometimes a word looks like a verb because its meaning is associated with action, but it functions as some other sentence part—quite often as the subject or a modifier. Take the word *work*, for example, which is an action word but which can serve as a subject, a verb, or a modifier.

> SUBJECT   *Work* is important to most people.
>
> VERB   People *work* for reasons other than pay.
>
> MODIFIER   The five-day *work* week may become obsolete.

To distinguish between *work* as a verb and *work* as some other sentence part, try putting an article (*a, an,* or *the*) in front of the word; if the sentence still makes sense, then the word is probably functioning as some other sentence part, but if the sentence does not make sense with the article included, the word is functioning as a verb.

> SUBJECT   [*The*] Work is important to most people.
>
> VERB   People [*the*]   work for reasons other than pay.
>
> MODIFIER   *The* five-day work week may become obsolete.

The verb determines the kind of complement that the sentence will have: either a word or words that receive the action of the verb or a word or words that say something about the subject.

Transitive Verbs   Many verbs serve as transitive verbs; they pass their action along to the object or objects. (See also **1b(1)**.)

> TRANSITIVE   Fortunately, people can change their careers. [Can change what?
>
> *Careers* receives the action of the verb.]

TRANSITIVE An internship showed me the need to change my career plans.

[Showed whom what? *Me* and *need* receive the action of the verb.]

Intransitive Verbs   If, on the other hand, the verb does not pass its action along to the complement, it is referred to as an *intransitive verb*. One type of intransitive verb is complete in itself; it has no complement.

INTRANSITIVE The internship ended. [The verb, *ended*, is complete in itself; it

needs no complement.]

Another type of intransitive verb, the *linking verb*, introduces material in the predicate that gives more information about the subject. The most common linking verbs are *be* (*is, are, am, was, were, has been, have been, will be*, and so on), *seem, appear*, and verbs that refer to the senses, such as *taste, look*, and *feel*.

LINKING VERB I was grateful for the internship program. [*Was* links the subject

with a complement, *grateful*, that says something about the sub-

ject.]

Position   The verb (underlined twice) is usually the second main part of a sentence; however, in questions, emphatic sentences, or sentences beginning with *there* or *it*, the verb may come first or may come before the subject (underlined once).

USUAL ORDER   Interns *can gain* valuable work experience.

QUESTION   *Can* interns *gain* valuable work experience?

EMPHATIC   Valuable *is* the experience that interns can gain.

THERE   *There is* valuable experience that interns can gain.

Form   Verbs can change their form to show number (one or more) and tense (the time of the action, occurrence, or state of being). Singular verbs in the present tense usually end in *s* or *es*, and past tense verbs usually end in *d* or *ed*. (The dictionary shows all unusual changes in verb form.)

A person usually shows a natural inclination to work with people or with things. [singular number; present tense]

People *show* their preferences in many ways. [plural number; present tense]

She *has decided* on a career in counseling.   [past tense shown by *d* ending of main verb; singular number shown by helping verb, *has*]

They *have selected* accounting as their major.   [past tense shown by *ed* ending of main verb; plural number shown by helping verb, *have*]

Auxiliary (Helping) Verbs   Often the main verb—which shows the action, occurrence, or state of being—is accompanied by one or more helping verbs—usually forms of *be* (*is, are, was, were, has been, will be,* and so on) or *has, have, do, can,* or *could* (see the Appendix for a more complete list of helping verbs). The helping verb or verbs (also called *auxiliary verbs*) may come immediately before the main verb or may be separated from the main verb.

Fortunately, people today *can change* their careers.   [The helping verb, *can,* immediately precedes the main verb, *change.*]

They *do* not *have* to remain in the same career forever.   [The helping verb, *do,* is separated from the main verb, *have,* by *not.*]

Have you *found* your career yet?   [The helping verb, *have,* is separated from the main verb, *found,* by the subject, *you.*]

Notice that a verb such as *have, has, be, can,* and *do* works either as the main verb of the sentence or as a helping verb. In the second example above, *have* is the main verb; in the third example, it is the helping verb.

Note: The helping verb, like the main verb, may be a part of a contraction: *can't* find (*cannot* find), *she's* coming (she *is* coming), *we've* gone (we *have* gone).

Verb + Particle   The main verb may also be accompanied by a particle—a word (or words) like *to, in, with, up,* and *of* that adds to or changes the meaning of the main verb.

We *put* our names on the list of applicants for the job.   [main verb]

We *cannot put up with* the company's delay much longer.   [The main verb, *put,* is accompanied by a helping verb, *can,* and the particles *up* and *with.*]

Compound Verbs   Often a sentence has two verbs connected by *and, but, or,* or *nor.*

We *applied for* summer work but *did* not *hear* from the company for a month.
We *waited* and *waited* for some word.

Deduct 4 for each incorrect item in the list.

Identifying Verbs   Exercise 1-2

NAME _____ SCORE _____

DIRECTIONS   The following famous quotations about work illustrate the various functions of verbs—to express action, occurrence, or state of being. The subject of each verb
is already underlined once; you should underline each verb twice. (Most sentences have
more than one verb.) Then make a list of the twenty-four verbs that you have located
in these quotations.

EXAMPLE
Work is the refuge of people who have nothing better to do.   —OSCAR WILDE

1. I never forget that work is a curse—which is why I've [I have] never made

   it a habit.   —BLAISE CENDRARS

2. Apparently we all work for ourselves, but in reality we are always working

   for others.   —DR. WILLIAM STEKHEL

3. A society in which everyone works is not necessarily a free society and may

   indeed be a slave society.   —ELEANOR ROOSEVELT

4. A human being must have occupation if he or she is not to become a nui-

   sance to the world.   —DOROTHY L. SAYERS

5. I thought [work] was a very bad thing that the human race had invented

   for itself.   —AGATHA CHRISTIE

6. When a man tells you that he got rich through hard work, [you] ask him

   whose.   —DON MARQUIS

7. [You] never give away your work. People don't [do not] value what they

   don't [do not] have to pay for.   —NANCY HALE

8. I'm [I am] a great believer in luck, and I find the harder I work the more

   I have of it.   —THOMAS JEFFERSON

SENTENCE SENSE

LIST OF VERBS

1. forget
2. is
3. is
4. have ('ve) made
5. work
6. are working
7. works
8. is
9. may be
10. must have
11. is
12. thought
    was

13. had invented
14. tells
15. got
16. ask
17. give
18. do
19. do
20. have
21. am ('m)
22. find
23. work
24. have

Identifying Helping Verbs and Particles   Exercise 1–3

NAME _____ SCORE _____

DIRECTIONS   In the following sentences the main verbs are underlined twice. Find the helping verbs and particles that go with these main verbs and also underline them twice. Then write the entire verb or verbs in the blank.

EXAMPLE
People should study the job market and match up their skills with the available

positions.   *should study, match up* _____

1. Often a person will hear of a job opening from friends or acquaintances.

   will hear _____

2. You might also find out about a job through the Help Wanted section of

   the newspaper.   *might find out* _____

3. Public or private employment agencies will also assist the job hunter. ___

   will assist _____

4. A public employment agency does not require payment for its services; a

   private agency, on the other hand, usually does charge a fee.   *does*

   require, does charge _____

5. Once you learn about a good opening, you will want to contact the em-

   ployer or personnel director immediately.   *learn,*

   will want _____

13

6. The applicant for the job should either <u>write</u> a letter or <u>call</u> for an interview

   with the potential employer. _____ *should write,*

   _____ *(should) call*_____

7. Because an application <u>will</u> <u>provide</u> the employer with a first, and usually

   a lasting, impression of the candidate, you <u>must</u> always <u>take</u> the time to

   make yours perfect. _____ *will provide, must take*_____

8. For most jobs, your letter of application <u>will</u> certainly <u>be</u> your letter of in-

   troduction. _____ *will be*_____

9. Your letter <u>should</u> <u>describe</u> those skills you have that qualify you for the

   job. _____ *should describe*_____

10. In the last paragraph of your letter, you <u>should</u> <u>ask</u> for an interview and

    <u>should</u> <u>provide</u> your telephone number. _____ *should ask,*_____

    _____ *should provide*_____

Main Verbs, Helping Verbs, and Particles

Exercise 1–4

NAME _____ SCORE _____

DIRECTIONS   In the following sentences the subjects have been underlined once. Underline the complete verbs twice—that is, the main verbs and, if there are any, the helping verbs and particles. Some sentences have compound verbs. Write the complete verb or verbs for each sentence in the blank.

EXAMPLE
The applicant may send in a résumé with the letter of application.

_____*may send in*_____

1. Sometimes the résumé is brought to the interview rather than sent in ahead

   of time. ____*is brought, sent in.*_____

2. A résumé describes in outline form the applicant's education, special skills,

   and job experience. ____*describes*_____

3. Most job applicants can usually confine their résumés to one or two pages.

   _____*can confine*_____

4. Your name, address, and telephone number will normally appear at the top

   of the résumé. ____*will appear*_____

5. The educational record and employment background of an applicant, as

   well as certain other information—activities and honors—make up the body

   of the résumé. ____*make up*_____

15

6. Your résumé should also provide the names of three to five references.

   should provide

7. These references should certainly know your qualifications for the job.

   should know

8. Have you ever put together a résumé? _have put together_

9. A résumé should be typed out and looked over carefully before it is dupli-

   cated or mailed out. _should be typed out,_

   looked over

10. The most effective résumés have been typeset and printed by a professional

    printer. _have been typeset, printed_

Deduct 5 for each blank incorrectly filled.

Forms of Verbs

Exercise 1–5

NAME _____ SCORE _____

DIRECTIONS   In each of the following sentences, one verb has been omitted. Fill in the blank with the present tense (present time) of the verb that appears in parentheses after the sentence. The subjects of the sentences are printed in italics.

EXAMPLE

Many college *courses* ___*present*___ theory rather than applied practice.   (presented)

Putting theory into practice ___*comes*___ with the job.   (came)

1. *People* ___*think*___ of their work in different ways.   (thought)

2. Many *arguments* ___*occur*___ over the importance of work.   (occurred)

3. Some *people* ___*feel*___ that their families are more important than their jobs.   (felt)

4. *Others* ___*see*___ their careers as the most important part of their lives.   (saw)

5. "All *work* and no *play* ___*makes*___ Jack a dull boy" is a familiar saying.   (made)

6. "*Idle hands are the devil's workshop*" ___*is*___ another well-known expression.   (was)

7. Other *people* ___*assert*___ that work is just something that people do to make the money they need to do the important things in life.   (asserted)

8. One *person* ___*says*___ that work is life itself.   (said)

9. The *importance* of work ___*depends*___ on a person's values. (depended)

10. For every one hundred lazy workers there___*is*___ at least one *workaholic*. (was)

11. Most *people* in the work force___*fall*___ somewhere in between these two extremes. (fell)

12. Still, most *people* ___*spend*___ many hours a day at work. (spent)

13. A *workaholic*, however, ___*finds*___ it difficult to stop working. (found)

14. The *workaholic* ___*stays*___ on at the office long after the end of the eight-hour day. (stayed)

15. The workaholics' *characteristics* ___*include*___ an inability to accept failure, guilt about their level of productivity, and almost constant worry about performance. (included)

16. For the workaholic, all *relationships* and leisure *activities* ___*become*___ unimportant when measured against success at work. (became)

17. Such a *person* rarely ___*enjoys*___ a vacation. (enjoyed)

18. Most *workaholics* ___*die*___ before they reach retirement age. (died)

19. *Heart attacks* among workaholics ___*are*___ extremely common. (was)

20. There ___*are*___ more *workaholics* than most of us realize. (was)

Verbals   Like verbs, verbals express action, occurrence, or a state of being. And the endings they have—*ing, ed,* and *en*—are the same endings that verbs may have. Here, for example, are four verbal forms for the verb *take:*

> *taking, taken, having taken, to take*

(Notice that *taking* and *taken,* when accompanied by helping verbs, are true verbs: *are taking* and *have taken,* for example.)

Finally, like verbs, verbals are often followed by words that complete their meaning.

> *Taking* my **time,** I found just the job I wanted.   [Taking what? *Time* completes the meaning of the verbal.]
> *Having taken* a vocational aptitude **test,** I was better able *to plan* a **career.**   [Having taken what? *Test* completes the meaning of the first verbal. To plan what? *Career* completes the meaning of the second verbal.]

But in spite of its similarities to a true verb, a verbal cannot serve as the verb of a sentence. Consider, for example, this sentence with its verb *have taken.*

> We have taken our time.

Notice that when a verbal replaces the verb, the word group is no longer a sentence. (See also **2a**.)

> we *taking* our time
> we *having taken* our time
> we *to take* our time

Thus whenever there is a verbal (or verbals) in a sentence, there must also be a main, or true, verb.

> *Taking* our time, we filled out the application carefully.

> *Having taken* our time, we answered each question completely.

> *To take* our time we carried our applications home *to fill out.*

Recognizing Verbs and Verbals   Exercise 1–6

NAME _____ SCORE _____

DIRECTIONS   Here are ten famous quotations about work. The verbals have been printed in italics. Find the true verbs and underline them twice. In the first blank, write the verbal or verbals; in the second, write the verb or verbs.

EXAMPLE
Working with people is difficult, but not impossible.   —PETER DRUCKER

_____*Working*_____   _____*is*_____

1. Next to *doing* a good job yourself the greatest joy is in *having* someone else

   do a first-class job under your direction.   —WILLIAM FEATHER

   _____*doing, having*_____   _____*is, do*_____

2. A great many people have . . . asked how I manage *to get* so much work

   done and still keep *looking* so *dissipated*.   —ROBERT BENCHLEY

   *to get done, looking, dissipated*   _*have asked, manage, keep*_

3. Many men are hard workers: they're [they are] always looking around *to*

   find something for others *to do*.   —EVAN ESAR

   _____*to find, to do*_____   _____*are, are looking around*_____

4. *Thinking* and *fretting* about work to be done often use up more energy than

   completing the actual task.   —F. FREDERICK SKITTIE

   *thinking, fretting, completing*   _*to be done, use up*_

5. If there is one thing better than the thrill of *looking* forward, it is the exhilaration that follows the *finishing* of a long and exacting piece of work.

    —ALEC WAUGH

    <u> looking, finishing </u> <u> is, is, follows </u>

6. No man is obliged *to do* as much as he can do; a man is *to have* part of his life to himself. —SAMUEL JOHNSON

    <u> to do, to have </u> <u> is obliged, can do, is </u>

7. Work expands so as *to fill* the time available for its completion.

    —NORTHCOTE PARKINSON

    <u> to fill </u> <u> expands </u>

8. Anyone can do any amount of work *provided* it isn't [is not] the work he is supposed *to be doing* at that moment. —ROBERT BENCHLEY

    <u> provided, to be doing </u> <u> can do, is, is supposed </u>

9. We work *to become*, not *to acquire*. —ELBERT HUBBARD

    <u> to become, to acquire </u> <u> work </u>

10. I go on *working* for the same reason that a hen goes on *laying* eggs.

    —H. L. MENCKEN

    <u> working, laying </u> <u> go on, goes on </u>

1b Learn to recognize subjects, objects, and complements.

1b(1) Learn to recognize subjects of verbs.

A sentence that has a verb but no stated subject is a command. In a command, the subject is understood to be *you*, though it is not actually written down.

[You] Fill out the application form and return it to the personnel director.

In all other kinds of sentences, the subject is stated, even in the shortest of sentences.

I quit!

Function   The subject is who or what the sentence is about. Once you have located the verb in a sentence, all you need to do then is to ask who or what is *doing, occurring,* or *being.* Your answer will be the complete subject. To find the simple subject, ask specifically who or what the verb is talking about.

Many important rewards are derived from work.   [What are derived? *Many im-*

portant rewards. What specifically are derived? Not "many important" but *re-*

wards.]

One of my friends wants a high income more than anything else.   [Who wants?

One of my friends. Who specifically wants? Not "of my friends" but *one.*]

It is important to be able to find the simple subject in a sentence so that you can make the number of the verb and the subject the same. If you mistake "friends" as the subject of the last example above, you will probably make the verb plural—"want"—and thus make an error in agreement because the simple subject is *one* and the verb must be singular (*wants*) to agree with it in number. (See also section **6**.)

Compound Subjects   Like the verb, the subject of a sentence may be compound. The parts of the compound subject are connected by a word like *and, but, or,* or *nor* (printed in boldface below).

Income, recognition, **and** *adventure* are three goals sought by workers.
Not *income* **but** *adventure* is my main concern now.

Noun Subjects   A majority of simple subjects are nouns, words that name persons, places, things, and ideas. Since people first appeared on the earth, they have been interested in nouns. We are told that the first job Adam had was to name the things he saw in the Garden of Eden: *sky, bird, flower, tree, apple, snake.* (Adam's name, of course, was a noun, too, as was the name of Eve.)

Modern people are still giving names to things. As soon as something new comes along, we rush to give it a name: *Skylab, astronaut, détente, rock and roll, Amtrak.*

Types of Nouns   Proper nouns begin with capital letters and name particular people, places, things, and ideas: *Columbus, New World, Mayflower, Thanksgiving, Declaration of Independence.* Common nouns are not capitalized; they are everyday names for general classes of people, places, things, and ideas: *explorer, continent, ship, holiday, capitalism.* Both common and proper nouns are often made up of more than one word: *tennis court, mother-in-law, oil well, Holy City, Bill of Rights.*

Many nouns name things that can be touched; these are called concrete nouns: *contract, report, insurance, corporation.* Other nouns refer to matters that cannot be touched; these are called abstract nouns: *praise, safety, satisfaction, plan, hostility.*

As you can see, we need nouns to say almost anything, even to speak a nonsense sentence like "*Peter Piper* picked a *peck* of pickled *peppers.*"

Noun Signals   Certain words signal that a noun is coming. Articles (*a, an, the*) and possessive pronouns (*my, your, his, her, its, our,* and *their*) are followed by nouns.

> **The** *supervisor* gave us **a** *copy* of **our** latest *reports.*

Form   Nouns change their endings to show two things: plural number and possession. When we name more than one of anything, we usually add an *s* or *es* to show that the noun is plural. (Remember that verbs act in just the opposite way: an *s* or *es* ending means that the verb is singular.)

> I wrote one report; Ethan wrote two reports.
> I read one memo; Ethan read two memos.
> I hired one woman; Ethan hired two women.
> I have one brother-in-law; Ethan has two brothers-in-law.   [Note that the chief word, *brother*, shows the sign of the plural.]

The dictionary shows you the plural for all nouns that form their plurals in some way other than the addition of *s* (for example, *man→men, calf→calves, sheep→sheep*).

Singular nouns add an apostrophe and an *s* ('*s*) to show possession, or ownership: *Ethan's job* or *Ethan's house* (we do not write *Ethan house* or *Ethan job*). The possessive noun is placed in front of the person, place, thing, or idea possessed.

If the possessive noun is plural, we usually add only the apostrophe:

jobs' requirements	teachers' salaries	guests' arrival
potatoes' roots	cities' problems	wolves' howling

But if the plural of the noun does not end in *s* (*women, children,* and *alumni,* for example), we add **'s** to form the plural possessive:

women**'s** rights   children**'s** absences   alumni**'s** contributions

When a compound noun is made possessive, the last word shows the sign of the possessive case:

sons-in-law**'s** jobs   the King of England**'s** biography

Note: When we give a noun the possessive form, whether singular or plural, we change it to a modifier—a descriptive or qualifying word. (You will study modifiers in **1d**.)

Recognizing Nouns   Exercise 1-7

NAME _____ SCORE _____

DIRECTIONS   Use *a*, *an*, and *the* to decide which of the following words are nouns; if a word sounds right with *a*, *an*, or *the* in front of it, write its plural form in the blank. If it does not, the word is not a noun; in that case, leave the blank empty. (If you are uncertain how to make the plural of the noun, consult your dictionary. When no plural form is given, the noun forms its plural in the usual way—by adding an *s* or *es*. See also **18d[5]**.)

EXAMPLES
into   _____

laugh   *laughs*

1. potato	*potatoes*		13. ski	*skis*
2. believe			14. on	
3. story	*stories*		15. right	*rights*
4. such			16. with	
5. artist-in-residence	*artists-in-residence*		17. carton	*cartons*
			18. some	
6. wolf	*wolves*		19. child	*children*
7. big			20. happy	
8. penny	*pennies*		21. account	*accounts*
9. belief	*beliefs*		22. percentage	*percentages*
10. sock	*socks*		23. slowly	
11. boss	*bosses*		24. blessing	*blessings*
12. bagful	*bagfuls*		25. object	*objects*

27

SENTENCE SENSE

DIRECTIONS   Use a possessive pronoun—*our*, for example—to decide which of the following words are nouns. If a word sounds right with *our* in front of it, write its plural in the blank. If it does not sound right with *our* in front of it, leave the blank empty because the word is not a noun. Use your dictionary to help you form the plurals of nouns that do not follow the usual pattern of adding *s* or *es*.

1. toy _toys_

2. remedy _remedies_

3. receive _____

4. cargo _cargos or cargoes_

5. fox _foxes_

6. only _____

7. separate _____

8. moth _moths_

9. mosquito _mosquitoes or mosquitos_

10. bus _buses or busses_

11. company _companies_

12. church _churches_

13. patio _patios_

14. reception _receptions_

15. crisis _crises_

16. fulfill _____

17. industry _industries_

18. ox _oxen_

19. brother-in-law _brothers-in-law_

20. business _businesses_

21. compute _____

22. tendency _tendencies_

23. monkey _monkeys_

24. bench _benches_

25. excellent _____

Deduct 4 for each blank incorrectly filled.

Making Nouns Possessive   Exercise 1-8

NAME _____ SCORE _____

DIRECTIONS   Rewrite each of the following word groups so that the second noun is placed in front of the first one. Give the possessive form to the noun you placed first. (Remember that by making the noun possessive, you change it to a modifier.)

EXAMPLES
goals of a person   *a person's goals*

benefits of jobs   *jobs' benefits*

1. work of the tellers   *the tellers' work*

2. evaluation of the committee   *the committee's evaluation*

3. reports of the environmental
   commissioner   *the environmental commissioner's reports*

4. location of a company   *a company's location*

5. jobs of the fathers-in-law   *the fathers-in-law's jobs*

6. office of the personnel
   director   *the personnel director's office*

7. opinions held by people   *people's opinions*

8. raise given to the employee   *the employee's raise*

9. results of the market survey   *the market survey's results*

10. the refund of a customer   *a customer's refund*

11. reports of experts   *experts' reports*

12. addresses of employers   *employers' addresses*

13. interests of an applicant   *an applicant's interests*

14. word processor of the writer   *the writer's word processor*

15. demands of the labor union   *the labor union's demands*

16. locations of the cities   *the cities' locations*

17. training of the workers   *the workers' training*

18. takeover of the two corporations   *the two corporations' takeover*

19. discussions of the unions   *the unions' discussions*

20. experiment of the scientist   *the scientist's experiment*

21. stock owned by investors   *investors' stock*

22. facilities belonging to IBM   *IBM's facilities*

23. plan of the contractor   *the contractor's plan*

24. choices made by the employees   *the employees' choices*

25. concern of laboratory technologists   *laboratory technologists' concern*

Deduct 5 for each blank incorrectly filled.

Recognizing Simple Subjects

Exercise 1-9

NAME _____ SCORE _____

DIRECTIONS   The complete subject in each of the following sentences is italicized. Find the simple subject that tells specifically who or what the verb (underlined twice) is speaking about. Underline the simple subject with one line and write it in the blank. (Remember that a simple subject may be compound.)

EXAMPLES

A *poorly prepared job* <u>candidate</u> entered the office.   *candidate*

This *person's* <u>résumé</u>, *with its many typographical errors*, was difficult to read.   *résumé*

1. The sloppy *clothes that the applicant* wore created an unfavorable first impression.   *clothes*

2. *Both the person and the résumé* looked untidy.   *person, résumé*

3. Poor *preparation for the interview* also did not help to improve the candidate's image.   *preparation*

4. *The job applicant's vague, halting replies to the interviewer's questions* were other problems.   *replies*

5. *The main requirements for the job that the applicant sought* were neatness and self-confidence.   *requirements*

6. *This particular person's interview with the personnel director* lasted just ten minutes.   *interview*

7. Needless to say, *this inappropriately dressed and poorly prepared applicant* did not get the job.   *applicant*

8. *The things on which people base their decision about whom to offer a job* often relate to first impressions.   *things*

9. *Many well-qualified people* may apply for a job.   *people*

10. *The person who is determined to land a good job* must carefully prepare for each interview.   *person*

11. *The self-confidence and fluency gained by careful preparation* will help any job applicant.   *self-confidence, fluency*

12. *A neatly filled-out application, a carefully typed résumé, and a businesslike appearance* are three especially valuable assets for any job applicant.   *application, résumé, appearance*

13. *Various methods of preparing for an interview* can benefit any job seeker.   *methods*

14. *One way to get ready for an interview* is to make a list of questions the interviewer might ask.   *way*

15. *The effort devoted to rehearsing possible answers to such questions* will generally pay off.   *effort*

16. *Another thing that the applicant might do* is to write out an autobiography.   *thing*

17. *The details included in the autobiography* usually provide answers to questions one may be asked.   *details*

18. *The interests and abilities of the applicant* come out in the autobiography.   *interests, abilities*

19. *These two important areas* are usually covered during an interview.   *areas*

20. *Some especially well-prepared applicants* have actually staged mock interviews.   *applicants*

Mastering Noun Subjects and Verbs   Exercise 1–10

NAME _____ SCORE _____

DIRECTIONS   Rewrite the subject and verb parts of the following sentences, changing the simple subjects and verbs from singular to plural or plural to singular. Underline the subjects with one line and the verbs with two lines.

EXAMPLE
A person trains for a job in various ways.

People (or Persons) train for

1. Students acquire skills (for example, typing and bookkeeping) through high-school and college courses.

Student acquires

2. Classes sometimes require outside work in the field of the student's intended occupation.

Class requires

3. For example, would-be teachers do student teaching during the last year of college.

teacher does

4. Prospective computer repair technicians also participate in apprenticeships.

technician participates

5. The on-the-job experiences in the field show the trainee what his or her future job is really all about.

experience shows

6. Sometimes after the internship the apprentices change occupational goals.

apprentice changes

7. More often, the intern decides to continue with his or her chosen career.

interns decide

8. Sometimes the student gets additional training in a specialized occupation through a summer job.

students get

9. Summer positions often pay little or nothing at all, but give valuable experience.

position pays

10. Thus the trainees are rewarded twice: in money and in extra, hands-on experience.

trainee is rewarded

Pronoun Subjects   Besides the noun, the pronoun is the other common type of simple subject. The use of pronouns avoids the unpleasant and often tedious repetition of nouns; substituting pronouns for some of the nouns will also add variety to your sentences. The skillful use of pronouns will help you avoid repetitious sentences such as

> The *manager* reads *reports*.
> The *manager* evaluates the information the *reports* provide.
> The *manager* bases the *manager's* decisions on the *report's* recommendations.

Clearly, that discussion of decision making would have been much improved if the writer had used pronouns—words that substitute for nouns.

> The *manager* reads *reports*.
> *She* evaluates the information that *they* provide.
> *She* bases *her* decisions on *their* recommendations.

Function   Pronouns take the place of nouns. The meaning of a pronoun is clear only when the reader is sure what noun is being referred to (usually called the pronoun's *antecedent* or its *referent*). For this reason, careful writers always make sure that each pronoun they use has an easily identifiable antecedent.

> NOUNS   All graduating *seniors* must take a one-hour *course* in "How to Get a Job."
>
> PRONOUNS   *They* must take *it* so that *they* will be prepared for job interviews. [*They* refers to *seniors; it* refers to *course.*]

Types of Pronouns   Unlike the almost limitless number of nouns, there are only a certain number of pronouns. The most frequently used ones are called personal pronouns: *I, me, you, he, him, she, her, it, we, us, they,* and *them.* As their name indicates, these pronouns refer to people or to living things.

Other pronouns refer only to things: *something, nothing, everything,* and *which,* for example. A few pronouns can refer to either persons or to things: *one, each, most, some, many, all, both,* and *that.*

A few important pronouns that you will study in depth later—*who, whom, which, that, what, whose, whoever,* and *whomever*—help to expand sentences. These pronouns sometimes serve as the subjects of their own word clusters; and they, too, take their meaning from the nouns that they refer to.

> The students *who* take this course are well prepared for their job interviews.
> [*Who* is the subject of the verb *take;* it refers to the noun *students.*]
> This course, *which* is offered several times a semester, is invaluable to students.
> [*Which* is the subject of the verb *is offered;* it refers to the noun *course.*]

These same pronouns may be used to ask questions—and are called interrogative pronouns when they are so used (in which case they need not always refer to particular nouns).

Who is your supervisor?
What is your job?

Form   Unlike nouns, pronouns do not form their plural by adding *s* or *es*. Instead, *I* becomes *we*; *he, she,* and *it* become *they*. One personal pronoun—*you*—does not change form at all to show plural number. Other pronouns can only be singular: for example, *each* and *one*; still others can only be plural: for example, *both* and *many*.

A few pronouns, like nouns, form their possessive by adding an *'s*: someone*'s* hat, everyone*'s* concern, anyone*'s* hope. All personal pronouns, however, have a distinct form for the possessive case: *my, mine; your, yours; his; her, hers; its; our, ours;* and *their, theirs*. And personal pronouns, unlike nouns, change their form to show whether they are being used as subjects or as objects of verbs (receivers of the action of the verb).

SUBJECT   *He* asked James for a raise.

OBJECT   James gave *him* his raise last month.

Deduct 8 1/3 for each incorrect pronoun. ✱

Pronouns as Replacements for Nouns   Exercise 1–11

NAME _____ SCORE _____

DIRECTIONS   Work with the following paragraph to substitute pronouns for at least twelve of the nouns or noun phrases to reduce the weak repetition. All of the nouns in the paragraph have been underlined to help you locate them. Remember not to create confusing antecedent problems; make sure that each pronoun that you use has a clear antecedent.

As a child Vincent Maher dreamed of being a policeman. ~~Vincent Maher~~ *He* tried other jobs, but ~~other jobs~~ *they* did not satisfy ~~Maher~~ *him*. ~~Vincent Maher~~ was cut out to be a policeman, and ~~Vincent Maher~~ *he* finally became a ~~policeman~~ *one*. Police work totally satisfied ~~Maher~~ *It*. Police work made ~~Vincent Maher~~ *him* feel necessary to people even though ~~people~~ *they* often ridiculed ~~Maher~~ *him*. ~~People~~ *They* called ~~Maher~~ *him* a bigot and a hypocrite, but Maher saw himself only as a human being with a job to do. ~~Vincent Maher~~ *He* tried not to judge people as superficially as ~~people~~ *they* judged ~~Vincent Maher~~ *him*. Maher preferred to work in poor neighborhoods because the people there especially needed ~~Maher~~ *him*. In white middle-class neighborhoods ~~Maher~~ *he* was expected to write parking tickets and scold people when the ~~people's~~ *their* dogs defecated on the grass. Maher did not become a policeman to do this kind of work. All ~~Maher's~~ *his* life Maher worked compulsively, both during and after hours, to become a detective. But being a detective was a goal ~~Vincent Maher~~ *that (or it or this)* ~~Vincent Maher~~ *he* never achieved.

✱ *Students' answers will vary depending on the nouns they choose to replace. This key identifies one possible series of nouns a student might replace.*

Deduct 10 for each incorrectly filled blank.

Recognizing Pronoun Subjects   Exercise 1–12

NAME _____ SCORE _____

DIRECTIONS   The verbs in the following sentences have been underlined twice. Underline all subjects with one line, and write the pronoun subjects in the blanks. Most sentences have more than one subject.

EXAMPLE
The jobs that require writing skills are many.   *that*

1. Who needs writing skills?   *who*

2. Virtually everyone must do some writing.   *everyone*

3. You and I will probably have desk jobs.   *You, I*

4. That means writing reports, letters, and memos.   *That*

5. Some careers that are very different from so-called desk

   jobs also require writing skills.   *that*

6. An electrician, who may spend the night working on

   power lines broken during a storm, must fill out a report

   at the end of the job.   *who*

7. Hardly anyone today escapes the job of writing.   *anyone*

8. My friend, who is a park ranger, has published more

   books than I have as a textbook author.   *who, I*

9. As often as not, the writing skills determine who gets a

   particular job.   *who*

10. On the job, someone is often promoted on the basis of

    ability to handle paperwork effectively.   *someone*

Deduct 5 for each incorrect subject (the first blank).

Mastering Subjects: A Review   Exercise 1–13

NAME _____ SCORE _____

DIRECTIONS   All verbs in the following sentences are underlined twice. You are to underline once the noun or pronoun subjects that tell who or what is doing, occurring, or being. Then write the subject in the first blank and the verb in the second blank. (Remember that a sentence may have a compound subject and/or verb.)

EXAMPLE
Studs Terkel's book, *Working*, explores attitudes about work.

_____*book*_____   _____*explores*_____

1. In his book, Terkel looks at how our work affects our lives.

_____*Terkel*_____   _____*looks*_____

2. His interesting book reports workers' feelings about their jobs.

_____*book*_____   _____*reports*_____

3. The workers Terkel interviewed express themselves honestly.

_____*workers*_____   _____*express*_____

4. Each person in the book feels strongly about his or her work.

_____*person*_____   _____*feels*_____

5. Some of the workers simply endure their jobs in order to live.

_____*Some*_____   _____*endure*_____

6. Others have found great fulfillment in their work.

_____*Others*_____   _____*have found*_____

7. Terkel's interviewees are all searching for meaning in life.

_____*interviewees*_____   _____*are searching*_____

8. These people all hope to be remembered for something.

_____*people*_____   _____*hope*_____

9. A few of them view their work as a way of achieving a kind of immortality.

few   _view_

10. Many, though, simply try to get through each day.

Many   _try_

11. The unhappy workers in Terkel's book see themselves as machines or ob-

jects.   _workers_   _see_

12. Usually included in their descriptions of their roles is the word *robot*.

word robot   _is included_

13. There are more unhappy workers than happy ones.

workers   _are_

14. Does this fact come as a surprise to you?

fact   _Does come_

15. Or are you also pessimistic about work providing people with satisfaction?

you   _are_

16. A few of the workers take pride in their jobs.

few   _take_

17. A bookbinder and a fireman both speak of the satisfaction of saving some-

thing.   _bookbinder, fireman_   _speak_

18. The many people interviewed came from all walks of life.

people   _came_

19. Both blue-collar and white-collar workers speak out in Terkel's book.

workers   _speak out_

20. Even a prostitute has her say in *Working*.

prostitute   _has_

1b(2) Learn to recognize objects and other kinds of complements.

Ask the subject and verb "who?" "whom?" or "what?" to find the complement of a sentence. If a sentence provides an answer when you follow the subject and verb with *whom* or *what*, the sentence has a complement or complements.

NO COMPLEMENT   Our workday ends at 4:30.   [Workday ends whom or what?

There is no answer in the sentence. The words that follow the

verb answer a different question—"when?"]

COMPLEMENT   Our schedule gives us a head start on the afternoon traffic.

[Our schedule gives whom? *Us.* Gives us what? *A head start.*]

Sometimes a sentence may have a complement that remains unstated.

The trainee understood.   [A complement may be added to this sentence because

the verb, *understood*, is a *transitive verb*, one that can take an object: The trainee

understood the manual.]

Function   A complement (or complements) that follows a *transitive verb* is a word (or words) to which the verb's action is transferred or passed along. There are three types of complements that may follow transitive verbs: *direct objects, indirect objects,* and *object complements.*
Direct objects are the most frequent complement to follow a transitive verb.

DIRECT OBJECT   My supervisor, Mr. Tom McMahon, manages twenty employees

in our laboratory.   [The direct object, *employees,* shows whom

the verb, *manages,* is acting upon.]

Direct objects can also be accompanied by an indirect object, which precedes it, or by an object complement, which follows it.

INDIRECT AND   He gives us careful instructions for each experiment.   [The
DIRECT OBJECTS

first object, *us,* is the indirect object. The second object, *in-*

structions, is the direct object. An indirect object shows *to* or

for whom (or what) the action is done.]

DIRECT OBJECT
AND OBJECT
COMPLEMENT

Attention to instructions made the lab a safe place to work.

[The object complement, *a safe place to work*, describes the

direct object, *lab.*]

Note: Some verbs such as *give, buy, send, call, consider,* or *find* may have a direct or an indirect object.

If a complement (or complements) follows a linking verb (forms of *be* and verbs such as *see, taste, feel, appear,* and *look*), the complement refers back to the subject of the sentence. These *subject complements* refer to, identify, or qualify the subject. Subject complements that rename the subject are either nouns or pronouns (also called *predicate nominatives* or *predicate nouns*); those subject complements that describe the subject are adjectives (also called *predicate adjectives*).

SUBJECT COMPLEMENT

The lab manager is enthusiastic. [*Enthusiastic* is a predi-

cate nominative giving more information about the sub-

ject, *manager.*]

SUBJECT COMPLEMENT

The lab equipment looks modern. [*Modern* is a predicate

adjective describing the subject, *equipment.*]

Note: Often you must be able to pick out the exact complement or complements in a sentence in order to avoid making mistakes in the form of the pronoun or the modifier. (See also sections **4** and **5**.)

Basic Formula   Now you have the basic formula for a sentence:

SUBJECT—VERB—(and usually) COMPLEMENT(S)

Deduct 3 1/3 for each incorrect underlining and each blank incorrectly filled.

Recognizing Complements   Exercise 1–14

NAME _____ SCORE _____

DIRECTIONS   In the following sentences underline the simple subject once, the verb twice, and the simple complement three times. Write *subject* in the blank if the complement (or complements) refers to the subject; write *object* if the complement (or complements) receives the action of the verb. If there is no complement, write a zero (*0*) in the blank.

EXAMPLE
The student visited her counselor.   *object*

Ellen Arnold is the student's counselor.   *subject*

1. At first, the student feels apprehensive.   *subject*

2. He wants a job with the recreation department.   *object*

3. The application form for the job frightens him.   *object*

4. The counselor seems courteous and pleasant to the

   student.   *subject*

5. She helps him with his application.   *object*

6. Her manner gives him confidence.   *object*

7. The counselor shows him similar applications with

   the spaces filled in.   *object*

8. The job search process begins to make sense.   *0*

9. The student finds these sample applications

   helpful.   *object*

10. His own application blank no longer looks so

    threatening.   *subject*

11. The counselor has shown him the way to deal with

    the forms.   *object*

12. With his counselor's help, he can now fill it out with confidence.   *object*

13. He will not be intimidated by forms of any kind.   *subject*

14. The student has found the counselor's help invaluable.   *object*

15. Who helped you with your first application forms?   *object*

Recognizing Subjects, Verbs, and Complements: A Review

Exercise 1–15

NAME _____ SCORE _____

DIRECTIONS   In the following sentences underline the simple subject once, the verb twice, and the simple complement or complements three times. Remember that one or more of the sentence parts may be compound.

EXAMPLES

The State Employment Service offers the unemployed information about jobs in their area.

What information do you need?

1. At the State Employment Service, people can obtain useful material that lists available jobs.

2. The agency charges people who come there no fee.

3. The State Employment Service is a branch of the United States Department of Labor's Employment Service.

4. Counselors working at the Employment Service assist teenagers, recent college graduates, and many other people.

5. The tests that the applicants take identify their interests and abilities.

6. Often counselors recommend training programs through which applicants can develop needed skills.

7. The primary objective of the Employment Service is the placement of individuals in suitable jobs.

8. What use have you made of the State Employment Service?

9. People interested in temporary employment will also find help at the State Employment Service.

10. For example, the agency finds young people summer jobs in the area.

11. One special program of the Employment Service offers graduating seniors and school dropouts a placement service.

12. This special service only certain state employment offices have.

13. Have you ever visited the Job Information Service?

14. It furnishes people computerized lists of jobs available in the immediate area.

15. Through the Job Information Service, applicants will also find jobs in other areas of the country.

1c Learn to recognize all the parts of speech.

Now that you have learned about the basic structure of a sentence, you are ready to begin working with all of the elements that combine to give a sentence its meaning. The following chart lists the various functions words can perform in a sentence and the types of words that perform each function.

Function	Kinds of Words
Naming	Nouns and Pronouns
Predicating (stating or asserting)	Verbs
Modifying	Adjectives and Adverbs
Connecting	Prepositions and Conjunctions

The next chart summarizes the parts of speech that you will study in detail in the rest of this section (except for interjections).

Part of Speech	Uses in Sentences	Examples
1. Verbs	Indicators of action, occurrence, or state of being	Tom *wrote* the report. Mary *evaluated* the stocks. They *are* executives.
2. Nouns	Subjects and objects	*Kay* gave *Ron* the *list* of *clients*.
3. Pronouns	Substitutes for nouns	*He* will return *it* to *her* later.
4. Adjectives	Modifiers of nouns and pronouns	The *detailed* prospectus is the *convincing* one.
5. Adverbs	Modifiers of verbs, adjectives, other adverbs, or whole clauses	presented *clearly* a *very* interesting study *entirely* too long *Indeed*, we are ready.

Parts of Speech	Uses in Sentences	Examples
6. Prepositions	Words used before nouns and pronouns to relate them to other words in the sentence	*in* a hurry *with* no thought *to* them
7. Conjunctions	Connectors of words, phrases, or clauses; may be either coordinating or subordinating	reinvest *or* sell before the meeting *and* after it *since* the sale of the stock
8. Interjections	Expressions of emotion (unrelated grammatically to the rest of the sentence)	*Good grief!* *Ouch!* *Well,* we tried.

1d Learn to recognize phrases and subordinate clauses.

You are already familiar with a group of words that may function as the verb of a sentence—the verb phrase (*will be writing*) and the verb with a particle (*put up with*). Other word groups may function as the subject or object (**1d(1)** below) or as modifiers (**1d(2)**).

1d(1) Learn to recognize phrases and subordinate clauses used as subjects and objects.

SUBJECT *Keeping a careful record of expenses* was a part of our job.

OBJECT We decided *to keep a log of our daily expenditures.*

SUBJECT AND OBJECT *Whoever examined our log* could find *what we had spent our money for each day.*

The main types of word groups that function as subjects and as objects are verbal phrases and noun clauses.

Verbal Phrases   A phrase is a series of grammatically related words (words grouped together) that lacks a subject, a predicate, or both. The verbal phrase is the kind that most frequently functions as a subject or object. The main part of the verbal phrase is the verbal itself—a word that shows action, occurrence, or state of being as a verb does but that cannot function as the verb of a sentence (see page 19). You may remember from your study of verbs and verbals in **1b(1)** that verbals usually end in *ing, ed, en,* or are preceded by *to* . The verbal, along with the other words in the phrase, can function as a subject, an object, or as a subject complement, just as an individual noun or pronoun can.

NOUN   *Machines* have eliminated many jobs.   [subject]

VERBAL PHRASE   *Using machines in the place of workers* has eliminated many jobs.   [subject]

NOUN   Machinery has increased the *efficiency* of many jobs.   [direct object]

VERBAL PHRASE   Machinery helps *to increase the efficiency of many jobs.*   [direct object]

NOUN   Their business was *agricultural equipment sales.*   [subject complement]

VERBAL PHRASE   Their business was *selling agricultural equipment.*   [subject complement]

Noun Clauses   A clause is a series of related words (words grouped together) that has both a subject and a verb. One kind of clause, referred to as a *main clause* or an *independent clause*, can stand alone as a sentence. The other, called a *subordinate clause* or a *dependent clause*, may function as a noun—either a subject or object—or as a modifier in a sentence. (**1d(2)** discusses the use of phrases and subordinate clauses as modifiers. In fact, they are more commonly used as modifiers than as subjects or objects.) As nouns, subordinate clauses usually are introduced by one of these words: *who, whom, whose, which, that, whoever, whomever, what, whether, how, why,* or *where.* These introductory words are clause markers; they are printed in boldface in the following examples.

NOUN   An *applicant* must fill out an application.   [subject]

NOUN CLAUSE   **Whoever** *wants a job* must fill out an application.   [subject]

NOUN   Applicants' responses to the questions often show their *skills* as writers.   [direct object]

NOUN CLAUSE   Applicants' responses to the questions often show **whether** *they can write well or not.*   [direct object]

OR

                    Applicants' responses to the questions often show **how** *well they can write.*   [direct object]

NOUN   The group's *findings* pleased their boss.   [subject]

NOUN CLAUSE   **What** the group found out *pleased their boss.*   [subject]

NOUN   He observed the factory *workers.*   [object]

NOUN CLAUSE   He observed **what** the factory workers did.   [object]

Like verbal phrases, noun clauses can also function as subject complements.

NOUN   The group's interest was *industry.*

VERBAL PHRASE   The group's interest was *evaluating industry.*

VERBAL PHRASE   The group's interest was *to evaluate industry.*

NOUN CLAUSE   Their belief was ***that*** *more agencies should evaluate industry.*

Recognizing Phrases and Clauses
Used as Subjects and as Complements   Exercise 1–16

NAME _____ SCORE _____

DIRECTIONS   In the first of each of the following pairs of sentences, the complete subject is underlined once or the complete object is underlined three times. In the second sentence of each pair, underline once the clause or phrase that functions as the subject or underline three times the clause or phrase that functions as the object. Then in the blank identify the phrase or clause with a *P* or *C*.

EXAMPLE
Future growth is important when one plans a career.

Knowing future growth possibilities is important when one plans a career.

_____*P*_____

1. For the next decade, some corporations project fewer employees.

   For the next decade, some corporations project that they will employ fewer

   people.   _____*C*_____

2. An exact forecast for a specific occupation is difficult.

   Forecasting employment opportunities exactly for a specific occupation is

   difficult.   _____*P*_____

3. Changes in national policy determine the growth rate of certain areas of

   employment.

   Changes in national policy determine whether certain areas of employment

   will grow.   _____*C*_____

4. For example, the government might decide that an area of scientific re-

   search should receive more funding.

   For example, the government might decide to give more funding to an area

   of scientific research.   _____*P*_____

5. The expanded government-sponsored program would increase the demand for scientists and laboratory personnel.

   The government's sponsoring of an expanded research program would increase the demand for scientists and laboratory personnel.   _____*P*_____

6. Predictions about employment are based on certain assumptions.

   Predicting employment is based on certain assumptions.   _____*P*_____

7. When experts make employment projections, they generally assume a peacetime economy.

   When experts make employment projections, they generally assume that the country will not be involved in a major war.   _____*C*_____

8. The changes that a war might bring about no one can accurately predict.

   What changes would occur as a result of war no one can accurately predict.   _____*C*_____

9. Stability in other areas of the economy is also a basic assumption.

   That other areas of the economy will remain stable is also a basic assumption.   _____*C*_____

10. People's basic attitudes about work, education, income, and leisure must remain unchanged.

    That people's attitudes about work, education, income, and leisure will not change is another basic assumption.   _____*C*_____

1d(2) Learn to recognize words, phrases, and subordinate clauses used as modifiers.

A modifier is a word or word group that describes, limits, or qualifies another word or word group, thus expanding the meaning of the sentence. A sentence made up only of the two main parts (the basic pattern of subject + predicate) is always short and direct, but it may lack the information necessary to be entirely clear, as the following sentence illustrates:

The <u>applicant</u> <u>had</u> <u>qualifications</u>.

Almost any reader would want to know "what applicant" and "qualifications for what." The basic formula is not very satisfying in this example. The addition of modifiers makes the sentence more exact in meaning. Adjectives modify nouns or pronouns; adverbs modify verbs, adjectives, other adverbs, and sometimes whole sentences. A single word, a phrase, or a subordinate clause can function as an adjective or as an adverb.

ADJECTIVES   The *best* applicant *for the job that the interviewers saw today* was

Jane Troy.

[All three adjectival modifiers (a word, a prepositional phrase, and a subordinate clause) qualify the subject, *applicant*.]

ADVERBS   *At the interview's end*, the personnel director *briefly* talked *about the site visit while the candidate listened.*

[The first adverbial modifier (a prepositional phrase) qualifies the whole sentence. The second (a word), the third (another prepositional phrase), and the fourth (a subordinate clause) all modify the verb, *talked*.]

Often you can combine two choppy sentences into a single, more effective sentence by making the essential information in one an added modifier in the other.

TWO SENTENCES	The report was poorly written. It was rejected by the manager.
COMBINED	The *poorly written* report was rejected by the manager.
TWO SENTENCES	The report contained several noticeable errors in grammar and spelling. It probably had not been proofread carefully by the writer.
COMBINED	*Since it contained several errors in grammar and spelling*, the report probably had not been proofread by the writer.
THREE SENTENCES	The manager examined the first page of the report. He did not bother to read any farther. The report did not represent careful work on the part of the writer.

COMBINED   *After the manager had examined the first page of the report, he did not bother to read any farther because it did not represent careful work on the part of the writer.*

Single-Word Modifiers   Nearly all sentences have one or more articles—*a, an,* and *the*—which modify nouns or elements functioning as nouns. In addition to *a, an,* and *the,* most sentences contain other words that modify various elements.

> A *large* increase in employment is expected in the field of landscape architecture. [*Large* modifies *increase.*]
> The increase is *largely* due to the *continued* interest in *city* and *regional environmental* planning. [*Largely* modifies *due; continued* modifies *interest; city, regional,* and *environmental* modify *planning.*]

Punctuation   Single-word modifiers are punctuated only if they are placed in an unusual position in the sentence or if they modify the whole sentence.

> *Attractive,* the grounds for the building contribute to a happy work environment. [usual position; *the attractive grounds*]
> *Surprisingly,* no employee objects to the long walk through the trees to enter the building. [*Surprisingly* modifies the whole sentence.]

Two modifiers in succession are usually punctuated when there is no *and* between them if *and* is understood. Where no *and* would fit, no comma is used.

> The *large, well-landscaped* grounds surrounding the building make the work environment pleasant. [You could say "large and well-landscaped grounds."]
> *Beautiful flower* gardens are also nearby. [You would not say "beautiful and flower gardens"; *beautiful* modifies *flower gardens,* not just *gardens.*]
> *Both large* and *small* plants line the street curving up to the building. [You would not say "both and large plants."]

(See also **12c.**)

Deduct 4 for each blank incorrectly filled and 4 for each incorrect reason.

Using Single-Word Modifiers

Exercise 1-17

NAME _____ SCORE _____

DIRECTIONS   In each blank write the required modifier or modifiers that fit smoothly into the sentence. Punctuate with commas where necessary. After each sentence explain the reason for punctuating or not punctuating each modifier you have added.

EXAMPLE
Two modifiers describing *lines*

The ___*long*___ , ___*slow*___ lines at the Placement

Bureau discouraged the students waiting to sign up for interviews.

Reason: *There are two modifiers in succession with and omitted.*

1. A modifier describing the attitude of the student *Dejected* ,

_____ one of the students turned away.

Reason: *Modifier is out of its usual position — "One of the dejected students."*

2. A modifier describing *job*

The long lines made him think he would never find a ___*good*___

job.

Reason: *Modifier is in its usual place.*

3. A modifier of *words*

He would require ___*strong*___ words of encouragement in order not to give up.

Reason: *Modifier is in its usual place.*

4. A modifier of *needed* and a modifier of *help*

He ___*certainly*___ needed to get ___*practical*___ help from his advisor.

Reason: *Modifiers are in their usual places.*

5. A modifier of the entire sentence and a modifier of *alternatives*

___*Naturally*___, he hoped his professor could offer some ___*worthwhile*___ alternatives.

Reason: *"Naturally" modifies the whole sentence; modifier is in its usual place.*

6. Two modifiers describing *advice*

The professor's advice, ___*specific*___ and ___*detailed*___, helped the student to refocus his job search.

Reason: *Modifiers are out of their usual position—"specific and detailed advice." There is no comma between the modifiers because of the use of "and."*

Using Single-Word Modifiers   Exercise 1–17 (continued)

7. A word modifying *other*

   His advisor told him there were _____*many*_____ other places

   to look for jobs besides the Placement Bureau.

   Reason: *Modifier is in its usual place.*

8. Two modifiers describing *job*

   The student wanted a _*satisfying*_ , _*well-paying*_

   job.

   Reason: *There are two modifiers in succession with __and__ omitted.*

9. A modifier of the entire sentence

   Undoubtedly, he would have to contact companies on his

   own.

   Reason: *"Undoubtedly" modifies the whole sentence.*

10. A modifier of *intended* and a modifier of *sections*

He also ___*certainly*___ intended to read the ___*entire*___
Help Wanted sections of several newspapers from the cities where he
hoped to work.

Reason: *Both modifiers are in the usual places.*

Phrases as Modifiers   You learned in **1d(1)** that a phrase is a series of grammatically related words that lacks a subject, a predicate, or both. Three types of phrases are commonly added as modifiers: appositives, prepositional phrases, and verbal phrases.

Appositives   An appositive is a word or phrase that identifies, explains, or supplements the meaning of a noun or pronoun that it is placed next to. Usually the appositive follows the noun or pronoun it identifies or explains. Appositives are set off by commas—or sometimes by dashes or a colon (see section **17**)—except on the few occasions when they are essential to the meaning of the noun or pronoun they refer to (see **12d**).

> *Megatrends, a best-seller about business,* has influenced people's thinking about the corporate world.   [The appositive, *a best-seller about business,* explains what *Megatrends* is.]
>
> Mr. Coulthard, *the business professor,* assigns *Megatrends* as required reading. [The appositive, *the business professor,* explains who Mr. Coulthard is.]

The appositive allows the writer to combine ideas that would otherwise be stated in two sentences.

TWO SENTENCES   *Megatrends* is a best-seller about business. It has influenced people's thinking about the corporate world.

APPOSITIVE ADDITION   *Megatrends, the best-seller about business,* has influenced people's thinking about the corporate world.

Prepositional Phrases   The prepositional phrase is the most frequent type of phrase modifier added to the sentence. It begins with a preposition—a word like *in, on, between,* or *to*—and ends with a noun, a pronoun, or an *ing* verbal: *in* the report, *on* the desk, *between* the machines, *to* everyone, *without* our knowing.

A prepositional phrase used to modify one word within a sentence is usually not punctuated. But a prepositional phrase that modifies the entire sentence is usually set off by a comma or commas (the comma may be omitted after a prepositional phrase that begins a sentence if no misreading would result).

MODIFIER OF NOUN   They read the book *about business law.*

MODIFIER OF VERB   They discussed the book *over the next week.*

MODIFIER OF SENTENCE   They examined, *in fact,* every case study carefully.

MODIFIER OF SENTENCE   The case studies, *in addition to the theory,* are necessary to teach how business law works in practice.

MODIFIER OF SENTENCE   *In a case study,* a specific law is illustrated by a real-world example.

Verbal Phrases   A verbal phrase includes a verbal (see page 19) and the other words related to it—usually a modifier or modifiers and an object.

> *Applauding the speaker enthusiastically,* the audience rose to their feet. [The verbal, *applauding,* is followed by an object, *speaker,* and a modifier, *enthusiastically.*]
> *To show its appreciation,* the audience remained standing until the speaker had left the platform. [The verbal, *to show,* is followed by an object, *appreciation,* and a modifier, *its*]

Adding a verbal phrase allows the writer to combine ideas that would otherwise be stated in two separate sentences.

TWO SENTENCES   The audience applauded the speaker enthusiastically. They rose to their feet.

VERBAL PHRASE ADDITION   *Applauding the speaker enthusiastically,* the audience rose to their feet.

Punctuation   Verbal phrases used as modifiers are usually punctuated by commas, whether they appear at the beginning, in the middle, or at the end of sentences.

BEGINNING   *Having limited herself to five main points,* the speaker finished her presentation in fifteen minutes.

MIDDLE   The speaker, *having limited herself to five main points,* finished her presentation in fifteen minutes.

END   The speaker finished her presentation in fifteen minutes, *having limited herself to five main points.*

Placement   Verbal phrases used as modifiers must be placed so that they clearly modify one word in the sentence, usually the subject. If the writer puts a verbal phrase in the wrong place or includes no word for the phrase to modify, the verbal phrase is called a dangling modifier (see also section **25**). A dangling modifier is sometimes laughable and is always confusing.

DANGLING MODIFIER   *Having always enjoyed books,* the library was where Dean chose to work. [*Dean,* not *the library,* enjoyed books.]

CLEAR MODIFIER   *Having always enjoyed books,* Dean chose to work in the library.

DANGLING MODIFIER   *While flying over Washington, D.C.,* the government buildings were an amazing sight. [There is no word for the verbal phrase to modify.]

CLEAR MODIFIER *While flying over Washington, D.C.,* I found the government buildings an amazing sight. [The verbal phrase now has a word to modify—*I.*]

Note: The verbal phrase can also function as an appositive.

EXAMPLE His goal, *to start his own business,* is still a long way off.

Using Appositives   Exercise 1–18

NAME _____ SCORE _____

DIRECTIONS   Combine each of the following pairs of sentences by making the essential information in one an appositive in the other. Place the appositive next to the noun it identifies or explains, and punctuate the appositive with commas (**Note:** Sometimes the appositive may precede the noun it identifies.)

EXAMPLE
Paralegal writers can carry out much of the routine work in a law office. Paralegal writers are professionals who have become more numerous in recent years.

Paralegal writers, professionals who have become more numerous in recent years, can carry out much of the routine work in a law office.

1. A paralegal writer is often a college graduate who has obtained additional training in the field. The paralegal is involved in conducting specialized research and other fact-finding activities for attorneys.

    A paralegal writer, often a college graduate who has obtained additional training in the field, is involved in conducting specialized research and other fact-finding activities for attorneys.

2. The paralegal is a skilled writer. The paralegal often must communicate with clients, judges, and opposing attorneys.

    A skilled writer, the paralegal often must communicate with clients, judges, and opposing attorneys.

63

3. The paralegal helps the attorney to prepare cases. The paralegal is often the person who composes rough drafts of complicated legal documents.

The paralegal, often the person who composes rough drafts of complicated legal documents, helps the attorney to prepare cases.

4. The attorney depends on the paralegal to do much of the initial information-gathering work for a case. The attorney is the person who must evaluate the evidence in the case.

The attorney, the person who must evaluate the evidence in the case, depends on the paralegal to do much of the initial information-gathering work for a case.

5. The lawyer is responsible for planning and developing the work on a case. The lawyer makes all of the final decisions.

The lawyer, responsible for planning and developing the work on a case, makes all of the final decisions.

Using Appositives   Exercise 1–18 (continued)

DIRECTIONS   The appositive often says as much as a longer construction does. Reduce the number of words in each of the following sentences by making the *who* or the *which* clause into an appositive. Cross out the words to be eliminated and add commas wherever necessary. Below the original sentence, write the appositive that results from your revision, including any needed commas.

EXAMPLE

The number of liberal arts majors,~~who are~~ students in fields such as history, English, and philosophy, entering technical occupations has increased in the past decade.

, students in fields such as history, English, and philosophy,

1. Students majoring in these disciplines,~~which were~~ traditionally viewed as ones for teachers rather than business persons, are currently in high demand as future employees in "high tech" fields.

   , traditionally viewed as ones for teachers rather than business persons,

2. Highly specialized technical corporations,~~which were~~ the ones that formerly interviewed only graduates in such fields as computer science, mathematics, and engineering, now seek out liberal arts majors, principally for their strong communication skills.

   , the ones that formerly interviewed only graduates in such fields as computer science, mathematics, and engineering,

3. One such company—EDS,~~which is~~ involved in developing customized software systems, provides its newly hired liberal arts majors with up to two years' technical on-the-job training.

   , involved in developing customized software systems,

4. On a recent campus tour, one of the EDS recruiters, ~~who is~~ a former English major, paid a special visit to the English Department to publicize their program.

   , a former English major,

5. The prospective employee ideally brings with him or her two attributes, ~~which are~~ an ability to write clearly and effectively and a good foundation in a technical subject.

   , an ability to write clearly and effectively and a good foundation in a technical subject.

Using Prepositional Phrases   Exercise 1–19

NAME _____ SCORE _____

DIRECTIONS   In the blanks on the left, indicate whether the italicized prepositional phrase in each of the following sentences modifies a sentence part (*P*) or modifies the entire sentence (*S*). Punctuate with commas those prepositional phrases that modify entire sentences. In the blanks on the right, write the italicized prepositional phrases and include the punctuation marks that you have added for the phrases that modify entire sentences.

EXAMPLES

To many people's surprise, the area of health care delivery is not as limited as they

had believed.

_____*S*_____   _*To many people's surprise,*_

More and more people enter branches *of this field* every year.

_____*P*_____   _*of this field*_

1. *In fact*, a student with an associate's degree can enter the health care delivery field.

_____*S*_____   _*In fact,*_

2. Most college dental hygiene or respiratory therapy programs provide on-the-job training *for their students.*

_____*P*_____   _*for their students.*_

3. People preparing for careers in these fields receive valuable training *as they work* with patients.

_____*P*_____   _*as they work*_

4. *Besides reading about how things should be done* students watch experienced teaching staff deliver the treatments they study.

_____*S*_____   _*Besides reading about how things should be done*_

5. People in these occupations express a high level of satisfaction *with their jobs.*

    _____P_____ _____with their jobs_____

6. Other types of medical practitioners will also be needed in increasing numbers *during the coming decade.*

    _____P_____ _____during the coming decade_____

7. *As the baby boom generation ages and requires additional health care* more and more jobs will open up in the health care professions.

    _____S_____ _____As the baby boom generation ages and requires additional health care_____

8. Many Americans work harder *at staying* in good health.

    _____P_____ _____at staying_____

9. Some people think of our contemporary times *as the Fitness-Conscious Era.*

    _____P_____ _____as the Fitness-Conscious Era_____

10. Moreover, concern about fitness is growing among people *of all ages and occupations.*

    _____P_____ _____of all ages and occupations_____

Deduct 10 for each incorrect combination.

Using Verbal Phrases

Exercise 1-20

NAME _____ SCORE _____

DIRECTIONS   Each of the following sentences has a verbal phrase written after it. Rewrite the sentence using the verbal phrase as a clear modifier. Be sure to include the punctuation needed. (Often, verbal phrases may be inserted in more than one place in their sentences.)

EXAMPLE
Industries may be divided into two categories.   looked at from a broad perspective

Looked at from a broad perspective, industries may be divided into two categories.

1. One type of industry involves the production of goods.   expected to show little growth in the next ten years

    Expected to show little growth in the next ten years, one type of industry involves the production of goods. or One type of industry, expected to show little growth in the next ten years, ...

2. The growth rate of industries providing goods is not expected to increase as dramatically as that of those providing services.   currently employing less than one-half of all workers

    Currently employing less than one-half of all workers, the growth rate of industries providing goods is not expected to increase as dramatically as that of those providing services.

3. Some industries produce both goods and services.   not so easily categorized

    Some industries, not so easily categorized, produce both goods and services. or Not so easily categorized, some ...

4. Service-producing industries include such divisions as government, transportation, public utilities, finance, insurance, and real estate.   requiring more and more college graduates

    Service-producing industries, requiring more and more college graduates, include such divisions as government, transportation, public utilities, finance, insurance, and real estate. or Requiring more and more college graduates, service-producing industries ....

5. Citizens of the United States demand more service industries than ever before.   to keep up their standard of living

   To keep up their standard of living, citizens of the United States demand more service industries than ever before. or Citizens of the United States, to keep up their standard of living, demand....

6. Government at the state and local levels has shown the largest growth of all
   service-producing industries.   having increased by about 90 percent in the
   last twenty years

   Government at the state and local levels, having increased by almost 90 percent in the last twenty years has shown the largest growth of all service-producing industries. [The verbal phrase may also be placed at the beginning or end of this sentence.]

7. State and local government is expected to need more and more college-
   trained employees.   to meet the public's demand for education, health,
   and protective services

   State and local government is expected to need more and more college-trained employees to meet the public's demand for education, health and protective services. or State and local government, to meet....

8. Employment at the federal level of government will not be so readily available during the coming decade.   increasing by only a small percentage in
   the last twenty years

   Increasing by only a small percentage in the last twenty years, employment at the federal level of government will not be so readily available during the coming decade.

9. You can determine the service areas that hold the most promise for future
   employment.   studying graphs that show projected rates of growth

   Studying graphs that show projected rates of growth, you can determine the service areas that hold the most promise for future employment.

10. Health services are expected to expand more rapidly than any others.   to
    satisfy the public's demand for more and better health care

    To satisfy the public's demand for more and better health care, health services are expected to expand more rapidly than any others. [Other arrangements of this sentence are acceptable.]

Subordinate Clauses as Modifiers   In **1d(1)** you studied one kind of subordinate clause—the noun clause, which can function as a subject or object. (As you may remember, a subordinate clause contains both a subject and a verb, but, unlike a main clause, cannot stand by itself as a sentence because of the subordinator that introduces it.) Other kinds of subordinate clauses—the adjective clause and the adverb clause—act as modifiers.

Adjective Clauses   Adjective clauses are introduced by a subordinator such as *who, whom, that, which,* or *whose*—often referred to as *relative pronouns.* A relative pronoun relates the rest of the words in its clause to a word in the main clause, and, as a pronoun, also serves some noun function in its own clause, often as the subject. (Remember that a clause, unlike a phrase, has both a subject and a verb.)

> Another field *that interests students* is health science.   [The relative pronoun *that* relates the subordinate clause to the main clause, *field*, and also serves as the subject of the verb, *interests*, in its own clause.]

An adjective clause follows the noun or pronoun that it modifies. It cannot be moved elsewhere without confusing either the meaning or the structure of the sentence.

> CORRECT PLACEMENT   The best-paying occupations, *which students are most likely to want*, are listed in various directories.
>
> INCORRECT PLACEMENT   The best-paying occupations are listed in various directories *which students are most likely to want.*
>
> CONFUSING STRUCTURE   *Which students are most likely to want*, the best-paying occupations are listed in various directories.

Sometimes the relative pronoun is omitted when the clause is short and no misreading could result.

> WITH RELATIVE PRONOUN   Zoo management is a career *that* few students have considered.
>
> WITHOUT RELATIVE PRONOUN   Zoo management is a career few students have considered.

An adjective clause may be either restrictive or nonrestrictive. A restrictive (defining) clause is not punctuated because it limits the meaning of the words it follows and is, consequently, essential to the meaning of the sentence. A nonrestrictive (nondefining) subordinate clause, on the other hand, is punctuated, usually with commas, because it is not essential to the meaning of the sentence. When used as a relative pronoun, the word *that* usually introduces a restrictive (defining) subordinate clause.

> RESTRICTIVE CLAUSE   The person *who decides to be a farmer* faces many hardships.   [The clause defines or identifies the kind of person who faces many hardships.]

NONRESTRICTIVE CLAUSE   My nearest neighbor, *who is a farmer*, faces many hardships. [The word *neighbor* is identified or defined by the modifier *nearest*.]

RESTRICTIVE CLAUSE   My neighbor is not discouraged by the hardships *that he endures*. [The word *that* introduces a restrictive clause.]

Adverb Clauses   An adverb clause is introduced by a subordinator such as *since, when, if, because, although,* or *so that* (see the Appendix for a list of the most commonly used subordinators). Like the adjective clause, the adverb clause adds another subject and verb (and sometimes other elements) to the sentence. But unlike the relative pronoun that introduces the adjective clause, the subordinator of an adverb clause does not function as a main part of its own clause. The adverb clause usually modifies the verb of the main clause, but it may also modify an adjective or adverb in the main clause.

If economists could only capture the economy in a bottle, they could explain it more accurately. [The subordinator, *If*, introduces the adverb clause, which modifies the verb *could explain*.]

Economists are seldom as confident *as they appear*. [The subordinator, *as*, introduces the adverb clause, which modifies the adjective *confident*.]

Nevertheless, economists can predict changes in the economy better *than anyone else can predict them*. [The subordinator, *than*, introduces the adverb clause, which modifies the adverb *better*.]

Adverb clauses may be added to a sentence at various places. When an adverb clause is added in front of a main clause, it is followed by a comma; when it is added in the middle of a main clause, it is usually set off by commas (a comma at the beginning and end of the clause); when it is added after a main clause, it is usually unpunctuated.

BEGINNING   *When our country was first settled*, almost every worker was a farmer.

MIDDLE   Almost every worker, *when our country was first settled*, was a farmer.

END   Almost every worker was a farmer *when our country was first settled*.

In general, subordinate clauses introduced by clause markers like *which, that, who, whom,* and *whose* may be added to sentences only after the words they modify; otherwise, the clauses are misplaced modifiers.

Deduct 5 for each incorrect combination and 5 for each blank incorrectly filled.

Using Subordinate Clauses

Exercise 1–21

NAME _____ SCORE _____

DIRECTIONS   A subordinate clause appears after each of the following main clauses (sentences). Combine the subordinate clause with the main clause, using commas whenever necessary. If the subordinate clause may be added at more than one place, write a check mark (✔) in the blank at the right.

EXAMPLES

College graduates will continue to face stiff competition in most occupations. If present trends continue,   _____✔_____

Many students train for their professions in two-year colleges. who do not want a B.S. or a B.A. degree   _____

1. The number of students entering junior and community colleges is increasing rapidly. because these colleges can successfully train students for many occupations in two years or less.   _____✔_____

2. The outlook for jobs during the 1990s will vary according to the occupation. although there is a general shortage of openings for graduates of both four-year and two-year colleges *   _____✔_____

3. A need for graduates in most engineering fields is expected. if past trends continue   _____✔_____

4. On the other hand, there is a surplus of graduates. who are trained in political science and philosophy.   _____

5. Obviously, students must pay careful attention to the changing demands of the job market. if they expect to find suitable work after graduation.   _____✔_____

6. Today's students must think of marketing their skills. who want jobs   _____

7. Careful planning must be a part of a student's education. , which considers the skills in demand on the job market   _____

8. Thus students must choose their subjects carefully. when they are scheduling their classes for the semester or quarter.   _____✔_____

* *Note that a dependent clause introduced by although is usually punctuated even if it is added to the end of the sentence.*

9. Certain subjects, like composition, mathematics, and computer science, are a must/ since the skills they teach will be required in most occupations.

10. In the 1990s there will be jobs for all graduates/ who have trained themselves for the openings in the available occupations. _____

1e Learn to recognize main clauses and the various types of sentences.

Sometimes a writer has two or more related ideas to set forth. Depending on the relationship of the ideas and on the desired emphasis, the writer may choose to express the ideas in separate sentences or to combine them in one of several ways.

Types of Sentences   There are four types of sentences: *simple, compound, complex,* and *compound-complex.* Which of these types a given sentence is depends on the number of main and subordinate clauses it includes.

Simple Sentences   The simple sentence consists of only one main clause and no subordinate clauses. A simple sentence is often short, but not always, since one or more of the basic sentence parts—the subject, verb, or objects—may be compound and since many single-word and phrase modifiers may be attached to the main clause.

SIMPLE   Computers handle many routine office chores.

SIMPLE   **Once used only by scientists,** computers now help *to reduce the amount*

of repetitious work in the modern office.   [The main clause, or basic for-

mula, *Computers help reduce work,* has been expanded by the addition

of one adjective (underlined), one verbal phrase (in boldface), and three

prepositional phrases (in italics).]

SIMPLE   In the modern office, complicated word processing, routine accounting

work, and complex data processing all are done with a computer.   [The

subject is compound; single-word modifiers and prepositional phrases also

expand the main clause.]

Compound Sentences   A compound sentence consists of two or more main clauses (but no subordinate clauses) connected by a coordinating conjunction[*] (*and, but, or, for, nor, so, yet*) or by a conjunctive adverb^{**} (such as *thus* or *therefore,* and others listed in the Appendix) or other transitional expressions (such as *as a matter of fact* and others listed in the Appendix). In a compound sentence the connecting word (in boldface below) acts like a fulcrum on a seesaw, balancing grammatically equivalent structures.

COMPOUND   Computer experience will help a person get a clerical position, **but**

some people still refuse to learn this skill.   [The first main clause is

* *Coordinating conjunctions are always three letters or fewer in length.*
** *Conjunctive adverbs are always four letters or more in length.*

balanced by the grammatically equivalent second main clause. The

clauses are connected by the coordinate conjunction *but*.]

COMPOUND   Most businesses still keep records; **however,** employees must now use

computers to handle many filing jobs. [The conjunctive adverb,

however, balances the first main clause against the grammatically

equivalent second main clause.]

Caution: If you overdo the joining of main clauses with *and*, your style will be childish. Save the *and*'s for ideas that should be stressed equally. Use a subordinate clause and main clause when one idea is dependent upon another. Or use two separate sentences when there is no strong relationship between the two ideas.

CHILDISH   I went to college so that I could get a good job, and I wanted to find work writing for a large corporation. I thought I would like the challenge of preparing reports, and I knew I could communicate ideas clearly. I learned about technical writing in an English course, and I took advanced classes to gain the skills I needed to be a technical writer.

BETTER   I went to college so that I could get a good job. I wanted to find work writing for a large corporation. I thought I would like the challenge of preparing reports, and I knew that I could communicate ideas clearly. After I learned about technical writing in an English course, I took advanced classes to gain the skills I needed to be a technical writer.

You will notice that the better paragraph has only one sentence in which two main clauses are joined by *and*, whereas the childish paragraph has three such sentences.

Punctuation   Either a comma or a semicolon shows the reader that one main clause has ended and another is about to be added. The punctuation mark is written after the first main clause, just *before* the joining word. When two main clauses are joined by a coordinating conjunction (a word such as *and* or *but*), a comma is used. When the two main clauses are joined by a conjunctive adverb (a word such as *however*) or other transitional expressions (a phrase such as *for instance*), a semicolon is used. A comma normally follows the conjunctive adverb or other transitional expression. (However, this comma is sometimes omitted when it is not needed to prevent misreading.)

Finally, when no conjunction joins two main clauses, a semicolon is used.

AND   The opportunities for receptionists are expected to increase during the late 1980s, and this occupation, unlike file clerking, should not be affected by automation.

HOWEVER   Thousands of job openings are expected for cashiers during the next few years; however, future growth may slow because of the widespread use of automated checkout systems.

NO JOINING WORD   Some clerical occupations depend on people more than on machinery; job openings in these areas will be increasing rapidly during the 1980s.

Complex Sentences   A complex sentence consists of one main clause and one or more subordinate clauses. The subordinate clause in a complex sentence may function as the subject, an object, or a modifier. Like the compound sentence, the complex sentence contains more than one subject and more than one verb; however, at least one of the subject–verb pairs is introduced by a subordinator such as *what, whoever, who, when, or if* (in boldface below) which makes its clause dependent on the main clause.

COMPLEX   *Whoever has visited Epcot Center in Florida* has had a glimpse into the future. [The subordinate clause functions as the subject of the sentence.]

COMPLEX   *When we stop to think about it*, even the eighties resemble a "science fiction" world. [The subordinate clause functions as a modifier—as an adverb clause.]

Compound-Complex Sentences   A compound-complex sentence consists of two or more main clauses and at least one subordinate clause. Thus it has three or more separate sets of subjects, verbs, and sometimes objects.

COMPOUND-COMPLEX   No one can predict what the machines of the future will

do, but it is safe to say that businesses of the future will

undoubtedly rely heavily on the new machine technology.

Deduct 10 for each blank incorrectly filled. (Main clauses may be combined in more than one way.)

Combining Main Clauses   Exercise 1-22

NAME _____ SCORE _____

DIRECTIONS   Using the type of conjunction indicated and punctuating the resulting sentence correctly, combine the second main clause with the first one. (In some cases you will be asked to use no conjunction.) Cross out the period and insert the correct word or words and punctuation mark (or marks) at the end of the first main clause. In the blank write the joining word and punctuation that you have used. If you used no joining word or words, simply list the punctuation mark.

EXAMPLE
transitional expression

People who enjoy sales work can choose from a variety

of occupations. *; for example,* They can become insurance agents, real

estate brokers, or retail trade salesworkers.   *; for example,*

1. *coordinating conjunction*

Each year thousands of positions open up in real

estate sales. *and* Many beginners will have to transfer

to other occupations because of the competitive na-

ture of the occupation.   _____, *and* _____

2. *conjunctive adverb*

During the last half of the 1980s modeling agencies

offered over eight hundred openings a year. *; however,* The

glamour of this occupation certainly attracted

many more than eight hundred applicants.   _____ *; however,* _____

3. *conjunctive adverb*

Self-service gasoline stations have eliminated the

need for many attendants; *nevertheless,* Service stations still

place ads for service station attendants.   *; nevertheless,*

4. *transitional expression*

Projections indicate that some businesses will still

have openings for large numbers of salespeople.;

for example, The demand for computer salespeople will increase

greatly because of the growing popularity of home

and business computers.   *; for example,*

5. *use no conjunction*

Employment for route drives will probably not in-

crease during the coming decade; Neither will

openings for manufacturers' salesworkers.   _____;_____

Combining Main Clauses   Exercise 1-22 (continued)

6. *use no conjunction*

   Sales work provides opportunities for high school

   as well as college graduates,/ₚPeople who want to

   work for someone else as well as those who want

   to run their own businesses should consider this

   line of work.   _____ ; _____

7. *conjunctive adverb*

   consequently,

   Salespersons must enjoy meeting people,/Someone

   who feels uncomfortable around strangers or who

   does not understand the needs of others should not

   consider sales as a potential career.   *; consequently,*

8. *use no conjunction*

   Sales work probably requires more exceptional

   a

   character traits than any other occupation,/A good

   salesperson is imaginative, self-confident, ambi-

   tious, and energetic.   _____ ; _____

81

9. *coordinating conjunction*

Good salespersons understand people. *but* They also
understand the business community and good business practices.   ___, *but* ___

10. *transitional expression*

Many people in sales must be willing to travel;
in fact, Some salespeople spend as much as four or five
months of the year on the road.   ___; *in fact,* ___

Deduct 11 for each incorrectly constructed sentence.

Building Sentences   Exercise 1-23

NAME _____ SCORE _____

DIRECTIONS   From each of the following sets of phrases and/or clauses write a sentence (or sentences) of the specified type in the space provided. Where indicated, use the connecting word given in italics. Be sure to punctuate correctly the segments you join together.

EXAMPLE

COMPOUND

about combining them into one career

they do not know where to look for advice

many people have several interests

but

Many people have several interests, but they do not know where to look for advice about combining them into one career.

1. SIMPLE

this office can help a person investigate potential careers

students often neglect to consult their school's placement bureau

Students often neglect to consult their school's placement bureau. This office can help a person investigate potential careers.

2. COMPLEX

while students are in their first years of college

placement counselors can help them evaluate their goals

While students are in their first years of college, placement counselors can help them evaluate their goals.

3. COMPOUND-COMPLEX

there are tests that students can take

the placement office may also provide information

to identify their real interests

about internship opportunities

however

There are tests that students can take to identify their real interests; however, [this comma may be omitted] the placement office may also provide information about internship opportunities.

4. COMPLEX
   especially if a person wants
   summer jobs and internships are worth investigating
   to explore a new career possibility

   Summer jobs and internships are worth investigating, especially if a person wants to explore a new career possibility.

5. COMPOUND
   others only employ summer interns
   on a year-round basis
   many companies hire interns

   Many companies hire interns on a year-round basis; others only employ summer interns.

6. COMPOUND-COMPLEX
   to earn money
   interests some students
   to continue their education
   the co-op program that large companies offer
   it enables them

   The co-op program that large companies offer interests some students; it enables them to earn money to continue their education.

7. COMPOUND
   this training supplements the theoretical courses
   co-op students work at a full-time job
   that they have taken in school
   and

   Co-op students work at a full-time job, and this training supplements the theoretical courses that they have taken in school.

8. COMPLEX
   with schools offering technical degrees
   although not all colleges and universities have co-op programs
   most large corporations participate in this type of arrangement

   Although not all colleges and universities have co-op programs, most large corporations participate in this type of arrangement with schools offering technical degrees.

9. SIMPLE
   to hire permanent employees
   many companies like
   from among their former co-op students

   Many companies like to hire permanent employees from among their former co-op students.

2

Write complete sentences.

A sentence fragment is a nonsentence beginning with a capital letter and ending with a period. A sentence fragment is usually a phrase (a group of related words that lacks a subject and/or a verb) or a subordinate clause (a group of related words that has both a subject and a verb but that is introduced by a clause marker—a word such as *who, which, that, if, since,* or *because*).

> PHRASE   needing to prepare a report for your employer
>
> SUBORDINATE CLAUSE   when you need to prepare a report for your employer
>
> SENTENCE   You need to prepare a report for your employer.

Few people write isolated fragments; rather they write fragments as parts of a paragraph. They separate what should be sentence additions from the main clauses they belong with. Notice that the writer of the following has mistakenly separated what should be sentence additions from the main clause they belong with.

> *When you need to prepare a report for your employer.* You may panic at the assignment. *Realizing that your writing skills as well as your knowledge of your field will be examined carefully.*

When the italicized words are treated as additions to the main clause, and are punctuated with commas, the fragments are avoided.

> *When you need to prepare a report for your employer,* you may panic at the assignment, *realizing that your writing skills as well as your knowledge of your field will be examined carefully.*

Of course, the fragments may also be avoided by making the italicized words into main clauses themselves, but the writing that results sounds childish.

> You need to prepare a report for your employer. You may panic at the assignment. You realize that your writing skills as well as your knowledge of your field will be examined carefully.

Usually, then, the best correction for a sentence fragment is to connect it with the main clause it has been separated from. The exercises in this section will provide you with experience in making fragments into additions to main clauses and in correctly punctuating these additions.

Deduct 5 for each incorrect revision and 5 for each blank incorrectly filled.

Avoiding Phrase Fragments   Exercise 2–1

NAME _____ SCORE _____

2a To avoid fragments, connect verbal phrases, prepositional phrases, and ap·positives to the independent clauses with which they belong.

DIRECTIONS   Join the sentence fragment to the main or independent clause it has been separated from. Use a comma either before or after the fragment. (You will need to change the capitalization of one of the word groups.) In the blank write either *a* or *b* to show which word group is the fragment.

EXAMPLES
ᵃAn important part of many jobs, ᵇThe business report is usually

presented in written form.   *a*

ᵃMost reports are quite simple, ᵇRequiring no more than one page

of composition.   *b*

1. ᵃBecause most reports follow a general-to-specific format, ᵇThey present the main point of the report first and then the

   supporting facts.   *a*

2. ᵃUnlike reports which may sometimes end with the main

   point, ᵇBusiness letters nearly always state the main point

   first.   *a*

3. ᵃThe facts or supporting points of proof are listed first to help

   persuade the reader. ᵇIn a report that ends with recommenda-

   tions.   *b*

4. ᵃThe reader may be ready to accept the recommendation, ᵇHaving been prepared for it by the writer's presentation.   *b*

87

5. ᵃMany formal reports are written by professional technical writers within the corporation or by outside consulting firms./ ᵇOften for presentation to corporate executives, clients, or stockholders.   *b*

6. ᵃUnlike complicated formal reports./ ᵇShort informal reports are usually written by ordinary workers.   *a*

7. ᵃMany short reports help an individual or a group of individuals make a decision./ ᵇBy presenting the facts needed to support a recommendation or a conclusion.   *b*

8. ᵃBusiness reports help their readers make any number of decisions./ ᵇSuch as whether a procedure is practical or the project is feasible.   *b*

9. ᵃA report may help a writer to prepare a future report of a similar nature./ ᵇAs a permanent record to be kept on file.   *b*

10. ᵃBefore preparing any report./ ᵇThe writer should be clear about the purpose of the report.   *a*

Deduct 8 for each incorrect revision and 2 for each blank incorrectly filled.

Avoiding Phrase Fragments—Continued Exercise 2-2

NAME _____ SCORE _____

To avoid fragments, connect a list of items or the second part of a compound verb or compound direct objects to the main clause it belongs with.

DIRECTIONS   Join a list of items or the second part of the compound verb or compound direct object to the main clause it belongs with. Use no comma before the second part of the compound verb or compound direct object. Use a comma or a colon before a list that you attach to the main clause: use a comma if the list is introduced by a phrase like *such as;* use a colon if there is no introductory phrase. (You will need to change the capitalization of each word group that you join to the main clause.) In the blank, write *compound verb* if the fragment that you join to the main clause is the second part of the verb or *compound object* if the fragment that you join to the main clause is the second part of the object; write *list* if the fragment is a series of items.

EXAMPLES

Sources of information for reports can include data ob-

tained firsthand, ~~o~~r material obtained through gath-

ering and assembling the research done by others.   *compound object*

Information from primary sources is obtained in several

ways; ~~q~~uestionnaires, experiments, and surveys.   *list*

1. Information from primary sources is obtained first-

   hand. ~~A~~nd has not been analyzed by someone else.   *compound verb*

2. Gathering information from primary sources takes

   more time. ~~A~~nd costs more than consulting second-

   ary sources.   *compound verb*

3. Thus, when writing a report, you should consult

   secondary sources first. / ~~A~~nd should use them to

   avoid duplicating someone else's work.   *compound verb*

4. Secondary sources are found in three places; Libraries, research departments in some companies,
   and, occasionally, data-gathering firms.   *list*

5. There are many kinds of libraries available, Such
   as school, college, and municipal.   *list*

6. The information from sources may be taken in one
   of two ways. Copied word for word from books or
   articles or summarized.   *list*

7. You may obtain information about office equipment and supplies from several primary sources;
   By studying manufacturers' brochures, by observing other offices, and by attending sales and professional conventions.   *list*

8. As you collect your information, you will need to
   organize your findings, And evaluate them.   *compound verb*

9. If you do your research carefully, you may have
   more information than you need, Or more than
   your supervisor will care to read about.   *compound object*

10. Before writing a report you must decide on a final
    plan for presentation, As well as eliminate all the
    information that does not suit your plan.   *compound verb*

Deduct 5 for each incorrect revision and 5 for each blank incorrectly filled.

Avoiding Subordinate Clause Fragments Exercise 2-3

NAME _____ SCORE _____

2b To avoid fragments, connect subordinate clauses to the main clauses they belong with.

DIRECTIONS   Join the subordinate clause to the main clause it has been separated from. Use a comma after the subordinate clause if it comes before the main clause; use no comma if the subordinate clause follows the main clause unless it is introduced by the clause marker *although*. (You will need to change the capitalization of one of the clauses.) In the blank write either *a* or *b* to show which word group is the fragment.

EXAMPLES

ᵃBefore a report is requested, ᵇIts probable usefulness to the com-

pany should be considered.   *a*

ᵃUnnecessary reports should be eliminated, ᵇBecause they are expen-

sive and time-consuming to produce and distribute.   *b*

1. ᵃPrepared forms are often used. ᵇBecause routine reports are

   written frequently.   *b*

2. ᵃIf a company receives frequent inquiries about its products.

   ᵇA prepared form providing the information requested saves

   both time and energy.   *a*

3. ᵃSince definite information must be presented. ᵇPrepared

   forms are used in most medical fields.   *a*

4. ᵃPatients are usually asked to respond to a definite set of ques-

   tions. ᵇWhen they report for dental or medical checkups.   *b*

5. ᵃWhenever the dental or medical firm must supply insurance

   companies with details concerning claims. ᵇPatients' answers

   recorded on these standard forms may become the basis for

   longer, formal reports.   *a*

6. [a]Short routine reports usually can be handled in minutes. [b]Whereas formal reports often require a long time to prepare.   *b*

7. [a]While the forms of the reports may vary. [b]No report is useful unless the information it includes is accurate, objective, and carefully organized.   *a*

8. [a]Because who will read the report and the purpose it will serve determine the report's structure. [b]A writer must first determine the audience for the report.   *a*

9. [a]If similar reports have been completed in the past. [b]The writer should read them carefully before writing the new report.   *a*

10. [a]A past report can keep the writer from wasting a great deal of time. [b]Although, unfortunately, previous reports are often unavailable because they have been lost in someone's files.   *b*

Deduct 5 for each incorrect revision and 5 for each blank incorrectly filled.

Avoiding Subordinate Clause Fragments   Exercise 2–4

NAME _____ SCORE _____

DIRECTIONS   For the following sentences, join the subordinate clause to the main clause that it has been separated from. If the subordinate clause defines or limits in some way the meaning of the term it refers to, use no comma before it. If the subordinate clause simply adds useful but not necessary information about the term it refers to, use a comma before the clause marker. No comma should be used before the clause marker *that*. (See **1d(2)** or restrictive and nonrestrictive clauses.) (You will need to change the capitalization in each subordinate clause.) In the blank write the clause marker, if one is included, that signals the beginning of the subordinate clause fragment. (**Note:** Sometimes *that* is omitted when the subordinate clause is joined to the main clause.)

EXAMPLES

[a]As an employee of any business, you may be asked to write reports/

[b]That must be prepared according to certain specifications.   *that*

[a]If the request comes to you in written form, carefully note the au-

thorization, [b]Which should make clear the exact nature of the re-

port you are to prepare.   *which*

1. [a]After underlining all major points listed in the authorization,

   make a note of any questions. [b]That you have about what you

   are expected to do.   *that*

2. [a]To find the answers to your questions, it is appropriate to call

   or write the person. [b]Who requested the report.   *who*

3. [a]You may wish to follow up any telephone conversation with

   a memo. [b]That spells out the understandings you reached with

   the person who authorized the report.   *that*

4. [a]Let us assume that Ms. Phillips has written to you requesting

   a report. [b]Which should evaluate the effectiveness of recent

   ads for your company's new product line.   *which*

5. ^aAfter reading the request carefully, you find that you have several questions about the exact information wanted by Ms. Phillips. ^bWho is your immediate supervisor and also the manager of the company.

who

6. ^aYour first step would be to make a list of the questions. ^bThat you want her to answer.

that

7. ^aYour questions might concern the meaning of "recent" ads and the amount of detail that should be given about each one. ^bThat you plan to list.

that

8. ^aTo write an effective study, you consult any reports covering past years. ^bYour predecessors have prepared.

_____

9. ^aThen you call Ms. Phillips, ^bWho is happy to respond to any questions left unanswered by your reading of previous reports.

who

10. By doing your "homework," you save your supervisor the trouble of giving you information. ^bThat you could easily have found on your own.

that

Deduct 5 for each incorrect circle and 5 for each incorrect revision.

Avoiding Sentence Fragments: A Review Exercise 2-5

NAME _____ SCORE _____

DIRECTIONS   Each sentence or fragment in the following paragraphs is numbered. Circle the numbers of the ten fragments. Then connect the fragments to the main clauses they belong with. (In a few cases a fragment can be joined to either of two main clauses. Also, a few fragments occur in succession.) Change the capitalization and include commas and colons as needed.

¹Your final written report will probably fall into one of three categories. ②The memorandum, the letter, or the short informal report. ³The memorandum and letter forms are alike, ④Except that the letter is slightly more formal, ⑤And will probably be read by people outside the company. ⁶Most likely, though, the information you have gathered will be presented in the form of the short informal report, ⑦Which is usually no longer than ten pages. ⑧If, for example, your subject is limited to a consideration of advertising strategies, ⁹You should have little trouble organizing your material, ⑩Since the various types of ads can serve as the basis for your paragraphing.

¹¹Your report probably should include several sections: ⑫The title page, followed by the letter or memorandum requesting or authorizing the report, ⑬Or by a statement indicating who requested or authorized it. ¹⁴The first section of the body of the report states the purpose of the report clearly and concisely. ¹⁵The next section should give a summary of your findings, ⑯Including a description of the method or sources used to arrive at the conclusions, ⑰Such as surveys, questionnaires, direct observations, and research. ¹⁸Finally, you should present your recommendations, ⑲Which will include the ways in which you think the ads could be improved, together with information about the most successful ad

formats, their particular features, and how they are an improvement over the present advertising campaign. [20]Headings should be used within the body of the report to identify its three main divisions: purpose, findings, and recommendations.

3

Avoid comma splices and fused sentences.

When one main clause is added to another, either a comma or a semicolon is used between the main clauses whenever the main clauses are connected by a coordinating conjunction: *and, but, or, nor, so, for,* or *yet.*

Using a comma between main clauses not connected by a coordinating conjunction creates a comma splice error (also called a comma fault). Using no punctuation mark at all creates a fused sentence (also called a run-on sentence.)

COMMA SPLICE   Most people think of a report as a written document, in reality, employees present almost as many oral reports as written ones.

FUSED SENTENCE   Most people think of a report as a written document in reality employees present almost as many oral reports as written ones.

If the coordinating conjunction is omitted between main clauses, then a semicolon is placed between the main clauses. On the other hand, if a colon is used, the second clause generally explains the first one.

Most people think of a report as a written document; in reality, employees present almost as many oral reports as written ones.

Employees may present oral reports to a variety of people: they may be called on for oral presentations by their immediate supervisors, by the upper management of their companies, and even, on occasion, by the general public. [Here the second main clause does not present a related point but rather explains the idea of the first main clause.]

If the coordinating conjunction is replaced by another type of connecting word—a conjunctive adverb (*thus, then, therefore, however*) or a transitional expression (*on the other hand, in fact, for example, to sum up*)—the standard mark of punctuation between the main clauses is still the semicolon.

Most people think of a report as a written document; *however,* in reality, employees present as many oral reports as written ones.

Note: Remember that a conjunctive adverb or a transitional expression may be used as an added modifier in a main clause *rather than* as a connector between main clauses. In such a case, the conjunctive adverb or transitional expression is normally set off by commas: "Few employees, however, escape the task of preparing some written reports."

In addition to the use of the semicolon, there are two other ways to correct a comma splice or fused sentence: write two separate sentences or make one of the main clauses into a subordinate clause.

TWO SENTENCES Most people think of a report as a written document. In reality, employees present almost as many oral reports as written ones.

SUBORDINATION Although most people think of a report as a written document, in reality, employees present almost as many oral reports as written ones.

The exercises in this section will give you practice in correcting comma splices and fused sentences in all three ways: by using a semicolon or colon, by writing two separate sentences, and by subordinating one idea to another.

Avoiding Comma Splices and
Fused Sentences

Exercise 3–1

NAME _____ SCORE _____

3a Use a comma between main clauses *only* when connecting them with the coordinating conjunctions *and, but, or, nor, for, so,* or *yet.* If no coordinating conjunction is used, do one of the following: (1) use a semicolon (but only if the statements made by the two main clauses are closely related); (2) use a colon (but only if the second main clause explains the first); (3) make the two main clauses separate sentences, each beginning with a capital letter and ending with a period; (4) rewrite one of the main clauses to make it a subordinate clause addition to the other main clause.

Note: Be especially careful to avoid fused sentences and comma splices when dividing a quotation.

> "Prepare an oral report as carefully as you would a written one," my technical writing instructor advised. [Do not use a comma here.] "Be especially conscious of your audience in preparing an oral report."

DIRECTIONS In the following fused and comma-spliced sentences, insert an inverted caret (**V**) where two main clauses come together. Then correct the error in the way you think best. Write **;** in the blank if you use a semicolon to make the correction, **:** if you use a colon, **.** if you use two sentences, and *sub* if you make one of the clauses subordinate.

EXAMPLE
According to one survey, preparation of oral reports takes up 25.4%

of a worker's time $\overset{\text{V}}{;}$ preparation of written reports occupies 24.5%. _____;_____

1. Technicians write many descriptive reports $\overset{\text{V and}}{,}$ they often write

   several long analytical reports each year. _____,_____

2. For example, a computer systems troubleshooter usually sub-

   mits a report on the work completed on each call $\overset{\text{V J}}{,}$ the report

   describes the customer's problems and what was done to re-

   store the computer to service. _____._____

3. Descriptive reports about changes in product specifications

   are as essential to the company as the products themselves $\overset{\text{V}}{/;}$

they help workers in the field stay abreast of the latest techni-

cal innovations.   ————— , —————

4. In smaller companies, technicians write most of the descrip-

tive literature about the company's products ∨and they fre-

quently write the instructions that appear on labels and in

user's manuals.   ————— , —————

5. The second major kind of technical report is the analytical

one,∨ʲ.these documents may summarize and evaluate such

things as tests performed by the company.   ————— . —————

6. Computerized record keeping has not eliminated the need to

write analytical reports ∨in small companies technicians tabu-

late and report test results.   ————— ; —————

Since or Because
7. ʀeaders of technical reports want to see the facts stated clearly,
   ∧
you must be precise and choose your words carefully.   ——— *sub* , ———

8. Supervisors are often shocked by the poor spelling of their em-

ployees *m*many comment that their employees' spelling ranges

from "poor" to "atrocious."   ————— . —————

9. A report that has misspelled words in it is not well received

because
the misspelled words imply carelessness and cast doubt on the

report's accuracy.   ——— *sub* ———

10. "Companies will not tolerate technicians who cannot spell

correctly," one company president remarked,∨/;if a technician

misspells a common word in the description of a product, the

customer does not trust the product."   ————— ; —————

Avoiding Comma Splices and
Fused Sentences

Exercise 3–2

NAME _____ SCORE _____

3b Use a semicolon between two main clauses joined by conjunctive adverbs such as *however* or *therefore* or a transitional expression such as *for example* or *on the other hand*.

DIRECTIONS   In the following fused and comma-spliced sentences, insert an inverted caret (**V**) where the two main clauses come together. Then add a semicolon if no mark of punctuation is there; if a comma is there, cross it out and insert a semicolon. In the blank write the semicolon and the word or phrase that follows it, as well as any punctuation that follows the word or phrase.

EXAMPLE
The memo is the shortest, most direct form of business

communication; therefore, it is the form most fre-

quently used within companies.   *; therefore*

1. In a memo the conclusions or recommendations

   come first, nevertheless, the sequence of points

   should be determined by the writer's purpose.   *; nevertheless,*

2. The memo next briefly supplies important details

   about the conclusion, then it offers further assist-

   ance or information.   *; then*

3. A memo is short generally, it should seldom run

   more than two pages.   *; generally,*

4. A memo primarily supplies information thus it

   does not have to present recommendations.   *; thus*

5. Memos should be dated and should include head-

   ings usually, *To*, *From*, *Subject* (rather than *Re*),

   and *Date* introduce a memo.   *; usually,*

6. Information can, of course, be communicated
   orally⌄;however, a memo will provide a lasting
   record.

   ; however, _____

7. A spoken message may be ignored or forgotten⌄;in
   contrast, a memo demands attention and can be
   referred to again.

   ; in contrast,

8. A report in letter form often supplies the same information that a memo would ⌄;in fact, the more
   formal letter-report generally goes to readers outside the company.

   _____ *; in fact,* _____

9. A letter-report will often omit some parts of the
   standard business letter ⌄;for example, it may drop
   the inside address, the salutation, and the comple-
   mentary close.

   ; for example,

10. For ease of reading, the letter-report contains
    headings and subheadings⌄;furthermore, it may in-
    clude tables or other illustrations.

    ; furthermore,

Avoiding Comma Splices and
Fused Sentences: A Review

Exercise 3–3

NAME _____ SCORE _____

DIRECTIONS   In the following paragraphs insert an inverted caret (**V**) where two main clauses are incorrectly joined. Then correct the fused and comma-spliced sentences by writing in semicolons or colons, by adding a period and a capital letter to make two separate sentences, or by rewriting one of the sentences as a subordinate clause.

[1]A report writer must observe certain conventions of style. [2]First, and most important, a simple, straightforward presentation is essential *or since* poetic words and roundabout phrasing have no place in reports. [3]The main purpose of a report is to communicate information clearly; therefore, anything that interferes with clarity should be avoided. [4]Sentences in memos and reports are usually much shorter and less complex in structure than are those in other types of writing; again clarity, not variety, is the primary aim of a report writer.

[5]Report writers should avoid the personal or subjective approach. [6]They should avoid personal pronouns, especially the first person *I* or *we*. these pronouns often make the report appear to give only the writer's opinion rather than information presented by an objective reporter. [7]For example, it is weak to say, "We found errors"; however, you could say that "The investigators found errors."

[8]Furthermore, vague evaluations such as *expensive* and *superior* should be avoided because these words can mean different things to different readers. [9]A

writer must give concrete details, ~~and~~ the reader will make judgments based on *since or because*

the facts the report presents. [10]"This product is the most wonderful thing our

company has ever manufactured," one enthusiastic technician wrote, "it is a *l*

must for every household." [11]Needless to say, the supervisor reading the techni-

cian's report was not impressed with these subjective opinions, furthermore, the *F*

technician's gushy, biased description of the product's operation annoyed the

supervisor.

[12]Finally, like any other writer, a report writer must give credit for all facts

and ideas gained through the research of others; otherwise, the writer is guilty

of plagiarism, as serious an offense in business and industry as it is in college.

[13]Footnotes or source identifications, which are enclosed in parentheses within

the body of the report, must be included to acknowledge sources used to develop

the final report; of course, note pages and, usually, a bibliography section are *O*

provided at the end of the report.

4

Use adjectives and adverbs correctly.

In **1d** you learned how a modifier can make a word in the basic formula more exact in meaning.

> Writing a *good business* letter is *not* the *extraordinarily difficult* task *most* people feel that it is.

Without the modifiers—not to mention the articles—this sentence would not even have the same meaning, as is clearly shown when the sentence is written without any modifiers.

> Writing a letter is the task people think that it is.

The modifiers (*good, business,* and *most*) of the subjects (*letter* and *people*), the modifier (*not*) of the verb (*is*), the modifier (*difficult*) of the complement (*task*), and the modifier (*extraordinarily*) of another modifier (*difficult*) are all necessary to make the meaning of the sentence clear.

Adjectives   Modifiers of nouns and pronouns are called adjectives.

> Of all the types of *business* letters, the *most difficult* one for *most* people to write
>
> is the letter of introduction.

Note: The pronouns *everyone* and *everybody* are often modified by adverbs rather than adjectives because they are compound words made up of a pronoun (*one* and *body*) and an adjective (*every*): "*Almost* everyone can learn to write an effective business letter to a friend as well as to a stranger."

An adjective may also be used either as a *subject complement* or as an *object complement.*

Subject Complements   Adjectives used as subject complements follow linking verbs—mainly forms of *be* (*am, is, are, was, were, has been, have been, will be,* and so on) and verbs like *appear, seem, look, feel,* and *taste*—and describe or show something about the subject of the sentence. (Because they appear as part of the predicate, they are also called predicate adjectives.)

> SUBJECT COMPLEMENT   The supervisor is fair and reasonable.   [*fair* and *reason-*
>
> *able* describe the subject, *supervisor.*]

Note: Some subject complements are nouns: The computer is the *solution.*

Object Complements   Adjectives used as object complements are also found in the predicate, but they describe or refer to the direct object of the verb.

OBJECT COMPLEMENT   Our boss finds competition healthy.   [The object complement, *healthy*, modifies the direct object, *competition*.]

Note: Some objective complements are nouns: Our boss considers us a *team*.

Adverbs   Adverbs modify verbs or modify other modifiers, verbals, a phrase, a clause, or even the rest of the sentence in which they appear.

A business letter written to a friend or an acquaintance is *quite often highly* informal.   [*Often* modifies the verb *is; quite* modifies the adverb *often;* and *highly* modifies the adjective *informal.*]

Writers often have special difficulty with sentences that include linking verbs and their modifiers and other verbs that function as linking verbs.

In sentences with linking verbs (*be, seem,* and so forth), or verbs sometimes used as linking verbs (for instance, *feel* or *look*), it is especially important to determine whether a modifier refers to the verb or to the subject. If it refers to the verb, an adverb must be used; if it refers to a subject, an adjective must be used.

When the modifier refers to a verb like *be, seem, feel,* or *look* rather than to the subject, an adverb, not an adjective, is used.

The client read *hurriedly* through the contractors' bids.   [*Hurriedly*, an adverb, modifies the verb, *read.*]
The client looked *hurried* as he searched through the contractors' bids.   [*Hurried*, an adjective, modifies the subject, *client.*]

Form   Both adjectives and adverbs change their form when two or more things are being compared. An *er* on the end of a modifier or a *less* or *more* in front of it indicates that two things or groups of things are being compared (the comparative degree); an *est* on the end of a modifier or a *least* or *most* in front of it indicates that three or more things or groups of things are being compared (the superlative degree). Some desk dictionaries show the *er* and *est* ending for those adjectives and adverbs that form their comparative and superlative degrees in this way (for example—old, old*er*, old*est*). Most dictionaries show the changes for highly irregular modifiers (for example—good, *better, best*). As a rule of thumb, most one-syllable adjectives and most two-syllable adjectives ending in a vowel sound (*tidy, narrow*) form the comparative with *er* and the superlative with *est*. Most adjectives of two or more syllables and most adverbs form the comparative by adding the word *more* and the superlative by adding the word *most*.

COMPARATIVE DEGREE   Writing a business letter to a customer is *more difficult* than writing a personal letter to a friend.

SUPERLATIVE DEGREE   The *most difficult* letter to write is the one requesting a job interview.

Caution: Many dictionaries do not list the *er* or *est* endings. Double-check if you are uncertain.

Note: For many adjectives the choice of *er* and *est* or *more* and *most* is optional.

The work grows *more and more* easy as time passes.

OR

The work grows *easier and easier* as time passes.

**Distinguishing Between Adjective
and Adverb Modifiers**   Exercise 4–1

NAME _____ SCORE _____

4a Use adverbs to modify verbs, adjectives, and other adverbs.

4b Use adjectives as subject or object complements.

DIRECTIONS   In each of the following sentences, choose the form of the word that would be considered appropriate in business and professional correspondence and reports. Cross out the incorrect choice; write the correct one in the blank. To help you decide which choice is correct, the word or words modified are underlined. (If you are uncertain about the part of speech of the underlined word or of the modifiers, consult your dictionary.)

EXAMPLE
(Almost, ~~Most~~) every employee must write many busi-

ness letters each year.   *almost*

1. Writing one's first business letter can be a (~~terrible~~,

terribly) intimidating experience.   *terribly*

2. Most people feel (hesitant, ~~hesitantly~~) about writ-

ing business letters.   *hesitant*

3. Procrastinating about writing a letter usually

makes a writer's job more (unpleasant, ~~unpleas-~~

~~antly~~).   *unpleasant*

4. Good writers (~~general~~, generally) write when an

event is still current.   *generally*

5. You should (~~usual~~, usually) try to make notes about

what you want to say.   *usually*

6. A letter that is (~~real~~, really) clearly written prob-

ably means its writer took the time to revise. *really*

7. A courteous business person <u>will</u> (careful, carefully) <u>plan</u> exactly what to say before writing. *carefully*

8. Letters from customers (most, <u>mostly</u>) <u>often</u> request answers to their questions. *most*

9. Any unnecessary delay in answering an important
   letter can make a customer <u>react</u> (angry, angrily). *angrily*

10. You are judged by employers as well as by cus-
    tomers on how (<u>rapid</u>, rapidly) you <u>respond</u> to
    their requests. *rapidly*

Deduct 5 for each blank incorrectly filled and 5 for each word or words incorrectly underlined.

Using Comparative and
Superlative Modifiers

Exercise 4–2

NAME _____ SCORE _____

4c Modifiers usually are changed to their comparative form (comparing two things) either by the addition of *er* to the end of the modifier or by the addition of *more* in front of it. Modifiers usually are changed to their superlative form (comparing three or more things) by the addition of *est* to the end of the modifier or by the addition of *most* in front of it. (See also **18d(3)**.)

DIRECTIONS   In each of the following sentences, cross out the incorrect form or forms of the modifier within the parentheses. In the blank, write whether you selected the comparative or the superlative form of the modifier. The word that the modifier refers to is underlined. (If you do not know how to form the comparative or superlative form of the modifier, consult your dictionary.)

EXAMPLE

You will write letters (~~frequentlier~~, more frequently) than reports.   *comparative*

1. Convincing customers that they matter is one of the (~~expensivest~~, most expensive) goals a business has.   *superlative*

2. These days many businesses "talk" to (fewer, ~~more few~~) customers in person than in letters.   *comparative*

3. For that reason it has become (~~importanter~~, more important) than ever to write effective letters.   *comparative*

4. Although a telephone call can take the place of some letters, many people still feel (better, ~~more better~~) seeing things set down in writing.   *comparative*

5. A letter provides the reader with the clearest, (~~exactest~~, most exact) record of what the company has agreed to do.   *superlative*

6. If legal questions arise later, a letter will show the judge (~~clearlier~~, more clearly) exactly what went on.   *comparative*

7. For this reason, the writer must use the (clearest, ~~most clear~~) possible words to avoid misunderstandings from occurring later.

    superlative

8. Most good writers think of clarity and conciseness as the two (~~more essential~~, ~~essentialist~~, most essential) qualities of good business letters.

    superlative

9. The three (~~more important~~, most important) things that a business letter should do are to get the reader to do what you want, to give the reader information, and to build goodwill.

    superlative

10. Business writers who accomplish these goals can expect to be (~~successfuller~~, more successful) than writers who forget to consider their readers.

    comparative

5

Use the correct form of the pronoun to show its function in a sentence.

As you learned in section **1**, a noun or pronoun may change form to indicate the way it works in a clause. The form of the noun or pronoun, referred to as its *case,* may be *subjective* (if it functions as a subject), *objective* (if it functions as an object), or *possessive* (if it shows ownership or possession). Nouns change their form for only one case—the possessive. (See also section **15**.)

Certain pronouns change their form for each case; you must be aware of these various forms in order to make the function of these pronouns immediately clear in your writing.

Subjective	Objective	Possessive
I	me	mine
we	us	our, ours
he, she	him, her	his, her, hers
they	them	their, theirs
who, whoever	whom, whomever	whose

Subjective Case   The subjective case is used for subjects of verbs and for subject complements.

> *She* answers all letters of complaint.   [subject of verb]
> The best writer in the firm is *she.*   [subject complement]

Note: You may sometimes find it more comfortable to avoid using the pronoun as a complement: "*She* is the best writer in the firm." OR "The best writer in the firm is *Mary.*"

Objective Case   The objective case is used for both direct and indirect objects, for objects of prepositions, and for both subjects and objects of infinitives.

> The customer called *me* about his problem with our product.   [direct object]
> He gave *me* his opinion about what should be done to improve the product.
>   [indirect object]
> He sent the unused portion of the product to *me.*   [object of preposition]
> He asked *me* to refund his money.   [subject of infinitive *to refund*]
> He wanted to tell *me* about his difficulty in using the product.   [object of infinitive
>   *to tell*]

Possessive Case   The possessive case is generally used before a gerund—a verbal that ends in *ing*—and acts as a noun. But a participle also sometimes has an *ing* ending. The possessive case is used before a gerund, which acts as a noun, but not before a participle, which acts as an adjective.

GERUND   I got tired of *his* criticizing my company's product.   [*Criticizing* acts as a noun, the object of the preposition *of*.]

PARTICIPLE   I found *him* unrelenting in his attack on our product.   [*Unrelenting* acts as an adjective, modifying *him*.]

Deduct 10 for each blank incorrectly filled.

Case Forms of Pronouns

Exercise 5-1

NAME _____ SCORE _____

The subjective case (*I, we, he, she, they, who, whoever*) is used for subjects and subject complements; the objective case (*me, us, him, her, them, whom, whomever*) is used for objects of verbs and verbals, for objects of prepositions, and for both subjects and objects of infinitives (for example, *to go, to be*); the possessive case (*my, our, his, her, their, whose*) is generally used to modify a gerund.

SUBJECTIVE   OBJECTIVE   OBJECTIVE
He expected *us* to hire *him*.

SUBJECTIVE   POSSESSIVE   OBJECTIVE
She heard about *his* criticizing the product from *us*.

OBJECTIVE   POSSESSIVE   POSSESSIVE
We regret *their* not being able to attend *your* meeting.

DIRECTIONS   In the following sentences cross out the incorrect case form or forms within parentheses and write the correct form in the blank. List your reason for your choice in the space provided after the sentence. (After your answers have been checked, you may find it helpful to read them aloud several times to accustom your ear to the sound of the correct case forms.)

EXAMPLE
He told (~~she~~, her) that the product had passed many demanding

tests.   *her*

Reason: *object of verb*

1. Only (she, ~~her~~) is qualified to answer the letters.   *she*
   Reason: *subject*

2. No one but (~~she~~, her) knows the history of the product.   *her*
   Reason: *object of preposition*

3. One customer told her about (you, your) trying to make the
   product burn.   *you or your*
   Reason: *object of preposition or possessive before a gerund*

4. It was (she, ~~her~~) who sent the report to the attorneys about the flammability study's poor results. *she*

Reason: *subject complement*

5. She sent (~~they,~~ them) a well-reasoned indictment of the product's safety record. *them*

Reason: *indirect object of verb*

6. Her letter was convincing enough to make (~~he,~~ him) file his complaint. *him*

Reason: *object of infinitive*

7. It was necessary for (~~he,~~ him) to revise his interpretation of what had happened at the plant. *him*

Reason: *subject of infinitive, but give credit for object of preposition for*

8. After observing (~~she,~~ her) for one day, we realized how much time an employee spends answering letters. *her*

Reason: *object*

9. Because her letters were so well written, all of (~~we,~~ us) who read them were impressed. *us*

Reason: *object of preposition*

10. (We, ~~Us~~) now believe that offering our employees training in business writing is a good investment of our time and money. *We*

Reason: *subject*

Pronouns in Compounds
and as Appositives

Exercise 5–2

NAME _____ SCORE _____

**5a A pronoun has the same case form in a compound or an appositive construc-
tion as it would if it were used alone.**

COMPOUND   Matthew and *I* took business writing courses taught by Mr. Rowe
CONSTRUCTIONS   and *her*.   [Compare with "I took courses taught by *her*."]

APPOSITIVE   *She*, the director of product information for a local firm, taught
CONSTRUCTIONS   *us* students what we needed to know about business writing.
                  [Compare with "*She* taught *us* what we needed to know about
                  business correspondence."]

DIRECTIONS   In the following sentences cross out the incorrect case form within parentheses and write the correct form in the blank. (To decide which case form is correct,
say aloud each part of the compound construction separately or say aloud the pronoun
without the appositive that follows it, as illustrated in the examples.)

EXAMPLES
(We, ~~Us~~) students took business writing. [*We took*

   business writing.]   *We*

The best writers in the class were (she and he, ~~her and~~

   ~~him~~).   [*The best writer in the class was she; the best*

   writer in the class was he.]   *she and he*

1. Our teacher taught (us, ~~we~~) students how to write

   many types of business letters.   *us*

2. (We, ~~Us~~) students learned a lot from working with

   sample letters.   *We*

3. The samples helped to clarify the format of a busi-

   ness letter for (~~the rest of the class and I,~~ the rest   *the rest of the*
                                                               class and me
   of the class and me).

4. Because we had taken the business writing class,

   (the other students and I, ~~the other students and~~   *the other*
                                                               students and I
   ~~me~~) now feel that we can write well.

5. By the end of the term, it was clear that (Julie and he, ~~Julie and him~~) knew how to write a courteous refusal letter.

Julie and he

6. (James and she, ~~James and her~~) gained practice writing sales letters to prospective clients.

James and she

7. (He, as well as she; ~~Him, as well as her,~~) had had experience placing and responding to orders for merchandise.

He, as well as she

8. Furthermore, the business writing course taught (~~James and she~~, James and her) how to write requests for information or assistance.

James and her

9. Finally, writing and answering claim and complaint letters seemed easier to (~~Sara and I~~, Sara and me).

Sara and me

10. Because they had had training in the correct way to write business letters and reports, the best writers that the company hired were (she and he, ~~her and him~~).

she and he

Pronouns in Subordinate Clauses
and with *Self* Added

Exercise 5-3

NAME _____ SCORE _____

5b The case of a pronoun depends on its use in its *own* clause.

> I think I know *who* should be chosen. [Although *who* begins the clause that is the object of *I know*, in its own clause *who* is the subject of the verb *should be chosen*.]

> It is she *whom* we should choose. [In its own clause, *whom* is the object of the verb *should choose*.]

Self is added to a pronoun only when a reflexive or an intensive pronoun is needed.

> I *myself* will answer the letter. [intensive pronoun: intensifies *I*]
> I wrote a letter to *myself*. [reflexive pronoun: reflects back to *I*]
> He wrote a letter to *me*. [NOT *myself*; neither intensive nor reflexive]

Note: *Hisself, theirselves, it self,* and *its self* are nonstandard forms of *himself, themselves,* and *itself.*

DIRECTIONS In the following sentences cross out the incorrect case form or forms within parentheses and write the correct form in the blank.

EXAMPLE
He was the personnel director for (~~who~~, whom) every-

one had the highest regard. _____*whom*_____

1. The students asked him (~~who~~, whom) they should

   talk to about job opportunities within his com-

   pany. _____*whom*_____

2. The personnel director said that they should first

   write to (him, ~~himself~~) for information and for ap-

   plication forms. _____*him*_____

3. Because they must talk about (~~them~~, themselves,

   ~~theirselves~~), most students find application letters

   difficult to write. _____*themselves*_____

4. On the other hand, the standard application (~~it-

   self~~, itself) and the résumé seem less intimidating

   than the application letter. _____*itself*_____

5. The students for (~~who,~~ whom) business writing has been a part of their studies are often the best-prepared job seekers.

whom

6. It was their business writing instructor (who, ~~whom~~), they remembered, told them that good writing skills would help them to acquire their first job.

who

7. When they were told the number of people in the company to (~~who,~~ whom) their letters would be sent, they realized how much their writing really would represent them.

whom

8. Anthony remarked that the practice résumé he had written for class was especially useful to (him, ~~himself, hisself~~) in his search for a job.

him

9. A correctly organized application letter and résumé say to (~~whoever,~~ whomever) reads them that the writer understands correct business writing form and style.

whomever

10. Well-written letters make (whoever, ~~whomever~~) reads them consider the writer in a professional and businesslike light.

whoever

Mastering Case: A Review Exercise 5-4

NAME _____ SCORE _____

DIRECTIONS   In the following sentences cross out the incorrect case form or forms within parentheses and write the correct form in the blank. Determine the use of the pronoun in its own clause before you choose the case form.

EXAMPLE

The personnel director is the employee within the company (who, ~~whom~~) usually answers letters from job applicants.

who

1. (~~Whoever~~, Whomever) a company wishes to interview will receive a written invitation to discuss the job opening.

Whomever

2. This letter contains specific information stating what the applicants need to know about the interview: (~~who~~, whom) they are to see, when and where the interview is to take place, and for what positions they are being considered.

whom

3. The letter lets the applicant know (~~who~~, whom) to contact in case of questions.

whom

4. Furthermore, applicants should know what (they, ~~them~~) should bring to the interview.

they

5. Finally, the letter tells applicants about any tests that will be given to (~~they~~, them, ~~themselves~~) at the time of the interview.

them

6. (~~They~~, Their, ~~Them~~) knowing what to expect will make it easier for applicants to do well in the interview.

Their

7. Applicants (~~who~~, whom) the company does not wish to interview will receive a polite letter of rejection.

whom

8. A good letter of rejection first thanks the applicant for her interest in the company and then explains that (she, her, hers) is not an application that they wish to consider further.

hers.

9. Finalists for a position often receive an invitation for a second visit: "(We, Us) at Wright Corporation would like to invite you to tour our plant."

We.

10. Even though a rejection letter will always disappoint its reader, the writers must still try to retain the goodwill of the applicants (who, whom) they are turning down for the job.

whom

6

Make a verb agree in number with its subject; make a pronoun agree in number with its antecedent.

For your ideas to be clearly stated, it is essential that all subjects and verbs agree in number; a singular subject requires a singular verb, and a plural subject requires a plural verb. (Remember that an *s* ending shows *plural* number for the subject but *singular* number for the verb.)

SINGULAR   A good business letter makes clear the response that is expected from

the recipient of the letter.

PLURAL   Good business letters make clear the responses that are expected from

the recipients of the letters.

In the same way, a pronoun agrees in number with the noun (or the other pronoun) it refers to, called its *antecedent*.

SINGULAR   A good business *letter* makes *its* purpose clear.

PLURAL   Good business *letters* make *their* purpose clear.

Mastering agreement requires that you be able to do three things: (1) match up the simple subject or subjects with the verb or verbs; (2) know which nouns and pronouns are traditionally singular and which are traditionally plural; and (3) identify the antecedent of a pronoun (the noun the pronoun refers to) so that you can determine the number of the antecedent.

6a Make a verb agree in number with its subject.

Simple Subjects   To make the subject and verb agree in number, you must be able to recognize the simple subject of a sentence as well as the verb. The simple subject is often surrounded by other words that are a part of the complete subject and that can easily be mistaken for the exact word or words that should agree in number with the verb.

SINGULAR   A device that encourages quick responses from recipients of request let-

ters is the stamped, addressed return envelope.   [The complete subject contains several plural nouns—*responses, recipients,* and *letters*—that must not be mistaken for the simple subject, which is singular.]

PLURAL   Devices that encourage a quick response from the recipient of a request letter include the stamped, addressed return envelope, a reply card with answers to check, and free prizes or other rewards for a prompt response.   [The complete subject contains several singular nouns—*response, recipient,* and *letter*—that must not be mistaken for the simple subject, which is plural.]

Be particularly careful about the subject-verb agreement in the following situations:

when the subject or the verb ends in *k* or *t:*

Often a business writer talks directly to the reader.

Journalists write guided by a different set of criteria.

when the subject is followed by a prepositional phrase or a subordinate clause:

The reason *for expecting* a response is obvious.

The reason *which was outlined in the correspondence,* is obvious.

when the subject follows the verb:

There are many daily *reports* from agencies of the government.

when the subject and subject complement do not have the same number (Usually you should rewrite the sentence, without using a form of *be,* to avoid the conflict in number.):

AWKWARD   Reports are one way to monitor progress within a company.

BETTER   Reports serve as one monitor of progress within a company.

Singular and Plural Nouns and Pronouns   Some noun subjects are traditionally singular, while others are traditionally plural. Those subjects that are traditionally singular include

(1) singular subjects joined by *or* and *nor* and subjects introduced by *many a:*

Neither the letter *nor* the advertisement requires a response.

Many a letter goes unnoticed.

(2) collective nouns regarded as a unit:

The *number* of request letters amazes me.

The *committee* has made its recommendation.

(3) nouns that are plural in form but singular in meaning:

The *news* creates a stir on Wall Street.

One hundred *miles* means *a long commute.*

(4) titles of works or words referred to as words:

Night Line features some of the best interviews on television.

Employee benefits is a term we use to mean *fringe benefits.*

Those subjects that are traditionally plural include

(1) subjects joined by *and:*

A letter *and* this memo have the same tone.

(2) a plural subject following *or* or *nor:*

Neither the manager *nor* his employees neglect correspondence.   [The verb agrees

with *employees,* the part of the subject it is nearer to.]

(3) collective nouns that do not act as a unit:

A *number* of corporations encourage their employees to return to school.

Certain nouns and pronouns are sometimes singular and sometimes plural, depending on their contexts in their sentences.

SINGULAR   A *group* of claim letters has been examined by management.   [Here

group is considered a unit.]

PLURAL   A *group* of employees are taking different actions in response to the company's latest stock option plan.   [Here *group* refers to many individuals, not to a unit.]

SINGULAR *Some* of this report is extremely well written.

PLURAL   *Some* of those reports are extremely well written.

Pronouns such as *each, either, neither, one, everybody, everyone, someone,* and *anyone* are traditionally singular; pronouns such as *both, few, several,* and *many* are traditionally plural.

6b Make a pronoun agree in number and gender with its antecedent.

A pronoun must agree in number and gender with the noun (or the pronoun) it refers to—that is, with its antecedent.

SINGULAR A clearly stated *request* is the *one* most likely to get action.

PLURAL   Clearly stated *requests* are the *ones* most likely to get action.

A pronoun agrees in number with its antecedent even when the antecedent is in a different clause. (Remember, however, that the *case* of a pronoun is determined entirely by its function in its own clause; see **5b**.)

SINGULAR A good business letter makes clear the *response that* is expected from the recipient of the letter.   [Notice that the verb *is expected* is singular because the antecedent of *that, response,* is singular.]

PLURAL   Good business letters make clear the *responses that* are expected from the recipients of the letters.   [Notice that the verb *are expected* is plural because the antecedent of *that, responses,* is plural.]

SINGULAR A *request that* is clearly stated is usually answered.   [*Request,* the antecedent of *that,* is singular; therefore *that* is also singular.]

PLURAL   *Requests that* are clearly stated are usually answered.   [*Requests,* the antecedent of *that,* is plural; therefore *that* is also plural.]

MASCULINE Emory represents *his* company well.

FEMININE   Juanita represents *her* company well.

Singular and Plural Antecedents   Some pronouns (like some nouns) are traditionally considered singular, whereas others are considered plural.

Pronouns such as *man, woman, person, everybody, one, anyone, each, either, neither, sort,* and *kind* are traditionally considered singular.

We try to give *each* of our products the promotion *it* deserves.

Naturally, *everyone* expects *his* own favorite to be the most popular.   [CONTRAST:

Many expect *their* own favorites to be the most popular.]

Each of the one hundred women surveyed was asked to send *her* reply promptly.

Note: Today most writers, and especially business writers, try to avoid sexism in the use of personal pronouns. Whereas most writers once wrote, "*Each* of us should do *his* best," they now try to avoid using the masculine pronoun to refer to both men and women. A careful writer avoids using pronouns that exclude either sex or that stereotype male and female roles.

NOT   A chief executive officer represents *his* company's interests.   [excludes females]

NOT   A chief executive officer represents *her* company's interests.   [excludes males]

BUT   Chief executive officers represent *their* companys' interests.   [includes both genders]

In other instances, writers inadvertently stereotype male and female roles:

The pilot flew to Los Angeles for *his* company.   [excludes female pilots]
The secretary turned in *her* annual report.   [excludes male secretaries]

To avoid sexism, some writers give both masculine and feminine pronoun references.

The negotiator represents the interests of *his or her* clients.

Other writers recast such sentences in the passive voice.

Clients' interests *are represented* by the negotiator.

Finally, to avoid using the pronoun altogether, some writers recast the sentence entirely.

The negotiator represents clients' interests.

The use of any of these options may change the meaning of your sentence; some work more smoothly than others. Many writers—and readers—consider the compound phrase *his or her* stylistically awkward; many also find the forms *his/her* and *he/she* ugly, impersonal, and bureaucratic.

Perhaps the easiest way to avoid sexism is to use plural pronouns and antecedents unless a feminine or a masculine pronoun is clearly called for, when *his* would definitely refer to a male employee or *her* to a female employee.

Negotiators represent the interests of *their* clients.

The most effective revisions include recasting the sentence in the plural or avoiding the use of the pronoun altogether. Pronouns such as *both, several, many,* and *few* are considered plural.

Few of the people surveyed said that *they* disliked the product.

Pronouns such as *all, any, half, most, none,* and *some* may be singular or plural, depending on their context (that is, depending on the rest of the sentence or paragraph in which they appear).

PLURAL   *All* of the people surveyed *have sent their* replies.

SINGULAR   *All* of the information *has served its* purpose.

Similarly, a collective noun, such as *staff, committee,* or *board,* may call for either a singular or plural pronoun, depending on whether—in its context—it signifies a unit or individual members.

SINGULAR   The *committee has completed its* report.

PLURAL   The *committee have gone* back to *their* various departments.

Caution: Avoid confusing or awkward shifts between singular and plural pronouns that refer to the same collective noun.

CONFUSING   The *committee has completed its* report and gone back to *their* various

departments.

CORRECTED   The *committee has completed its* report, and the *members have gone*

back to *their* various departments.

Deduct 10 for each blank incorrectly filled.

Subject and Verb Agreement   Exercise 6-1

NAME _____ SCORE _____

DIRECTIONS   In each of the following sentences underline the subject with one line (remember that a verbal may act as a subject); then match it with one of the verbs in parentheses. Cross out the verb that does not agree with the subject, and write in the blank the verb that does agree. (When all of your answers have been checked, read each sentence aloud, emphasizing the subject and verb.)

EXAMPLE

The purpose of persuasive letters (is, ~~are~~) to sell a product, an idea, or a service.   _____is_____

1. People who write persuasively (try, ~~tries~~) to win over readers.   _____try_____

2. Facts, figures, and logic generally (work, ~~works~~) best to convince skeptical readers.   _____work_____

3. Another way to sway readers (is, ~~are~~) to touch on their emotions.   _____is_____

4. These "sales" letters, like a persuasive essay, often (use, ~~uses~~) emotional appeals.   _____use_____

5. The writer's tactics (~~is~~, are) not obvious.   _____are_____

6. Exaggerated emotional appeals, however, sometimes (make, ~~makes~~) the reader grow irritated with the writer.   _____make_____

7. Successful writers generally (match, ~~matches~~) any emotional appeal they use to the special interests of the audience.   _____match_____

8. Writers of persuasive letters (~~has~~, have) to remember that uninvited mail can annoy people.   _____have_____

9. The biggest challenge that a writer of persuasive letters faces (is, ~~are~~) to make the reader want to keep reading.   _____is_____

10. As soon as the readers lose interest, such letters usually (get, ~~gets~~) thrown away.   _____get_____

Deduct 3 1/3 points for each subject or verb incorrectly identified and 3 1/3 points for each incorrect sentence.

Subject and Verb Agreement

Exercise 6-2

NAME _____ SCORE _____

DIRECTIONS   In the sentences that follow, first underline the subject with one line and the verb with two lines. Then rewrite each sentence, replacing the plural subjects and verbs with singular ones and the singular subjects and verbs with plural ones. Underline the subject of the new sentence with one line and the verb of the new sentence with two lines. You will also need to change the articles (*a, an,* and *the*) to make the sentences correct.

EXAMPLES

A persuasive letter usually arrives uninvited.

Persuasive letters usually arrive uninvited.

Readers have not requested such letters.

A reader has not requested such letters.

1. Writers of effective persuasive letters convince readers to look beyond the first few lines.

   The writer of effective persuasive letters convinces readers to look beyond the first few lines.

2. The opening line of a persuasive letter is extremely important.

   The opening lines of a persuasive letter are extremely important.

3. Persuasive writers generally follow a definite plan to gain the reader's attention.

   A persuasive writer generally follows a definite plan to gain the reader's attention.

4. An appeal to the reader's self-interest forms the opening of persuasive letters.

Appeals to the reader's self-interest form the opening of persuasive letters.

5. Openings promise certain rewards to the readers, such as health, popularity, success, or some other personal benefit.

An opening promises certain rewards to the readers, like health, popularity, success, or some other personal benefit.

6. Successful advertisements suggest effective ways to open a persuasive letter.

A successful advertisement suggests effective ways to open a persuasive letter.

7. The headline of an advertisement serves much the same purpose as the opening sentence of a persuasive letter.

The headlines of an advertisement serve much the same purpose as the opening sentence of a persuasive letter.

8. Headlines get the audience to pay attention to the rest of the advertisement.

A headline gets the audience to pay attention to the rest of the advertisement.

9. In successful advertisements and in persuasive letters, the benefits promised the audience are specified.

In successful advertisements and in persuasive letters, the benefit promised the audience is specified.

10. Readers favorably impressed by persuasive letters or advertisements want to buy the product they describe.

A reader favorably impressed by persuasive letters or advertisements wants to buy the product they describe.

Deduct 10 for each blank incorrectly filled.

Singular and Plural Noun Subjects

Exercise 6-3

NAME _____ SCORE _____

DIRECTIONS   In each of the following sentences underline the subject (or subjects, if compound) with one line and match it (or them) with one of the verbs in parentheses. Circle any key word or words that affect the number of the subject. Then cross out the verb that does not agree with the subject and, in the blank, write the verb that does agree.

EXAMPLE

(A)number of appeals (is, are) available to the persuasive

writer.   _____*are*_____

1. News that benefits the reader (capitalize, capital-

izes) on the reader's secret wishes.   _____*capitalizes*_____

2. "How will such products make my life better?" (and)

"Why should I buy this product?" (is, are) the

reader's main questions.   _____*are*_____

3. Either health (or) comfort (answer, answers) those

questions.   _____*answers*_____

4. Saving money (and) being a part of the "in crowd"

(is, are) other benefits a skillful writer can offer to

the reader.   _____*are*_____

5. Promises (and) tips, of course, also (get, gets) many

readers' attention.   _____*get*_____

6. A promise of something good (or) tips about finances

favorably (impress, impresses) a reader.   _____*impress*_____

7. (A) variety of other tactics (is, are) used to gain the

reader's attention.   _____*are*_____

8. Often new <u>information</u> (or) <u>satisfaction</u> of curiosity

(~~work,~~ works) as a "promise" made to the reader of

a persuasive letter.   *works*

9. "Completely new!" (and) "You've been selected!"

(capture, ~~captures~~) the reader's attention.   *capture*

10. The (group) of attention-getting words that persua-

sive writers typically rely on (is, ~~are~~) surprisingly

small.   *is*

Singular and Plural Noun
and Pronoun Subjects

Exercise 6–4

NAME _____ SCORE _____

DIRECTIONS   In the following sentences cross out the verb in parentheses that does not agree with its subject. Then enter the correct verb in the blank.

EXAMPLE

One of the most important things to do in persuasive

letters (~~are~~, is) to involve the reader quickly.   *is*

1. Most of us (~~wants~~, want) to receive the benefits
   promised by the opening line of a persuasive letter.   *want*

2. Few of us (~~reads~~, read) far if we do not see the
   value of the product or service for ourselves.   *read*

3. One who (writes, ~~write~~) successful persuasive letters will generally introduce the word *you* in the
   first few sentences.   *writes*

4. A number of different persuasive strategies (~~is~~, are)
   commonly employed to make readers imagine the
   benefits that they will soon be enjoying.   *are*

5. "Do you have a weight problem? Is this the day
   that you finally do something about it?" are opening lines that immediately (put, ~~puts~~) a reader into
   the picture.   *put*

6. The skillful writer of these ads (~~play~~, plays) on the
   American obsession with appearing to be fat.   *plays*

7. Charts then follow that (give, ~~gives~~) desirable
   weights for men and women.   *give*

8. Those who read this letter (check, ~~checks~~) to see
   how their weight compares with the ideals listed in
   the charts.   *check*

9. Both the male and the female reader (hope, ~~hopes~~)
to be considered thin in today's weight-conscious
society.

hope

10. The letter finally (~~show~~, shows) how the product
it advertises can help readers to achieve the ideal
weight level shown on the charts.

shows

Deduct 3 1/3 for each incorrectly marked pronoun, 3 1/3 for each incorrectly marked antecedent, and 3 1/3 for each blank incorrectly filled.

Pronoun and Antecedent Agreement

Exercise 6–5

NAME _____ SCORE _____

DIRECTIONS   In each of the following sentences, select the pronoun that agrees in number with its antecedent (**Note:** sometimes the antecedent comes *after* the pronoun that refers to it); cross out the incorrect pronoun, and write in the blank whether the pronoun is singular or plural. Finally, underline the noun (or nouns) functioning as the antecedent (or antecedents) of the pronoun you selected.

EXAMPLE

The writer and the designer of an advertisement work

together to plan (~~their~~, its) contents.   *singular*

1. These advertising specialists decide on the funda-

   mental persuasive strategy (~~he~~, they) will use.   *plural*

2. The artwork in an advertisement is very impor-

   tant; (it, ~~they~~) will catch a reader's eye.   *singular*

3. Even if the reader is not aware of (~~its~~, their) effect,

   big, flashy lettering and a well-drawn illustration

   can draw attention to an advertisement.   *plural*

4. Because the visual portion of the advertisement at-

   tracts the most attention, the writer and designer

   plan (it, ~~them~~) very carefully.   *singular*

5. The most important parts of the advertisement

   should be placed where readers will notice (~~it~~,

   them).   *plural*

6. Generally, <u>advertisements</u> will devote more space to pictures than to words in order to make (~~its~~, their) point.

plural

7. The pictures in the <u>advertisement</u> should not, however, distract the reader from (its, ~~their~~) text.

singular

8. If a writer needs to include the product's <u>cost</u>, (he, it, ~~they~~) will usually appear in small print near the end of the advertisement.

singular

9. Of course, if the <u>price</u> of a company's products is a selling point, then advertisement writers will emphasize (it, ~~them~~).

singular

10. Good letter writers wishing to sell products may use the same strategy—emphasize <u>cost</u> if (it, ~~they~~) helps them to sell the product.

singular

Deduct 5 for each incorrectly marked or missed pronoun and 5 for each incorrectly revised sentence.

Avoiding Sexism in the Use
of Personal Pronouns

Exercise 6-6

NAME _____ SCORE _____

DIRECTIONS   In each of the following sentences, underline those pronouns that incorrectly exclude either gender or that stereotype male or female roles. In the space provided, rewrite each sentence to eliminate the problem. **Note:** Use whichever strategy seems most appropriate and that does not distort the original meaning of the sentence.

EXAMPLE
In advertising, a client may not always be right, but his opinions should always be
listened to.

In advertising, a client may not always be right, but his or her opinions should always be listened to.

* 1. An advertising executive must certainly be sensitive to his clients' wishes.

2. When someone designs material to sell a product, she must also think of the advertisement's potential readers.

3. Of course, the writer wants his advertisements to sell the readers on the product, but not if it means deceiving them.

4. A health care product's advertisement may promise the customer something that it cannot give her.

* *Answers for these exercises will vary depending on the strategy the student uses.*

5. If <u>he</u> is told that a company can do something, the reader has a legal right to expect that what the advertisement says is true.

6. Losing a customer's goodwill is something that the conscientious writer wants to avoid, for <u>he</u> knows that lost customers equal lost revenue for clients.

7. A successful writer of persuasive letters never forgets that <u>his</u> reader's satisfaction is the most important consideration.

8. A writer who looks at what <u>he</u> says through a reader's eyes will create effective persuasive letters.

9. Now the reader of the letter offering discounts on vitamins will see how buying them will benefit <u>her</u> personally.

10. A writer who knows <u>his</u> product and audience well can motivate the reader to buy what the letter is selling.

Mastering Agreement: A Review

Exercise 6–7

NAME _____ SCORE _____

DIRECTIONS   In the following sentences underline the subject; then cross out the verb or pronoun in parentheses that does not agree with its subject or antecedent. Write the correct pronoun or verb in the blank.

EXAMPLE
Most successful advertisements (~~appeals~~, appeal) to

both our minds and our emotions.   *appeal*

1. Details (~~convinces~~, convince) our minds to buy

what our hearts desire.   *convince*

2. Everyone wants to rationalize (~~his, her~~, his or her)

desires.   *his or her*

3. The use of details in the persuasive letter (~~provide~~,

provides) the needed rationalization.   *provides*

4. If someone (~~want~~, wants) to buy a new car, that

person must be convinced that the car is really nec-

essary.   *wants*

5. The facts the advertisement lists (~~gives~~, give) the

reader proof that that particular car is "the one."   *give*

6. Effective kinds of information (~~includes~~, include)

physical features of the product, the reputation of

the company, and the performance data.   *include*

7. Another tool for persuading readers (is, ~~are~~) the

testimonial of a satisfied customer.   *is*

8. An <u>advertisement</u> for exercise equipment demonstrates still another strategy: showing (it, ~~them~~) in use.

_it_

9. Many an out-of-shape <u>person</u> buys an exercise bike hoping to see (~~himself, herself,~~ himself or herself, ~~themselves~~) transformed into a slender, fit person like the one in the advertisement.

himself or herself

10. Of course, any <u>claim</u> that a writer makes must be (one, ~~ones~~) the reader will believe to be true.

one

11. If a writer knows the facts, the legitimate <u>promises</u> that can be made about a product or service (~~is,~~ are) usually many.

are

12. As a persuasive writer, <u>you</u> must emphasize the facts about your product that give it an edge over (your, ~~their~~) competitor's.

your

13. A successful persuasive <u>letter</u> usually (asks, ~~ask~~) the reader to do something.

asks

14. The last <u>lines</u> of the letter (~~suggests,~~ suggest) that the reader send for more information or fill out a questionnaire or an application form.

suggest

15. <u>Writers</u> of persuasive letters must clearly state what action (~~he expects,~~ they expect) the reader to take.

they expect

16. Most persuasive letters (~~follows~~, follow) a set pattern: they capture a reader's attention, interest the reader in a product, and ask for some response. _follow_

17. Sentences and paragraphs in an effective persuasive letter are relatively short; (~~its~~, their) vocabulary is simple but mature. _their_

18. The company that the writer represents must also never seem to be talking down to (its, ~~their~~) potential clients. _its_

19. Both consideration and a courteous tone (~~wins~~, win) customers. _win_

20. As in any other kind of business letter, two of the main purposes of a persuasive letter (~~is~~, are) to promote the company's product and to build goodwill for the company. _are_

7

Master and use appropriate verb forms. Learn the main tenses of verbs.

Regular Verbs   Most verbs are called regular verbs; that is, the changes they undergo to show tense (or time) are predictable; *d* or *ed* is usually added to the end of the present tense to form the past tense and the past participle. All the tenses of verbs are formed from the three principal parts of the verb—present, past, and past participle—together with auxiliary (helping) verbs, such as *will* and *have*. Thus, a verb's ending (called its *inflection*) and/or the helping verb will allow you to determine that verb's tense. Although different systems are sometimes used to classify the number of verb tenses in English, the usual practice is to distinguish six tenses.

PRESENT I prepare the report.   [denotes action (or occurrence) at the present time]

PROGRESSIVE I am preparing . . .   [denotes action in progress at the present time]

PAST I prepared the report yesterday.   [denotes action in the past]

PROGRESSIVE I was preparing . . .   [denotes action in progress at a past time]

FUTURE I will prepare the report tomorrow.   [denotes action in the future]

PROGRESSIVE I will be preparing . . .   [denotes action in progress at a future time]

PRESENT PERFECT I have prepared the report many times.   [emphasizes completion in the present of action previously begun]

PROGRESSIVE I have been preparing . . .   [emphasizes progress to the present of action previously begun]

PAST PERFECT	I had <u>prepared</u> the report before the manager requested it. [emphasizes completion at a past time of action previously begun]
PROGRESSIVE	I <u>had been preparing</u> . . . [emphasizes progress until some past time of action previously begun]
FUTURE PERFECT	I <u>will have prepared</u> the report before the manager requests it. [emphasizes completion of an action by some future time]
PROGRESSIVE	I <u>will have been preparing</u> . . . [emphasizes progress of an action continuing until some future time]

Note: You may have noticed that other words besides the main verb and its auxiliaries can express time—for example, *yesterday, tomorrow,* and *before.* The future is frequently expressed by a form of the present tense plus a word like *tomorrow* and/or an infinitive.

I <u>am preparing</u> the report *tomorrow.*

I <u>am going</u> *to prepare* the report *tomorrow.*

Irregular Verbs   Irregular verbs do not form the past and past participle in the usual way; instead, they undergo various kinds of changes or, in a few cases, no change at all. (See the chart of frequently used irregular verbs in the Appendix.)

run, ran, run, running
choose, chose, chosen, choosing
burst, burst, burst, bursting

The dictionary lists all four parts of irregular verbs, usually at the beginning of the entry. The dictionary also lists all forms of regular verbs that undergo a change in spelling for the past, the past participle, or the present participle. This change in spelling is most frequently the substitution of *i* of *y,* the doubling of the last letter, or changing *y* to *id.*

try, tried, tried, trying
occur, occurred, occurred, occurring
pay, paid, paid, paying

Auxiliary Verbs   Auxiliary verbs are combined with the basic verb forms to indicate tense or voice (active or passive), for emphasis, to ask questions, and to express the negative. The following words are commonly used as auxiliaries:

have	be	will	may
has	am		might
had	are	can	must
	is		ought to
do	was	would	has to
does	were	should	have to
did	been	could	used to

For the purpose of this discussion of auxiliaries, consider the auxiliary verb *do.* The present tense *do* (or *does*) is used with the present tense form of a verb to express questions, for the negative, and for special emphasis.

Does she *prepare* reports well?   [a question]

She *does* not (OR *doesn't*) *prepare* reports well.   [a negative]

She *does prepare* reports well.   [special emphasis]

When *did,* the past-tense form of *do,* is used as an auxiliary with a main verb, the writer emphasizes past time even though the main verb remains in the present-tense form. This *did* form is used mainly for questions, for the negative, and for special emphasis.

Did she *prepare* the report yesterday?   [a question]

She *did* not (OR *didn't*) *prepare* the report yesterday.   [a negative]

She *did prepare* the report yesterday.   [special emphasis]

Learn the Uses of the Passive Voice.   Most sentences use verbs in the active voice; that is, the verb expresses an action carried out by the subject. Sometimes, however, a writer reverses the pattern, in which case the subject does not act but is acted upon; such a verb is in the passive voice.

To form the passive voice, place a form of the verb *be* in front of the past participle form of the verb (for example—*is prepared, was prepared, has been prepared, will be prepared*).

ACTIVE VOICE   The executives often prepare reports.

PASSIVE VOICE   Reports are often prepared by the executives.

As you probably noticed from the above examples, the object of a sentence with an active verb becomes the subject of a sentence with a passive verb. In a passive verb construction, the actual person or thing doing or responsible for the action is often identified by the use of a prepositional phrase beginning with *by* (as in the example of the passive voice above). Sometimes this "agent" is left unstated in the sentence.

Writers use the passive voice when they do not know the doer of the action ("Mr. McDowell's store *was robbed* last night") or when they want to emphasize the verb or the receiver of the action of the verb ("A report *is* sometimes *rewritten* three times before it *is submitted* to upper management"). Writers employ the passive voice sparingly because it sounds highly impersonal and sometimes deprives writing of emphasis (see also section **29**).

Note: Business writers find the passive voice most useful when they do not want to hurt the reader's feelings ("The motor *was left on*" instead of "You left the motor on") or when they do not wish to use the first person pronoun in formal report writing ("The cost *was estimated* to be $10,000" rather than "I estimated the cost to be $10,000").

Deduct 2 for each error in verb choice.
Regular and Irregular Verbs

Exercise 7-1

NAME _____ SCORE _____

DIRECTIONS   Mastering verb forms, especially irregular verb forms, requires memorizing them (just as you would memorize multiplication tables or chemical formulas) and accustoming your ear to the correct forms. The best way to learn verb forms, then, is through written and oral drill of the five forms of those verbs that cause difficulty: present, past, present or past perfect (both formed from the past participle), progressive, and the form with a word such as *did* as an auxiliary.

Using the models given as your example, create short sentences for the verbs and objects or modifiers listed. Use either *he* or *she* for your subject. (Consult your dictionary if you are unsure of the way to form any of the tenses.)

EXAMPLE
draw/illustration
PRESENT

She draws an illustration.

PAST

She drew an illustration.

PRESENT PERFECT

She has drawn an illustration.

PROGRESSIVE PRESENT

She is drawing an illustration.

did FORM OF PAST AS A QUESTION

Did she draw an illustration?

1. write/business letters
PRESENT

She writes business letters.

PAST

She wrote business letters.

PRESENT PERFECT

She has written business letters.

PROGRESSIVE PRESENT

She is writing business letters.

did FORM OF PAST FOR EMPHASIS

She did write business letters.

2. speak/highly of them

PRESENT

He speaks highly of them.

PAST

He spoke highly of them.

PRESENT PERFECT

He has spoken highly of them.

PROGRESSIVE PRESENT

He is speaking highly of them.

did FORM OF PAST IN THE NEGATIVE

He did not speak highly of them.

3. bring/the contracts

PRESENT

She brings the contracts.

PAST

She brought the contracts.

PRESENT PERFECT

She has brought the contracts.

PROGRESSIVE PRESENT

She is bringing the contracts.

did FORM OF PAST AS A QUESTION

Did she bring the contracts?

4. go/back to work

PRESENT

He goes back to work.

PAST

He went back to work.

PRESENT PERFECT

He has gone back to work.

PROGRESSIVE PRESENT

He is going back to work.

did FORM OF PAST FOR EMPHASIS

He did go back to work.

5. begin/to honor the rebate
   PRESENT

   She begins to honor the rebate.

   PAST

   She began to honor the rebate.

   PRESENT PERFECT

   She has begun to honor the rebate.

   PROGRESSIVE PRESENT

   She is beginning to honor the rebate.

   did FORM OF PAST IN THE NEGATIVE

   She did not begin to honor the rebate.

6. run/the computer
   PRESENT

   He runs the computer.

   PAST

   He ran the computer.

   PRESENT PERFECT

   He has run the computer.

   PROGRESSIVE PRESENT

   He is running the computer.

   did FORM OF PAST AS A QUESTION

   Did he run the computer?

7. sit/on the board of directors
   PRESENT

   She sits on the board of directors.

   PAST

   She sat on the board of directors.

   PRESENT PERFECT

   She has sat on the board of directors.

   PROGRESSIVE PRESENT

   She is sitting on the board of directors.

   did FORM OF PAST AS A QUESTION

   Did she sit on the board of directors?

8. choose/a career

PRESENT

He chooses a career.

PAST

He chose a career.

PRESENT PERFECT

He has chosen a career.

PROGRESSIVE PRESENT

He is choosing a career.

did FORM OF PAST IN THE NEGATIVE

He did not choose a career.

9. take/the discount

PRESENT

She takes the discount.

PAST

She took the discount.

PRESENT PERFECT

She has taken the discount.

PROGRESSIVE PRESENT

She is taking the discount.

did FORM OF PAST IN THE NEGATIVE

She did not take the discount.

10. cash/checks

PRESENT

He cashes checks.

PAST

He cashed checks.

PRESENT PERFECT

He has cashed checks.

PROGRESSIVE PRESENT

He is cashing checks.

did FORM OF PAST AS A QUESTION

Did he cash checks?

Deduct 10 for each error in verb choice.
Using Irregular Verbs   Exercise 7-2

NAME _____ SCORE _____

DIRECTIONS   The questions below use either *past tense* or *future tense* verbs with the auxiliaries *did* and *will* (the verbs are underlined twice). Answer those questions having past tense verbs with statements that use the past tense form of the verb without an auxiliary. Answer those questions that have future tense verbs with statements that use the present perfect tense with *already*. Consult your dictionary for the various forms of all verbs that you are unsure of.

EXAMPLES

PAST TENSE   Did they give a report?

Yes, they gave a report.

FUTURE TENSE   Will they shake the job candidate's hand?

They have already shaken the job candidate's hand.

1. Will the pressure burst the valve?

   The pressure has already burst the valve.

2. Did the expansion of the sales district grow to be a problem?

   Yes, the expansion of the sales district grew to be a problem.

3. Will the prices fall after the announced merger?

   The prices have already fallen after the announced merger.

4. Did the public interest rise after the new year?

   Yes, the public interest rose after the new year.

5. Will you speak to the reporter?

   I have already spoken to the reporter.

6. Did the worker finally take a break?

   Yes, the worker finally took a break.

7. Will the company pay its bills?

   The company has already paid its bills.

8. Did the explosion shake the building?

   Yes, the explosion shook the building.

9. Will the project begin on schedule?

   The project has already begun on schedule.

10. Did the attorney know of the exceptions?

    Yes, the attorney knew of the exceptions.

There are four main points to be aware of when you write the tense of a verb.

(1) Be sure to put *ed* on the end of all past tense regular verbs (unless they end in *e*—in which case, simply add *d*).

When the company developed problems, a troubleshooter was requested.

Caution: Do not omit a needed *d* or *ed* because of pronunciation.

NOT His presentation *prejudice* them against him.

BUT His presentation *prejudiced* them against him.

NOT She *talk* with her supervisor.

BUT She *talked* with her supervisor.

(2) Be sure not to confuse the past tense with the past participle form.

The troubleshooter was carefully chosen [NOT *chose*].

The troubleshooter began [NOT *begun*] his investigation

(3) Be sure not to give an irregular verb the *ed* ending.

The whistle blew [NOT *blowed*] loudly at noon.

The employees knew [NOT *knowed*] what the whistle meant.

(4) Be especially careful with troublesome verbs like *lie* and *lay*, *sit* and *set*, and *rise* and *raise*.

Notice that *lie* and *sit* are alike: they signify a *state* of resting and do not take objects. Notice also that *lay* and *set* are alike: they signify the *action* of placing, and they do take objects.

He lay [NOT *laid*] down on a couch in his office.

He had sat [NOT *had set*] too long on a hard chair.

Finally, notice that while *rise* does not take an object, *raise*, on the other hand, does.

Stock prices rose [NOT *raised*] during the last month.

Verbs That Cause Difficulties

Exercise 7-3

NAME _____ SCORE _____

DIRECTIONS   After each of the following sentences the present form of a verb is given. In the blank within the sentence and also in the blank at the right, write the tense called for by the meaning of the sentence. Consult your dictionary if you are uncertain about the other forms of a verb.

EXAMPLE
Managers are frequently ___*asked*___ to

evaluate written reports.   (ask)   ___*asked*___

1. Once a report or letter is ___*assigned*___,

careful writers consider their audience.   (assign)   ___*assigned*___

2. A report that is ___*begun*___ without

much planning will make a poor impression.

(begin)   ___*begun*___

3. When you ___*sit*___ down to write a

report, select words that the reader is likely to un-

derstand.   (sit)   ___*sit*___

4. The words used are ___*drawn*___ from

the reader's familiar vocabulary.   (draw)   ___*drawn*___

5. The successful technical report is ___*written*___

using little jargon.   (write)   ___*written*___

6. A great deal of research has been ___*done*___

to determine what makes writing clear.   (do)   ___*done*___

7. The writer reports whatever has ___*occurred*___

simply and concisely.   (occur)   ___*occurred*___

8. No writer should use fifteen words to communicate

   an idea when only ten are ___*required*___. ___*required*___

   (require)

9. Recommendations ___*given*___ in

   clear, concise sentences are easier to understand.

   (give)   ___*given*___

Special Problems with Verbs   Exercise 7–4

NAME _____ SCORE _____

Make the tense of a verb in a subordinate clause or of a verbal relate logically to the tense of the verb in the main clause.

> She rested for a few minutes after she *had finished* the year-end report.   [The action of the subordinate verb, *had finished*, occurred before the action of the main verb, *rested*.]
>
> *Having finished* the year-end report, she was able to begin other projects.   [The perfect form of the verbal, *having finished*, shows action completed before the action of the main verb, *was*.]
>
> He would have wanted *to complete* the project.   [Use the present infinitive after a verb in the perfect tense.]
>
> He would want *to complete* the project.   [The present infinitive may be used after a verb that is not in the present tense.

Caution: Avoid switching tenses needlessly in a sentence. (See also **27a**.)

Use the subjunctive mood to express a condition contrary to *fact* (often introduced by *if*); to state a wish; and to express a demand, a recommendation, or a request in a *that* clause.

> If we were given an extra week, we *might finish* this report on time.
>
> They wished they *were* better report writers.
>
> Your supervisor insisted that you *be given* this assignment.

Use the present tense to state facts or ideas that are generally regarded as being true.

> A clearly presented report *shows* the reader the answers.
>
> Hast *makes* waste.

DIRECTIONS   In the following sentences cross out the incorrect form of the subordinate verb or verbal in parentheses and write the correct form in the blank.

EXAMPLE

After Julio (~~studied~~, had studied) his first draft, he found many words that he could omit.

had studied

1. Julio wanted (to write, ~~to have written~~) as clearly and concisely as possible.

   to write,

2. When he finished his report, he found that he (~~included~~, had included) many unnecessary words.

   had included

3. Remembering to eliminate useless words, Julio (~~deletes~~, deleted) "in regard to" and wrote "regarding."

   deleted

4. He ought (~~to say~~, to have said) "since" instead of "in view of the fact that."

   to have said.

5. "If I (~~was~~, were) the reader of this report," Julio thought, "I would not want to waste time with meaningless words."

   were

6. After he (~~inspects~~, had inspected) his first draft even more carefully, he found many weak "there is" and "there are" sentences.

   had inspected.

7. In one paragraph, he (~~wrote~~, had written), "There is a product available," when he should have said, "A product is available."

   had written

8. "This report requires that my words (~~are~~, be) carefully chosen," Julio reminded himself.

   be

9. He realized that it is generally wise (to choose, ~~to have chosen~~) the shortest wording possible.

   to choose.

10. (~~Working~~, Having worked) hard to eliminate wordiness, Julio found the final draft easier to complete.

    Having worked

Mastering Verbs: A Review   Exercise 7-5

NAME _____ SCORE _____

DIRECTIONS   In the following sentences cross out the incorrect form of the verb in parentheses and write the correct form in the blank.

EXAMPLE
Writers who have (~~chose~~, chosen) their verbs with care

make their points clearly.   *chosen*

1. One place many writers (get, ~~have got~~) into trouble
   is with word choice, especially verbs.   *get*

2. Like spelling errors, verb errors (~~will rise~~, will
   raise) doubts about a writer's accuracy.   *will raise*

3. When I began writing business reports, I (~~use~~,
   used) to like long sentences.   *used*

4. I was (~~advise~~, advised) to be concise, even with
   verbs.   *advised*

5. I had (~~suppose~~, supposed) they made me sound in-
   telligent, but they only made my writing wordy.   *supposed*

6. One type of wordiness is (~~cause~~, caused) by the use
   of long verbal phrases.   *caused*

7. Some writers are (~~tempt~~, tempted) to use wordy
   verbal phrases such as *be in receipt of* instead of
   the less-stuffy *received*.   *tempted*

8. When you have the choice, the simpler, clearer
   verbs should be (~~select~~, selected).   *selected*

9. Many reports have been (~~wrote~~, written) that
   could have communicated the same point with
   fewer words.   *written*

10. The use of long verbal phrases has often (~~lead~~, led)
    to confusion for the reader.   *led*

11. The verbs *get* and *make* are sometimes (~~use,~~ used) too frequently by poor writers.

        used

12. Many managers have (~~shook,~~ shaken) their heads at the number of *gets* found in a report.

        shaken

13. One such report (began, ~~begun~~): "After we get through investigating all products now available, we will get a look at the ones still under development."

        began

14. Because active verbs result in more concise, informative sentences, report writers have generally (~~choose,~~ chosen) them over passive verbs.

        chosen

15. A passive verb is "slow" because it always (~~require,~~ requires) an additional verb, a form of *be,* and often a *by* phrase.

        requires

16. No definite rules can be (~~sit,~~ set) for when it is appropriate to use the passive voice.

        set

17. However, a formula can be (~~lay,~~ laid, ~~lain~~) out: passive verbs can be used when the doer of the action is not known.

        laid

18. If the doer of the action is not (~~saw,~~ seen) as more important than the receiver of the action, then a passive verb is appropriate.

        seen

19. *The store gave each customer a ten-percent discount* emphasizes the store's action, whereas *Each customer was (~~gave,~~ given) a ten-percent discount* emphasizes the customer.

        given

20. One thing that my teacher (~~claim,~~ claimed) was essential was to proofread carefully to make sure that all verb tenses were correct.

        claimed

MANUSCRIPT FORM   ms 8

8

Follow acceptable form in writing your paper. (See also section **35**.)

Business letters, memorandums, and reports have definite formats, which are illustrated in section **35**. The format for an essay written in college varies according to the length of the paper. The average college writing assignment usually requires no more than the essay itself and sometimes an outline and a title page. A research paper, on the other hand, may include a title page, an outline, the text, an endnote page or pages, and a bibliography.

Whether you are writing for college or a career, the most important advice to remember about format is to follow the directions given by your instructor or your supervisor. Many instructors and supervisors refuse to read papers that do not follow the format guidelines that they have specified.

Usually a college instructor's guidelines for manuscript preparation include the points discussed in this section.

8a Use proper materials.

If you handwrite your papers, use wide-lined, $8\frac{1}{2} \times 11$-inch theme paper (not torn from a spiral notebook). Write in blue or black ink on one side of the paper only.

If you type your papers, use regular white $8\frac{1}{2} \times 11$-inch typing paper (neither erasable bond nor onion skin). Use a fresh black ribbon, double-space between lines, and type on one side of the paper only. Avoid fancy typefaces such as a script or all-capitals.

Note: In business writing, handwritten documents are generally not acceptable.

8b Arrange your writing in clear and orderly fashion on the page.

Margins   Theme paper usually has the margins already marked. With unlined paper, be sure to leave about one-inch margins on all sides (except for page numbers).

Indentions   Indent the first lines of paragraphs uniformly: about an inch in handwritten copy and five spaces on the typewriter. Leave no long gap at the end of any line except the last one in a paragraph.

Paging   Use Arabic numerals (1, 2, and so forth)—without parentheses or periods—in the upper right-hand corner to mark all pages.

Heading   Instructors vary in what information they require and where they want this information placed. Usually papers carry the name of the student, the course title and number, the instructor's name, and the date. Often the number of the assignment is also included. This information should be placed one inch from the top and one inch from the left edge of the page, double-spacing after each line.

Title　　Center the title and double-space between the lines of a long title. Use neither quotation marks nor underlining with your title. Capitalize the first word of the title and all other words except articles, coordinating conjunctions, prepositions, and the *to* in infinitives. Leave one blank line between the title and the first paragraph. (Your instructor may ask you to make a title page. If so, you need not rewrite the title on the first page of the paper unless your instructor asks you to do so.)

Punctuation　　Never begin a line of your paper with a comma, a colon, a semicolon, a dash, or an end mark of punctuation; never end a line with the first of a pair of brackets, parentheses, or quotation marks.

Binding　　Unless directed to do otherwise, secure the pages of your paper with a paper clip; do not use staples, pins, or plastic folders.

Note:　Business reports are often punched and secured in a folder with prongs. Avoid plastic report covers having slide-on spines since pages easily pop out of this type of holder.

8c Write, type, or print out your manuscript for easy and accurate reading.

Avoid fancy handwriting flourishes or crowded lines. If your instructor allows you to cross out mistakes, do so neatly. If such corrections become so numerous that the page looks messy or is difficult to read, recopy it. You may prefer to use correction fluid or erasable ink to fix mistakes so that your finished product will create a good impression. If you type, be sure that your ribbon is reasonably fresh and that the type is clean. If you make errors, correct them neatly with correction tape or fluid. Whether writing or typing, do not use erasable bond paper; it smears and looks messy.

　　If you use a word processor to produce your paper, check with your instructor first to see if the typeface and paper that you plan to use are acceptable. Daisy wheel and laser printers produce letter-quality print that is always acceptable. With a dot matrix printer, however, make sure that it produces *p*'s, *q*'s, and *y*'s that descend below the line and *b*'s, *d*'s, and *t*'s that ascend above the line. Select the near-letter-quality mode on your printer or from your word processing program's printing options. The paper that you use should be good quality with perforations that tear cleanly on all edges. Finally, check to see that the printer's ribbon is fresh.

8d Whenever possible, avoid dividing a word at the end of a line. Make such divisions only between syllables and according to standard practice.

The best way to determine where to divide a word that comes at the end of a line is to check a dictionary for the syllable markings (usually indicated by dots).

In general, though, remember these guidelines: never divide a single-syllable word; do not carry over to the next line one letter of a word or a syllable like *ed;* divide a hyphenated word only at the hyphen. Keep in mind that an uneven right-hand margin is to be expected and that too many divisions at the ends of lines make a paper difficult to read.

8e Revise and proofread your manuscript with care.

For papers written out of class, be sure to go over your rough draft and revise it carefully. It is helpful to set the paper aside for several hours or even a day before you begin reworking it. Doing so will give you greater objectivity and make it easier for you to spot places in need of extra work.

Few people create good papers without revising their first draft. A carefully revised piece of writing takes work and concentration, but the time you spend on this part of the writing process will pay off in a more clearly expressed, well-organized final draft. When you need to make a change, draw a straight horizontal line through the part to be deleted and insert a caret (ʌ) at the point where the addition that is written above the line is to be made.

8f Keep a record of your revisions to help you improve your writing.

So that you can keep track of your progress and so that you will gain an understanding of what types of errors you routinely make and the problems that you frequently have, keep a list of the comments your instructor makes on your papers for future reference. Be sure to update your list frequently.

8g Use a word processor effectively.

A word processor can do much more for a writer than simply produce neatly formatted, typo-free printed pages—which isn't such a small benefit in and of itself! But for a writer wanting to get the most out of drafting and revision work, the word processor is a real breakthrough since such machines enable you to insert and delete even large blocks of material with ease. Thus, a writer who works with a word processor can tinker with a text until it is clear and effective without having to recopy or retype passages in order to do so.

Furthermore, your word processor's search feature will allow you to check a draft for such things as a repetition, weak use of the passive voice, and inconsistencies in terminology. A style-check program can evaluate your paper for many kinds of grammatical problems and other mannerisms that may cause readers difficulties, including wordiness and the use of sexist language. A spelling checker can scan your text for typographical errors, but be aware that no program can identify *misused* words—*it's* for *its,* or *there* for *their* or *they're,* for instance. If you are a poor speller, however, over time such a program can actually help you to improve your spelling.

Word processors also allow their users to create sophisticated-looking texts. They will number pages automatically, space lines as you wish them to appear, alter the number of lines per page, produce a variety of different type styles (italic, boldface, to name two), underline words and phrases, and number notes. *Unless* your printer can produce proportional spacing, do not have your word processor justify (make even) the right margin, for the resulting lines contain added spaces between words that make reading difficult.

A word processor is a genuine writing tool, but one that you must learn to use to its best advantage. These machines won't do your thinking for you, and they won't catch oversights that result from making a series of rapid deletions and insertions that leaves parts of the old version in odd places on the page. Used as a means to manipulate the text you have written, the word processor will help you to develop and improve as a writer. But because they *are* only machines, be sure to proofread all final drafts very carefully for inadvertent errors.

9

Learn to capitalize words in accordance with current practices. Avoid unnecessary capitals.

In general, capital letters are used for first words (the first word of a sentence, including a quoted sentence, a line of poetry, the salutation and complimentary close of a letter, and an item in an outline) and for names of specific persons, places, and things (in other words, proper nouns). A recently published dictionary is your best guide to current standards for capitalization and for the use of italics, abbreviations, and numbers.

The most important rules for capitalization are listed below, but you may find the style sheet on the next page as helpful as the rules.

9a Capitalize words referring to persons, places, things, times, organizations, races (option: Blacks or blacks), and religions, but not words that refer to classes of persons, places, or things. Capitalize geographic locations only when they refer to specific areas of the country (*the West Coast*) or the world (*the Near East*).

> Most of the doctors in the East attended the medical convention held in Atlanta, Georgia, last August.
> We are taking Business English 201 and also a course in report writing at the University of North Carolina.

9b In general, capitalize a title that immediately precedes (but not one that follows) the name of a person. Capitalize nouns that indicate family relationships when they are used as names or titles or are written in combination with names (*Uncle Ben*).

> My mother and her sister, my Aunt Nancy, met Professor Joseph Tate of the English Department and also the heads of several departments of Northern State College.

Note: Usage varies with regard to capitalization of titles of high rank and titles of family members.

> Michael Dukakis is governor (or Governor) of Massachusetts.

9c Capitalize the first word and the last word of a title, and all other key words (not *a, an,* or *the,* prepositions, coordinating conjunctions, or the *to* in infinitives).

> I think that *How to Write for the World of Work* is an excellent reference book for all occupational writers.

Note: When only a part of a sentence is quoted, the first word is not capitalized.

Exception: Titles in an APA-style reference list.

> Most experts agree that workers in the twenty-first century will demand "a bigger voice in decisions that affect their job performance."

9d Capitalize the pronoun *I*, the interjection *O*, most nouns referring to the deity (*the Almighty*), and words that express personification (*the Four Horsemen of the Apocalypse*).

9e Capitalize the first word of each sentence (including a quoted sentence).

> I told my boss, "The report will be in the mail tomorrow."

Style sheet for capitalization

SPECIFIC PERSONS   Shakespeare, Buddha, Mr. Keogh, Mayor Koenig

SPECIFIC PLACES   Puerto Rico; Atlanta, Georgia; Western Avenue; the West (BUT "he lives west of here"); Broughton High School

SPECIFIC THINGS   the Statue of Liberty, the Bible, History 304 (BUT history class), the First World War, Parkinson's disease, Sanka coffee

SPECIFIC TIMES AND EVENTS   Wednesday, July (BUT winter, spring, summer, fall, autumn), Thanksgiving, the Age of Enlightenment, the Great Depression (BUT the twentieth century)

SPECIFIC ORGANIZATIONS   the Peace Corps, the Rotary Club, Phi Kappa Phi

SPECIFIC POLITICAL AND MILITARY BODIES   State Department, the United States Senate, Republican Party, United States Army (BUT the army)

RELIGIONS AND BELIEFS   Judaism, Methodists, Marxism (BUT capitalism, communism)

WORDS DERIVED FROM PROPER NAMES   Swedish, New Yorker, Oriental rugs, Labrador retriever

ESSENTIAL PARTS OF PROPER NAMES   the Bill of Rights, the Battle of the Bulge, the New Deal

PARTS OF A LETTER   Dear Mr. Jacobs, Very truly yours

ITEMS IN AN OUTLINE   I. Parts of a letter
          A. Date
          B. Inside address

Deduct 3 1/3 for each blank incorrectly filled and 3 1/3 for each incorrect revision.

Capitalization   Exercise 9–1

NAME _____ SCORE _____

DIRECTIONS   A word or words in one of each of the following pairs should be capitalized. Identify the group that needs capitalization by writing either *a* or *b* in the blank.
Then revise the appropriate group of words.

EXAMPLE
(a) a class in ecology at our college

(b) ecology 1101 at washington state university   _b_

1. (a) drove to new mexico during christmas season

   (b) drove south during the holiday   _a_

2. (a) "what you really want from your job" in psychology today

   (b) an article in a popular magazine about psychology   _a_

3. (a) flying west to visit a university campus

   (b) a branch campus in the west   _b_

4. (a) gothic architecture

   (b) modern architecture   _a_

5. (a) the president of our company

   (b) president Lee Iacocca of chrysler corporation.   _b_

6. (a) wrote, "you have the contract."

   (b) wrote that you have the contract   _a_

7. (a) the god of the sun

   (b) the gods of the ancient greeks   _b_

8. (a) bought an apple computer

   (b) bought a computer for the home office   _a_

9. (a) the nineteenth century

   (b) the *a*ge of *R*eason   _b_

10. (a) the representative from our district

   (b) *R*epresentative *C*owles speaking during assembly   _b_

11. (a) the *B*lue *R*idge *m*ountains

   (b) the mountains of our southern counties   _a_

12. (a) *H*odgkin's disease

   (b) measles   _a_

13. (a) reading *m*egatrends

   (b) reading an interesting behavioral psychology essay   _a_

14. (a) a course in *F*rench

   (b) a course in business law   _a_

15. (a) the *G*erman *A*rmy during *W*orld *W*ar II

   (b) an army during the war   _a_

Capitalization   Exercise 9–2

NAME _____ SCORE _____

DIRECTIONS   Each of the following sentences contains words and word groups that require capitalization. First, underline once the letters that should be capitalized; then
rewrite the sentences with the appropriate words or word groups capitalized.

EXAMPLE
A friend of mine from south america is studying geology at columbia university this

summer.

A friend of mine from South America is studying geology at Columbia University this summer.

1. The wall street journal ran an interesting series several years ago entitled

"the new american corporation in a global economy."

The Wall Street Journal ran an interesting series several years ago entitled "The New American Corporation in a Global Economy."

2. secretary of state marilyn hodges said that the visiting dignitaries would

arrive on monday, march 15.

Secretary of State Marilyn Hodges said that the visiting dignitaries would arrive on Monday, March 15.

3. On wednesday the catholics in our firm took the day off to observe a reli-

gious holiday.

On Wednesday the Catholics in our firm took the day off to observe a religious holiday.

4. The president of our college and professor karen carmean of the decision sciences department spoke at a meeting of the academic computing association.

The president of our college and Professor Karen Carmean of the Decision Sciences Department spoke at a meeting of the Academic Computing Association.

5. ROLM corporation, a telecommunications-equipment company in la canada, california, provides a full recreational center for its employees.

ROLM Corporation, a telecommunications-equipment company in La Canada, California, provides a full recreational center for its employees.

6. This fall we hope to visit the shedd aquarium and the hancock building while we are vacationing in the midwest.

This fall we hope to visit the Shedd Aquarium and the Hancock Building while we are vacationing in the Midwest.

7. Many companies, like the nabisco corporation, have corporate headquarters in winston-salem, north carolina.

Many companies, like the Nabisco Corporation, have corporate headquarters in Winston-Salem, North Carolina.

8. The professor in business economics 203 said, "i hope you finish your term project during spring break."

The professor in Business Economics 203 said, "I hope you finish your term project during spring break."

10

Underline words that should be printed in italics.

To show which words should be printed in italics, use underlining. If your composition were to be set in type by a printer, the words that you have underlined would then appear in italic type.

Since some of the rules for the use of quotation marks and italics overlap, you may want to study section **16** together with this section. In general, italics are used for works that are contained under one cover, while quotation marks are used for works that are parts of longer works.

> The article "Importing a Recession" appeared in a recent issue of *Newsweek.*
> Flannery O'Connor's short story "The Life You Save May Be Your Own" is a part of the collection *A Good Man Is Hard to Find.*
> "The Imperial March" is from *The Empire Strikes Back.*

10a Italicize (underline) the titles of books, plays, films, radio and television programs, entire recordings, long poems (several pages), software programs, and titles of magazines, journals, and newspapers.

> *Dangerous Words: A Guide to the Law of Libel* can help you understand the power of the written word.
> *Wall Street,* a popular movie of the late 1980s, called attention to the corruption of some investment brokers.
> Archibald MacLeish wrote his play *J.B.* in verse.

Note: Italicize legal citations.

> In 1973 the Supreme Court ruled in the case of *San Antonio Independent School District v. Rodriguez* that property taxes could be used to finance public education.

10b Italicize (underline) foreign words and phrases that are not a part of the English vocabulary.

> Most people would not think wearing jeans, a sweatshirt, and tennis shoes to a job interview to be *très chic.* [In general, it is best to avoid a foreign term when an English equivalent is available.]

Note: Many words that were italicized as foreign—like *coup d'état* and *détente*—are now so frequently used that the italics have been dropped.

10c Italicize (underline) the names of specific ships, airplanes, satellites, and spacecraft as well as works of art.

> The space shuttle *Discovery* returned to space in 1988.
> She saw the *Mona Lisa* at the Louvre in Paris.

10d Italicize (underline) words, letters, and figures spoken of as such.

Remember that *misspelled* has two *s*'s and two *l*'s.

The word *petroleum* comes from two Latin words—*petra*, which means "rock," and *oleum*, which means "oil."

Note: Quotation marks may also be used to identify words used as such.

The word "petroleum" comes from two Latin words—*petra*, which means "rock" and *oleum*, which means "oil."

Deduct 5 for each incorrect underlining.

Italics   Exercise 10–1

NAME _____ SCORE _____

DIRECTIONS   In the following sentences underline the words or word groups that should be printed in italics.

EXAMPLE
The movie Silkwood shows what happens when one person tries to fight the system.

1. We went to see Nine-to-Five, a film about three secretaries.

2. Probably the most famous single ruling of the Supreme Court was handed down in 1954 in Brown v. Topeka Board of Education, which made segregation in the public schools unconstitutional.

3. Some people would argue that the Pilgrims' Mayflower was the first "company car."

4. I used to forget that in restaurant the first a is followed by a u.

5. Many people forget that the possessive pronoun has no apostrophe, and so they write it's when they mean its.

6. Bruce Springsteen's album Born in the USA contains many songs about working men and women.

7. The One-Minute Manager is a very interesting book about how to be an effective supervisor.

8. The* Atlanta Journal–Atlanta Constitution ran an interesting series of articles entitled "Working in the Year 2000."

9. My English class is reading The Jungle, Upton Sinclair's exposé of the meat packing industry.

10. Arthur Miller's play, Death of a Salesman, portrays a "little man" ground down by the system.

11. The term ergonomics, which means "fitting the work to the worker," has an ics on the end, as do many of the names of other applied sciences.

12. The first Russian spacecraft was called Sputnik.

*The is also acceptable.

13. The Smithsonian Air and Space Museum in Washington has the original airplane flown by the Wright brothers in 1903 as well as Charles Lindbergh's Spirit of St. Louis.

14. Surprisingly, Herman Melville's novel Moby Dick used the slang expression cool, a word made popular in the 1970s by the television character "The Fonz" of Happy Days.

15. The word advertise comes from the Middle English word advertisen, which means "to notify."

11

Follow current practices in the use of abbreviations, acronyms, and numbers.

Abbreviations are more common in business and technical writing than in other kinds of composition, but even there writers should take note of the following. First, a writer should only use those abbreviations that the reader is sure to understand. Second, a letter, memo, or report should never look as though it is overflowing with abbreviations. Finally, once an abbreviation has been introduced, the writer should use it consistently throughout the document.

Acronyms abound in almost any field; an acronym is a word made up of the first letters in a compound phrase—for instance, NASA, which stands for National Aeronautics and Space Administration. Few things are as annoying to a reader as an avalanche of these "invented" words. When you use an acronym, always write out the complete phrase or title the first time unless it is one that all your readers will understand.

Figures are commonly used in occupational writing except when a number is the first word in a sentence or when the number to be used is ten or under. In other kinds of writing, figures are used only when the numbers could not be written out in one or two words (for example, 150; 2,300; $250.00) or when a series of numbers is being reported.

11a Certain abbreviations are commonly used even for first references.

TITLES   Ms. (or Ms), Mr., Mrs., Dr.

Caution: Do not use redundant titles: Dr. H. U. Farr OR H. U. Farr, PhD [NOT Dr. H. U. Farr, PhD]

TIMES	a.m. (OR AM), p.m. (OR PM), BC, AD, E.S.T.
DEGREE	BS, MA, PhD, CPA
PLACES	USA, USSR
ORGANIZATIONS	TVA, UNICEF, HEW, FBI, NASA [Notice that the abbreviations for organizations require no periods.]
LATIN TERMS	etc. (and so forth), i.e. (that is), e.g. (for example), cf. (compare), vs. (versus) [Do not interchange *i.e.* and *e.g.*]

Note: Today the English forms (enclosed in parentheses) are generally preferred over their Latin equivalents.

11b Spell out the names of states, countries, continents, months, days of the week, and units of measurement.

> *Great Britain* (NOT *G.B.*), *New York* (NOT *N.Y.*) [except for long names, like
>   *USSR* for Union of Soviet Socialist Republics or *DC* for District of Columbia]
> *January* (NOT *Jan.*)
> *Wednesday* (NOT *Wed.*)
> nine *pounds* (NOT *nine lbs.*)
> *Washington* (NOT *WA* or *Wash.*) [It is appropriate to use the two-letter Post
>   Office abbreviations for states on envelopes and in the heading and return ad-
>   dress sections of business letters.]
> *and* (NOT *&*)

Note: Do not use & (the ampersand) except in copying official titles or names of firms: AT&T.

Note: Use appropriate postal abbreviations on envelopes:

AL	Alabama	KY	Kentucky	ND	North Dakota
AK	Alaska	LA	Louisiana	OH	Ohio
AZ	Arizona	ME	Maine	OK	Oklahoma
AR	Arkansas	MD	Maryland	OR	Oregon
CA	California	MA	Massachusetts	PA	Pennsylvania
CO	Colorado	MI	Michigan	PR	Puerto Rico
CT	Connecticut	MN	Minnesota	RI	Rhode Island
DE	Delaware	MS	Mississippi	SC	South Carolina
DC	District of Columbia	MO	Missouri	SD	South Dakota
FL	Florida	MT	Montana	TN	Tennessee
GA	Georgia	NE	Nebraska	TX	Texas
HI	Hawaii	NV	Nevada	UT	Utah
ID	Idaho	NH	New Hampshire	VT	Vermont
IL	Illinois	NJ	New Jersey	VA	Virginia
IN	Indiana	NM	New Mexico	WA	Washington (state)
IA	Iowa	NY	New York	WV	West Virginia
KS	Kansas	NC	North Carolina	WI	Wisconsin
				WY	Wyoming

11c Spell out *Street, Avenue, Road, Park, Mount, River, Company,* and other similar words used as a part of a proper name.

Abbreviations such as *Prof., Sen., 1st Lt.,* or *Capt.* should be used only before initials or full names (Prof. Rex H. Lankowski) and not before last names alone.

11d Spell out the words *volume, chapter,* and *page* and the names of courses of study.

> *chapter* 9 (NOT *ch.* 9)
> *biology* (NOT *bio.*)

11e Spell out the meaning of any acronym your reader may not know when you first use it.

The **R**ead **O**nly **M**emory (ROM) of the computer contains the routines that make it run. The ROM cannot be altered.

OR

The computer's ROM (Read Only Memory) is installed when it is manufactured.

11f Follow acceptable practices for writing numbers; be consistent.

The *forty*-hour workweek may soon be changed to *thirty-five* hours.
In 1976 our country was *200* years old; our state, *187;* and our county, *125.*

Note: When numbers are used infrequently in a text, writers usually spell out those that can be expressed in one or two words and use figures for all others. Business and technical writers generally use figures for all numbers above ten except when (1) a number occurs at the beginning of the sentence; (2) a fraction is used alone; or (3) the exact amount or number is not known.

The *40*-hour workweek may soon be changed to *35* hours.
One hundred years ago the average American worked about *fifty-five* hours a week, or *one-third* of the *168* hours in a week.

In documentation for reports and charts, certain abbreviations are commonly used: *p.* (page), *pp.* (pages), *col.* (column), *cols.* (columns), *no.* (number), *nos.* (numbers).

In special circumstances—for instance, in tables or footnotes, where space is limited—any abbreviation listed in a standard dictionary is acceptable.

Deduct 10 for each incorrect answer.

Abbreviations and Numbers   Exercise 11-1

NAME _____ SCORE _____

DIRECTIONS   Change any part of each of the following items to an abbreviation or a figure if the abbreviation or figure would be appropriate as a first reference in writing (not in tables or footnotes). Write your revision in the blank. If it would not be correct written as a number or figure, rewrite the item as it stands.

EXAMPLES
Three o'clock in the evening
3 p.m. or 3 P M

this Wednesday afternoon
this Wednesday afternoon

1. twenty-seven percent
27 percent

2. sixty-eight pounds, fourteen ounces
68 pounds, 14 ounces

3. Ridgeview Road at Ferris Boulevard
Ridgeview Road at Ferris Boulevard

4. nine hundred years before Christ
900 B C

5. page twelve of part five
page 12 of part five

6. Captain Brewster
Captain Brewster

7. Monte di Santi, Master of Science
Monte di Santi, M S

8. three hundred and sixty-five dollars
$ 365.00

9. the lieutenant governor of Idaho
the lieutenant governor of Idaho

10. the introductory chemistry classes in Rankin Hall
the introductory chemistry class in Rankin Hall

DIRECTIONS   Rewrite the following sentences to correct any errors in the use of abbreviations, acronyms, or numbers. If the sentence is correct, rewrite it as it stands.

11. After looking for nearly 6 hours, Martha found the figure seventy-five percent on page 126 of the book.

After looking for nearly six hours, Martha found the figure 75 percent on page 126 of the book.

12. Emory said he liked the advertisement & that he would buy the computer.

Emory said he liked the advertisement and that he would buy the computer.

13. The only tax shelter that Fred qualified for was an IRA (Individual Retirement Account).

The only tax shelter that Fred qualified for was an IRA (Individual Retirement Account).

14. The sales force generally meets the first Tues. in Mar. and Sept.

The sales force generally meets the first Tuesday in March and September.

15. The office is located at Sixty Locust St. in Boone, NC.

The office is located at 60 Locust Street in Boone, North Carolina.

16. I believe he said that Gen. Huntley's Feb. report is overdue.

I believe he said that General Huntley's February report is overdue.

17. The lawyer said that a Mich. firm submitted the lowest bid.

The lawyer said that a Michigan firm submitted the lowest bid.

18. Xavier will have been at IBM 25 years as of Jan. 28, 1989.

Xavier will have been at IBM twenty-five years as of January 28, 1989.

19. Their general practitioner (GP) is Dr. Theresa L. Braker, MD.

Their general practitioner (G.P.) is Dr. Theresa L. Braker. or Theresa L. Braker, M.D.

20. 370 customers ordered the product in the first fifteen days after it went on sale.

Three hundred seventy customers ordered the product in the first fifteen days after it went on sale.

Deduct 3 1/3 for each word or word group incorrectly revised.

Capitalization, Italics, Abbreviations,
Acronyms, and Numbers: A Review   Exercise 11-2

NAME _____ SCORE _____

DIRECTIONS   The following passages have been altered to include errors. Revise them
to reflect the correct use of capital letters, italics, abbreviations, acronyms, and numbers. (In the scoring, a word group counts as a single change.) Apply the business writing
principles discussed in **11f**.

T
tests over the years show that the average sentence length in successful pulp magazines

12   15
has been kept between ~~twelve~~ and ~~fifteen~~ words. The Reader's Digest average is consist-

and
ently between 14 and 17, ~~&~~ that of Time 17 to 19. Our count of 3-syllable words shows

3
the following averages for the same publications: True Confessions, ~~three~~ percent;

9   10
Reader's Digest, 8 to 9 percent; Time, ~~nine~~ to ~~ten~~ percent.   —ROBERT GUNNING, *The*

Technique of Clear Writing

    Career decision-making, whether it involves choosing or changing one's job,

M
is an important process. ~~m~~ost people spend more than 100,000 hours—one-sixth

Charles F.   B S   i
of their lives—at work. As ~~Chas. F.~~ Kettering, ~~bachelor of science,~~ the ~~I~~nventor

e   T
and ~~E~~ngineer, once said, "~~t~~he future is all we are interested in, because we are

O
going to spend the rest of our lives there. ~~o~~bviously, anything that takes up so

much of our lives should be carefully planned—to ensure a career directed by

c   c
~~C~~hoice rather than ~~C~~hance.   —DEAN L. HUMMEL, "What Should I Be When I Grow

Up?"

* *Gunning writes out these numbers, but business writers would use figures.*

Rangeley, ~~ME~~, is the home of ~~Tranet~~ (transnational network for appropriate alternative technologies). . . . TRANET's purpose is to link people, projects, & resources in the appropriate technical community. The network has ~~five hun-dred~~ members worldwide, publishes a quarterly newspaper, . . . maintains files on some ~~fifteen hundred~~ Appropriate Technology Projects & 10,000 individuals, has an extensive library, and is able to arrange many successful linkages.

—JOHN NAISBITT, *Megatrends: Ten New Directions Transforming Our Lives.*

THE COMMA

12 and 13

Let sentence structure guide you in the use of commas.

In speaking, you use pauses and changes in voice pitch to make the meaning of your sentences clear. In writing, you use punctuation marks in a similar way, especially as you make additions to the basic pattern. As you will recall from section **1**, the word order of a basic sentence follows a subject—verb—complement pattern:

SUBJECT VERB COMPLEMENT

The company president decided to fund the project.

Often, however, the sentences that you write will vary this basic pattern.

PATTERN *Addition,* subject—verb—complement.

After studying the report, the company president decided to fund the project.

PATTERN Subject, *addition,* verb—complement.

The company president, *after studying the report,* decided to fund the project.

PATTERN Subject—verb, *addition,* complement.

The company president decided, *after studying the report,* to fund the project.

PATTERN Subject—verb—complement, *addition.*

The company president decided to fund the project, *after studying the report.*

Five main rules govern the use of the comma. In the exercises that follow, each of these rules is explained and illustrated (**12a**, **12b**, and so forth). Cautions against the corresponding misuses are also provided (**13a**, **13b**, and so forth).

12a A comma follows a main clause that is linked to another main clause by a coordinating conjunction—*and, but, or, for, so, yet*. This construction is called a *compound sentence*.

PATTERN   MAIN CLAUSE, coordinating conjunction MAIN CLAUSE.

> Businesses submit written proposals to gain new contracts**,** *and* experienced writers have the responsibility for producing them.

Caution: Do not place a comma after a coordinating conjunction linking main clauses.

NOT   Businesses submit written proposals to gain new contracts, and**,** experienced writers have the responsibility for producing them.

Note: The semicolon may also be used when the two main clauses linked by the coordinating conjunction contain other commas.

> Businesses**,** and sometimes private individuals**,** submit written proposals to gain new contracts**;** and experienced writers**,** or teams of writers and technicians**,** have the responsibility for producing them.

13b(1) A comma is not used *after* a coordinating conjunction.

(Throughout this section, a circled comma ⊙ indicates a misuse of the comma.)

> Businesses submit proposals for many purposes, and ⊙ these documents follow a variety of formats.   [The comma comes *before*, but not *after*, the coordinating conjunction.]

13b(2) Nor is a comma used *before* a coordinating conjunction when only words, phrases, or subordinate clauses (rather than main clauses) are being linked.

TWO WORDS   Proposals vary in both length ⊙ and format.   [A comma is not used before a coordinating conjunction that links two words or phrases.]

TWO SUBORDINATE Because proposals are time-consuming to write ⊙ and be-
CLAUSES   cause they often treat complex problems, they require careful planning.   [A comma is not used before a coordinating conjunction that links two subordinate clauses.]

Deduct 5 for each incorrectly placed or omitted comma and 5 for each blank incorrectly filled.

Commas and Coordinating Conjunctions

Exercise 12/13–1

NAME _____ SCORE _____

DIRECTIONS   In the following sentences insert an inverted caret (**V**) before coordinating conjunctions that connect main clauses. Then insert a comma after the first main clause and write a comma and the conjunction in the blank. If a sentence having no commas is correct as it stands, write *C* in the blank to indicate that no comma is needed. If a sentence contains a misused comma, circle the comma; then place a circled comma (Ⓓ) in the blank.

EXAMPLES

People or companies submit written proposals,ᵛand these documents

explain what the company or person will do for someone and at

what price.   _,and_

Many times proposals total hundreds of pages, but short proposals

need to be thorough and specific too.   _C_

1. A good proposal convinces the reader that its writer under-

   stands the company's needs, and offers a practical solution to

   the problem.   _Ⓓ_

2. Your company may have specific guidelines for proposal writ-

   ing, so your document should conform to those requirements. _C_

3. A proposal must make clear what needs to be done, and how

   it will be accomplished.   _Ⓓ_

4. Details are important, and your proposal should include spe-

   cific time schedules and budgets.   _C_

5. But such details should be selected and organized, so that they

   do not overwhelm the reader.   _Ⓓ_

6. Personal qualifications may be important,ᵛso you may wish to

   include background about key personnel.   _,so_

7. One problem a proposal writer faces is "overkill,"ᵛbut your

   proposal must include enough information to be convincing. _,"but_

8. Sometimes a company or a client will ask you to investigate a

   problem,ᵛand they will require you to submit a proposal show-

   ing how your firm would solve it.   _,and_

9. An *unsolicited* proposal must persuade a company that it has a problem and it must convince them that you are the one to solve it.

　　　　　　　　　　　　　　　　　　　　, and

10. An unsolicited proposal is more difficult to write for you must devise your own pattern of organization.

　　　　　　　　　　　　　　　　　　　　, for

Deduct 5 for each incorrectly placed comma and 5 for each blank incorrectly filled.

Commas and Introductory Additions   Exercise 12/13–2

NAME _____ SCORE _____

12b A comma often follows adverb clauses that precede main clauses. A comma often follows introductory phrases (especially verbal phrases) and transitional expressions. A comma follows an introductory interjection (such as *oh*) or an introductory *yes* or *no*.

> *When our company received a request for a proposal,* we asked our best writer to prepare it.   [introductory adverb clause (for a list of common adverb clause markers, see *Subordinators* in the Appendix)]
> *Following the guidelines suggested by the company,* the writer prepared an excellent proposal.   [introductory verbal phrase]

A comma is often omitted after introductory prepositional phrases when no misreading would result. When an adverb clause comes at the end of a sentence, it is not usually preceded by a comma unless the clause is introduced by *although*.

> *Not long after,* the company received a positive response from the company that solicited the proposal.   [The comma prevents misreading.]
> Our company was chosen ⊙ *because the writer of the proposal had prepared an excellent presentation.*   [concluding adverb clause]
> The writer of the proposal sold our company's product, *although more than twenty other companies also presented proposals.*   [concluding adverb clause introduced by *although*]

DIRECTIONS   After each introductory element in the sentences below, either write a *C* to indicate that the sentence is correct as it stands or insert a comma where one is needed. Then write the *C* or the comma in the blank.

> EXAMPLES
> When you write an unsolicited proposal,you generally may choose
>
> your own format.   ___,___
>
> Quite often *C* an unsolicited proposal is presented in the form of a
>   O✳
> letter.   ___C___

1. Even when the proposal takes the form of a letter,captions or

   headings still identify major sections.   ___,___

2. In the abstract *C comma optional* the writer usually provides a summary of the
                    O
   proposal's contents.   ___C___

3. By using the first section of the report to summarize or sketch

   the main points,the writer tries to make the reader's job as

   easy as possible.   ___,___

✳ *The zero marks the point where a student is likely to insert an unnecessary comma.*

4. Instead of having to read the entire document,the reader can decide which sections of the report to concentrate on.   ___,___

5. In many ways⟨C⟩this abstract helps the reader to focus easily on the sections that follow.   ___C___

6. The key words in a section's first sentence often form the basis for a good heading,although that is not always the case.   ___,___

7. Remember, because you need to make the reports that you write easy to read, use clear, helpful headings for all sections.   ___,___,___

8. Producing an accurate proposal is extremely important, because it may be interpreted as a legal document.   ___C___

9. *C comma optional*
In court, you would be judged responsible for following through with everything promised in your proposal.   ___C___

10. Legally, you can be made to pay for the oversights in your proposal.   ___,___

**12c Commas are used to separate items in a series, including coordinate adjec-
tives (in pairs or series).**

A series is a succession of three or more parallel elements. Note the commas:

    1,   **2,**   and   **3**

English, *mathematics,* and *psychology* are all disciplines with important applica-

tions to nearly any career.

          1,   **2,**   and   **3**

The office is *pleasant to work in,* *easy to get to,* and *inexpensive to maintain.*

Adjectives are coordinate when they describe the same noun (or noun substitute)
in a parallel fashion—so that these adjectives could logically be joined by *and*
or *or* and so that their order could be reversed without loss of sense. *Pleasant,*
easy, and *inexpensive* in the preceding example are coordinate adjectives. Coordinate adjectives are also used in pairs:

        1,   **2**

They are *alert,* *energetic* employees.   [Note that the sequence could be reversed

and the comma replaced by *and:* They are *energetic and alert* employees.]

In all the preceding examples notice that the commas are used where the coordinating conjunction *and* would otherwise appear. (In a series, the last comma usually is accompanied by the coordinating conjunction rather than replacing it.

    1 and   **2** and   **3**

English *and* mathematics *and* psychology

       1   and   **2**   and   **3**

pleasant to work in *and* easy to get to *and* inexpensive to maintain

 1 and   **2**

alert *and* energetic

**13e Commas are not used between adjectives that are not coordinate (those
that could not be linked by *and*), before the first item or after the last item in a
series, or between *two* items linked by a coordinator.**

A modern , chrome , rocking chair stood in one corner. [The adjectives are
    not coordinate: their sequence cannot be reversed, nor can they logically be
    joined by *and.*]
The office did not lack such necessary equipment as , desk, file cabinets, and
    typewriters. [No comma is used before the first item in the series.]
Yesterday a supply center delivered a photocopy machine, a calculator, and a cellu-
    lar phone , to the office. [No comma is used after the last item in the series.]
Our office was both attractive , and functional. [No comma is used be-
    [*That* introduces a restrictive clause essential to identify *writing.*]

Commas and Items in a Series   Exercise 12/13-3

NAME _____ SCORE _____

DIRECTIONS Identify each series (or pair) that needs commas by writing *1, 2* or *1, 2, and 3* above the items and also in the blanks. Insert commas where they belong in the sentence and also between the numbers in the blank to show the punctuation of the pattern. Write *C* after each sentence that has no items in a series that need punctuation.

EXAMPLES

Almost everyone has to present a formal oral report. _____*C*_____

Oral reports are used to explain policies and procedures
¹ teach others what they need to know, and ³ persuade
others to accept the speaker's position. _____*1, 2 and 3*_____

1. You need to know how to prepare an oral report,
   how to make use of visual effects in the report, and
   how to deliver the report effectively. _____*1, 2, and 3*_____

2. Three of the main considerations in preparing oral
   reports are audience, occasion, and purpose. _____*1, 2, and 3*_____

3. You must consider whether the occasion for the report is business, social, or both _____*1, 2, and 3*_____

4. The same speech may be a huge success at one time
   and a dismal failure at another, depending on the
   occasion and the audience. _____*C*_____

5. A short report with touches of humor may be appropriate at a luncheon or dinner meeting. _____*C*_____

6. At a formal business meeting, however, a formal,
   detailed report would be called for. _____*1, 2*_____

7. Another aspect of the occasion is the place itself:
   the size of the room, the number of chairs, and the
   time of day. _____*1, 2, and 3*_____

8. A very effective oral presentation may be made to forty people in a room meant for thirty; but, in general, a report given to forty people in a room large enough to hold two hundred is destined for trouble.   _____C_____

9. If you plan to show slides, a filmstrip, or a movie, you must be sure that the room is equipped with the right kind of projector and screen.   _1, 2, or 3_

10. A cold, dimly lit room may also handicap a speaker.   _1, 2_

Commas and Restrictive and Nonrestrictive
Additions

Exercise 12/13–4

NAME _____ SCORE _____

12d Commas are used to set off nonrestrictive clauses and phrases (those that are not essential or necessary to the meaning of the terms they refer to) and other parenthetical elements.

> The North Carolina Technical Writers' Workshop, *which was held in Raleigh during August,* attracted middle management personnel from all over the state. [The *which* clause is not needed to identify *Workshop.*]
>
> The organizer of the Workshop, *Leo Bernstein,* was pleased with the turnout. [An appositive is usually nonrestrictive.]
>
> The new managers, *not to mention the experienced ones,* learned a great deal from the seminars. [*Not to mention* introduces a parenthetical element.]

Caution: Avoid the serious error of using only one comma to set off a nonrestrictive phrase or clause. When the second comma is not used, the writer seems to be separating the subject from the verb or the verb from the complement. (Remember that commas do not separate the parts of the basic sentence—subject–verb–complement—but rather show where additions that require punctuation have been made.)

NOT   The workshop *which met in August* ⎵ led to an immediate improvement in the reports that the managers wrote.

NOT   The workshop ⎵ *which met in August* led to an immediate improvement in the reports that the managers wrote.

BUT   The workshop, *which met in August,* led to an immediate improvement in the reports that the managers wrote.

Remember, then, to use two commas when a nonrestrictive or other parenthetical element appears in the middle of a sentence.

> The managers, fortunately for all concerned, praised the workshop's leaders.

When the explanatory phrase or clause ends a sentence, the second comma is replaced by the period.

> The managers praised the workshop's leaders, *I might add.*

When two sentences are joined, however, one of the two commas setting off a parenthetical element may be replaced by a semicolon.

> We were pleased with the training session; *I might add,* the managers praised the workshop's leaders.

197

13d Restrictive phrases and clauses (those that give information essential to the meaning of the terms they refer to) are not set off with commas. The circled commas in the following examples are incorrect.

The seminar Ⓐ in technical writing Ⓐ attracted participants from all over the country.   [The phrase identifies *seminar.*]
The professor Ⓐ *who planned the seminar* Ⓐ was surprised by the number of applications received.   [The *who* clause identifies *professor.*]
Much of the writing *that was done as a result of the seminar* was published.
   [*That* introduces a restrictive clause essential to identify *writing.*]

DIRECTIONS   In the sentences below, use commas to set off all nonrestrictive and parenthetical additions. Then in the blanks place (1) a dash followed by a comma (—,) if the nonrestrictive or parenthetical addition begins the sentence, (2) a comma followed by a dash (,—) if the addition ends the sentence, or a dash enclosed within commas (,—,) if the addition comes within the sentence. Write *C* if there is no nonrestrictive or parenthetical addition to set off.

EXAMPLE
Public speaking, like any skill, requires practice.   —, —,

1. Generally, unskilled speakers who do not prepare in advance
    will make many mistakes.   —,

2. The speech that demands the least preparation is the im-
    promptu speech.   *C*

3. Most speakers, even in formal business settings, prefer to deliver
    an extemporaneous speech.   —, —,

4. Just like other types of speeches, an extemporaneous speech de-
    mands skill and preparation.   —,

5. Although it is not memorized, a successful extemporaneous
    speech, as a rule, has been carefully planned.   —, —,

6. Written speeches, it should be noted, are frequently given at
    large business meetings.   —, —,

7. Listening to someone read a speech, especially a long one, can
    put some people to sleep.   —, —,

8. Giving a written speech requires a well-lighted room, a condi-
    tion that the speaker cannot count on.   —,

9. On the other hand, people like guides and tour leaders make
    use of memorized speeches.   —,

10. If you forget a word or phrase, a memorized speech can fail.   —,

Deduct 5 for incorrect punctuation of a sentence and 5 for each incorrectly filled blank.

Conventional Uses of Commas

Exercise 12/13-5

NAME _____ SCORE _____

12e Commas are conventionally used to set off a variety of constructions: (1) negative or contrasted elements, (2) words in direct address, (3) words that explain who is speaking in a direct quotation, (4) items in dates, addresses, and geographic locations, and (5) a letter's complimentary close (see section **35**).

The most common kind of speech is extemporaneous**,** *not written or memorized.* [A contrasted element is commonly introduced by *not.*]

*"Harold***,** would you be in charge of the presentation for the board of directors next Friday," *the sales manager asked***,** "that explains our new marketing program?" [A comma is used after the name of someone addressed directly; commas set off expressions like *he said* or *she asked* (unless a question mark or exclamation point is called for). See also section **16** for the placement of other punctuation in relationship to quotation marks.]

The annual convention of the Junior Chamber of Commerce will be held at *Laguna Beach***,** *California***,** on *March 16***,** *1990.*

Official documents and reports sometimes arrange dates differently; the punctuation will then vary from the usual practice: *14 August 1990.* However, the usual form in business letters would be *August 14***,** *1990.*

Note: If only the month and the year are given, no comma is necessary: *August 1990.*

Caution: No comma is used before the zip code in a postal address: *New York***,** *NY 10017.*

DIRECTIONS   Insert any needed commas in each of the following sentences. In the blank write the number that represents the reason you inserted the comma or commas: *1* for negative or contrasted elements, *2* for words in direct address, *3* for words that explain who is speaking, and *4* for items in dates, addresses, or geographic locations. Some sentences require more than one comma.

EXAMPLE
"Sara**,** could you come to our Chicago office for an interview?" the

personnel director asked.　　　　　　　　　　　　　　　_*2*_

1. Since July 1**,** 1989**,** the company asked job finalists to give brief

presentations to a small group of supervisors.　　　_*4*_

2. The company wanted Sara to see the plant**,** not just to look at

pictures.　　　　　　　　　　　　　　　　　　　_*1*_

3. "Please tell us something about your training as a technical

writer**,**" the personnel director told Sara.　　　　_*3*_

4. The personnel director asked her to be ready to give an extemporaneous speech, not a formal written one.   *1*

5. Sara decided to start by mentioning her internship at IBM in St. Louis, Missouri, that ran from January to May 1990.   *4*

6. Sara said, "My business writing course prepared me for the work that I did as an intern."   *3*

7. "I think," she continued, "I will discuss the types of technical reports that I now know how to write."   *3*

8. "And, Sara, could you please bring samples of your written work?" the personnel director asked.   *2*

9. "I had planned to bring copies of ads I wrote at IBM," Sara told the personnel director.   *2*

10. On Wednesday, August 8, 1990, Sara flew from Greensboro North Carolina, to Chicago, confident that her presentation would go well.   *4*

Deduct 3 for incorrect punctuation of a sentence and 2 for each blank incorrectly filled.

Mastering Commas: A Review   Exercise 12/13–6

NAME _____ SCORE _____

DIRECTIONS   Insert commas as they are needed in the following sentences. (Not all sentences require commas.) Then in the blanks write the number representing the reason for the comma or commas that you add to a sentence: *1* for main clauses linked by a coordinator, *2* for introductory elements, *3* for items in a series, *4* for nonrestrictive clauses and phrases and other parenthetical elements, and *5* for any other conventional uses. If you do not need to add a comma to a sentence, write *0* in the blank.

EXAMPLE
When you are asked to prepare a report, find out as much as you can

about your audience.   *2*

1. It is important to know who makes up your audience, and it
   helps to know how much understanding the audience has of
   the field about which you will be speaking.   *1*

2. If the audience is unfamiliar with your subject, you may need
   to give some background information.   *2*

3. It is wise to avoid technical vocabulary as much as possible
   whenever you are writing for a group of people who are unfamiliar with your subject.   *0*

4. People in your own field, on the other hand, will be able to
   follow a report that makes use of common technical words.   *4*

5. Professionals in your own field, who are likely to know the
   technical vocabulary associated with your subject, must be
   treated with respect.   *4*

6. You should not define simple technical terms, offer background
   information, or otherwise talk down to a reading audience that
   is already familiar with your subject.   *3*

7. If your reading audience is composed of friends and colleagues,
   your report can be less formal than if you are writing to
   strangers.   *2*

8. At the same time, writing for a group of friends and/or co-
   workers can be difficult.   *2 or 4*

9. An old saying states,"A prophet is not without honor save in his own country."   _5_

10. To a certain extent, this maxim applies whenever you must write for an audience that is familiar with you.   _2 or 4_

11. It is often more difficult to convince friends than strangers that you know what you are talking about.   _0_

12. You may need to use more evidence, not less, to convince an audience made up of friends and co-workers.   _4 or 5_

13. Since these readers know you quite well, they may not take your recommendations seriously unless you support those ideas with details.   _2_

14. Of course, a reading audience that does not know you can also present difficulties.   _2 or 4_

15. Such an audience may make harsh, unjustified judgments about you even before finishing your report.   _3_

16. These readers may, for example, decide that you are too inexperienced to be an expert.   _4_

17. When writing for an audience that does not know you, you should prepare a rather formal report.   _2_

18. You will be more likely to write an effective report if you know the kind of audience you are addressing, but sometimes it is not possible to analyze an audience carefully.   _1_

19. There are three suggestions, however, that can help you write to an audience.   _4_

20. You should be clear, argue logically, and support your claims with facts and details.   _3_

14

Use a semicolon between two related main clauses not joined by a coordinating conjunction, between two main clauses that are joined by a coordinating conjunction but which themselves contain commas, and between coordinate items to separate a series of items which themselves contain commas. Elements with semicolons between them should be of equal grammatical rank.

14a Use the semicolon between two main clauses not joined by a coordinating conjunction.

Often the semicolon between clauses is accompanied by a conjunctive adverb (such as *however*) or a transitional expression (such as *on the other hand*) that signals the exact relationship between the clauses. A semicolon can be used instead of a coordinating conjunction to join two main clauses if they are closely related. Usually, one of the clauses explains the other or stands in contrast to it.

> A formal speech is written down and memorized; an extemporaneous speech is planned but not written down.   [The content of the second main clause contrasts with the idea in the first clause; the semicolon acts as the balancing point between the first and the second clause.]

If the second clause explains the first clause, often a colon is more appropriate. (See **17d**.)

> An impromptu speech is just what the term suggests: it is an unplanned speech that is delivered on the spur of the moment.

Often the semicolon between clauses is accompanied by a conjunctive adverb (such as *however*) or a transitional expression (such as *on the other hand*) that signals the exact relationship between the clauses.

> A written speech tends to be very formal; an extemporaneous speech sounds more natural and spontaneous.
> A written speech is suitable for many occasions; however, it is likely to be very boring when read on social occasions.

Note: Remember that when a conjunctive adverb or a transitional expression is used *as an addition to* a main clause, it is often set off by commas.

> A written speech is suitable for some occasions; it is, *however,* likely to be very boring when read on social occasions.

This "addition" to the main clause can be moved to numerous places within the sentence.

A written speech is suitable for some occasions; it is likely, *however,* to be very boring when read on social occasions.

OR

A written speech is suitable for some occasions; *however,* it is likely to be very boring when read on social occasions.   [Note that when the conjunctive adverb immediately follows the semicolon, the semicolon absorbs the first comma.]

Caution: Be especially careful to use a semicolon between two main clauses not joined by a coordinator when direct quotations are involved.

"Prepare only an outline for a talk," the instructor suggested; "don't memorize a set of words."

14b   Use a semicolon to separate a series of elements which themselves contain commas.

The four types of speeches we studied were the written speech, which is read to the audience; the memorized speech, which is first written down and then learned verbatim; the extemporaneous speech, in which a plan, but not the exact words, is often sketched out as a guide;. and the impromptu speech, which is made without preparation or advance thought.

14c Do not use a semicolon between parts of unequal grammatical rank.

A semicolon should not be used between a clause and a phrase or between a main clause and a subordinate clause.

NOT   He gave an extemporaneous speech; usually the most effective kind.

BUT   He gave an extemporaneous speech, usually the most effective kind.   [A comma, not a semicolon, is used between the clause and the phrase.]

NOT   The speech sounded entirely natural; although it had been carefully planned.

BUT   The speech sounded entirely natural, although it had been carefully planned.   [A comma, not a semicolon, is appropriate between the main clause and the subordinate clause.]

Deduct 5 for each caret incorrectly placed and 5 for each blank incorrectly filled.

Semicolons Between Main Clauses   Exercise 14–1

NAME _____ SCORE _____

DIRECTIONS   In the following sentences insert an inverted caret (**V**) between main clauses and add the semicolon. In the blank, copy the semicolon and any conjunctive adverb or transitional expression that follows it. Be sure to include the comma with the expression if there is one. Write *C* if the sentence is correctly punctuated.

EXAMPLE
You may think that the application process ends when

you leave the interview; however, you still have more

to do.   *; however,* _____

1. At your interview, you thank the interviewer for

   talking with you; however, you should also write a

   thank-you letter.   *; however,* _____

2. Personnel directors are busy people; thus, a letter

   that rambles on will annoy your reader.   *; thus,* _____

3. Companies look for consideration in prospective

   employees; your thank-you letter shows that you

   have this quality.   _____ *;* _____

4. Interviews always seem too short; in fact, after you

   get home, you will probably think of several points

   that you should have made.   *; in fact,* _____

5. The thank-you letter provides you with an oppor-

   tunity to give more information; the company will

   never know those additional facts about you unless

   you mention them.   _____ *;* _____

6. A thank-you letter can remind the reader who you

   are, can continue your contact with the firm, and

   can allow you to elaborate on your qualifications.   _____ *C* _____

7. Of course, your thank-you letter should not sound

   pushy; it should not demand a response; it should

   not be "cute."   _____ *;* _____ *;* _____

8. You want the company to think that you will be a competent employee; therefore, use this letter to show how your skills meet the company's needs.

   ; therefore,

9. Once you mail your letter, sit back, wait patiently, and remember that no news is good news.

   C

10. Six weeks may seem a long time to wait for the company's response; nevertheless, companies often find it necessary to keep you waiting that long.

    ; nevertheless,

Deduct 5 for each caret incorrectly placed and 5 for each blank incorrectly filled.

Semicolons and Commas   Exercise 14-2

NAME _____ SCORE _____

DIRECTIONS   In each sentence use an inverted caret (**V**) to mark the spot where a comma or a semicolon should go. Insert the correct punctuation mark in the sentence and also write it in the blank. (One of the sentences will require two commas or semicolons.)

EXAMPLE

Speaking extemporaneously is the most popular way of giving talks; such speeches are planned but not memorized.   ___;___

1. The extemporaneous talk is planned and rehearsed, yet the speech's actual wording will vary from presentation to presentation.   ___,___

2. Extemporaneous speakers may prepare as much for their presentations as those who give written or memorized speeches; however, an extemporaneous speech never has a final, unchanging set of words.   ___;_,___

3. Because the phrasing does vary each time the extemporaneous speech is presented, the speaker is not as likely to sound monotonous, preachy, or uninvolved as he or she might when giving memorized or written speeches, yet the speaker has still carefully planned and rehearsed his or her presentation.   _,_,_,_;___

4. An extemporaneous speech can "instantly" be adapted to match the mood of the audience; for this reason, many plan for most occasions.   ___;_,___

5. The extemporaneous speech is a lifesaver if any of these conditions occur: the audience is enthusiastic, people look lost or puzzled, or someone interrupts by coming in late or asking a question.   ___,_,___

6. Extemporaneous speakers generally use minimal notes for their presentations, so they can move about the lecture area more freely than they could if they were giving a written speech.   ___,___

7. "What are you going to talk about for your oral report," my instructor asked; "what type of presentation do you plan to use?" $\underline{\quad\,;\;\;;\quad}$

8. "I'm going to give an extemporaneous speech that presents the employment opportunities available to public relations majors," I replied. $\underline{\quad\quad,\quad}$

9. My instructor seemed happy that I was going to speak extemporaneously, but he cautioned me to make certain that I was well prepared. $\underline{\quad\quad,\quad}$

10. An extemporaneous speech may not be written down; it is, however, carefully thought out. $\underline{\quad;\;\;,,\quad}$

15

Use the apostrophe to indicate the possessive case (except for personal pronouns), to mark omissions in contractions, and to form certain plurals.

Remember that the apostrophe, in most of its uses, indicates that something has been omitted.

> don't [do *not*]
> you're [you *are*]
> the class of '90 [the class of 1990]
> accountant's books [books *of, by,* or *for* an accountant]
> children's movies [movies *of* or *for* children]

15a The main use of the apostrophe is to indicate the possessive case (including that of acronyms).

Add either an *'s* or an *'* to form the possessive of nouns and some pronouns.

(1) Add the apostrophe and an s ('s) to a noun or indefinite pronoun to indicate the singular possessive case. (See the list of indefinite pronouns in the Appendix.)

> speaker's duty [singular possessive; duty of one speaker]
> everyone's duty [singular possessive of a pronoun]
> IBM's computer [singular possessive of an acronym]

Option: Although most writers add *'s* to all proper names ending in *s*, some authorities permit adding only the apostrophe:

> Mars' terrain OR Mars's terrain [singular possessive of a singular noun ending in *s*]

(2) Add the apostrophe (') to all plural nouns that end in s to indicate the plural possessive case. Add the apostrophe and an s ('s) to all plural nouns not ending in s to indicate the plural possessive case.

Always form the plural of the noun first. Then, if the plural of the noun already ends in *s*, add only the apostrophe to show the possessive case.

> speaker [singular]   speakers [plural]   speakers' [plural possessive]
> secretary [singular]   secretaries [plural]   secretaries' [plural possessive]

If the plural noun does not end in *s*, add the apostrophe and an *s* to show the possessive case.

> man [singular]   men [plural]   men's [plural possessive]
> woman [singular]   women [plural]   women's [plural possessive]

(3) Add the apostrophe and an s to the last word of compounds or word groups.

> sister-in-law**'**s office
> everyone else**'**s raise
> chairman of the board**'**s presentation

(4) Add the apostrophe and an s to each name to indicate individual ownership, but add it only to the final name to indicate joint ownership.

> Sam**'**s and Jane**'**s offices   [Sam and Jane have different offices.]
> Sam and Jane**'**s office   [Sam and Jane have the same office.]

15b Use an apostrophe to indicate omissions in contractions and in numbers. Remember to place the apostrophe exactly where the omission occurs.

> *It***'***s* [It *is*] the duty of the president of the class of **'**91 [1991] to open the vault.

Caution: The use of contractions is not common in writing unless a conversational tone is sought. For instance, contractions are often used in business letters to make the tone less formal; contractions would, however, not be used in formal business reports.

15c An apostrophe plus s ('s) may be used to form the plural of lowercase letters, figures, symbols, abbreviations, and words referred to as words.

> final k**'**s OR ks
> 1990**'**s OR 1990s
> V.F.W.**'**s OR V.F.W.s
> and**'**s OR ands

Caution: An apostrophe is never used for plural nouns that are not in the possessive case.

> They put up *signs* to direct *visitors* to the right *buildings*.   [NOT *signs's, visitor's, building's*]

15d The apostrophe is not used for possessive pronouns—*his, hers, its, ours, yours, theirs,* and *whose;* nor is it used for plural nouns not in the possessive case.

> *Whose* project is this—*yours* or *theirs?*
> The car lost *its* brakes.

Deduct 5 for each incorrect revision.

Apostrophes and the Possessive Case   Exercise 15–1

NAME _____ SCORE _____

DIRECTIONS   Rewrite each of the following word groups as a noun or a pronoun preceded by another noun or pronoun in the possessive case.

EXAMPLES
the salary of everyone
everyone's salary

the businesses owned by the Davises
the Davises' businesses

1. the designs on the dish
   the dish's designs

2. the reports of Martha and Emory
   Martha's and Emory's reports

3. entries in the index
   the index's entries

4. the floor plan of the executive office building
   the executive office building's floor plan

5. the reunion of the Barths
   the Barths' reunion

6. the history of our company
   our company's history

7. the refunds of the stockholders
   the stockholders' refunds

8. problems of today
   today's problems

9. the businesses owned by my father-in-law
   my father-in-law's businesses

10. the interpretations of the rules
    the rules' interpretations

11. the tax report of Mr. Jones
    Mr. Jones' or Mr. Jones's tax report

12. an address by the senator from Colorado
the senator from Colorado's address

13. the ships of Columbus
Columbus's or Columbus' ships

14. a patent belonging to Louise and Gene
Louise and Gene's patent

15. the column of the editor-in-chief
the editor-in-chief's column

16. the promotion of the women
the women's promotion

17. the formulas of the alloys
the alloys' formulas

18. slowdown of industry
the industry's slowdown

19. a presentation made by Walker Blevins
Walker Blevins' or Blevins's presentation

20. decisions made by him
his decisions

Mastering Apostrophes: A Review Exercise 15-2

NAME _____ SCORE _____

DIRECTIONS   In the following sentences add all the apostrophes that are needed. Then in the blank enter each word, number, or letter to which you have added an apostrophe. Be careful not to add needless apostrophes.

EXAMPLE
Ms. Franklin, the state of North Carolina's chief conservation advocate, spoke at the Boone town meeting last night.

Carolina's

1. Ms. Franklin's talk helped her audience understand its place in the conservation movement.

Franklin's

2. She pointed out that, in the 1990's, a city's inhabitants must work together to solve the problem of waste.

1990's or 1990s
city's

3. It's not simply that the town's job becomes one of waste management," Franklin said; "residents have to be involved, too."

It's
town's

4. "Recycling's not easy, but, for most areas, there are no ifs' or whens' about this problem," she went on.

Recycling's
ifs' or ifs
when's or whens

5. "This area's landfills now are reaching capacity, and it won't be long before they're full," Franklin warned.

area's
won't
they're

6. She pointed out that soon even towns with populations below the 100,000's will face such difficulties.

100,000's
or 100,000s

7. "All the Smiths and Jones of every town in the U.S. throw out tons of garbage each year; today's home owner is just as responsible for the problems as the large industries," she observed.

today's

8. In an effort to convince her listeners, she concluded with her best point: everyone's need to recycle materials.

everyone's

9. "Your hope—and your children's," Ms. Franklin
said, "will be to make your homes small recycling
centers."   *children's*

10. Ms. Franklin ended by repeating a timely slogan:
"Think globally, act locally"; she hoped it would
become her audience's motto as well.   *audience's*

16

Use quotation marks to set off all direct quotations, some titles, and words used in a special sense. Place quotation marks in proper relationship to other marks of punctuation.

Quotation marks allow you to let your reader know that you are directly quoting (repeating word-for-word) what someone else has written, said, or thought.

> "The board will review the proposal on Tuesday," the memo said.
> "I'll be there," I told my co-worker. But I thought to myself, "With my luck, I'll probably have to be out of town."

16a Use quotation marks (" ") for direct quotations and in all dialogue. Set off long quotations by indention.

(1) Use double quotation marks (" ") before and after all direct (but not indirect) quotations; use a single quotation mark (' ') before and after a quotation within a quotation.

INDIRECT QUOTATION He asked me if I would speak at the company's board meeting. [*If, whether,* and *that* frequently introduce indirect quotations.]

DIRECT QUOTATION He asked me, "Will you speak at the company's board meeting?" [The indirect quotation is made a direct quotation.]

DIRECT QUOTATION The program for the meeting noted that I was going to discuss "the effects of government regulations on the textile industry." [*The* is not capitalized because only a phrase is being quoted.]

Note: Use single quotation marks (' ') for quotation marks that appear within other quotation marks.

> "The conference 'The Global Marketplace' is going on at the same time as our board meeting," Arnold told me.

Caution: In direct quotations, reproduce all quoted material *exactly* as it appears in the original, including capitalization and punctuation. If the material you are quoting contains an error, insert the word *sic* within brackets immediately after the error (See **17g**).

> The report went on to say, "the pipe busted [sic] under the excessive pressure."

(2) In quoting dialogue (conversation), a new paragraph begins each time the speaker changes.

> "I guess I'll have to miss the conference," I said.
> "Had you planned to go before the board scheduled its meeting?" Arnold asked

me, knowing that I have a deep interest in international business and would be sorry to miss such a meeting.

"Well," I responded, " I mailed in my registration fees and application to be a panel moderator two months ago."

Note: Commas set off expressions like *he said* that introduce, interrupt, or follow direct quotations.

> The secretary said, "Mr. Jones can't come to the meeting either."
> "Mr. Jones can't come to the meeting either," the secretary said.
> "Mr. Jones," the secretary said, "can't come to the meeting either."

Caution: Remember that a divided quotation made up of two main clauses or two complete sentences must be punctuated with a semicolon or an end mark.

> "Every time they try to convene the review board, this happens," she said; "I have to find someone to go in his place."
>
> OR
>
> "Every time they try to convene the review board, this happens," she said. "I have to find someone to go in his place."

(3) Prose quotations that would require four or more lines of typing and poetry that would require four or more lines are indented from the rest of the text.

Prose   If the material that you quote is one paragraph or less, all lines of a long quotation (more than four lines) are indented ten spaces from the left margin and are double-spaced. When you quote two or more paragraphs, indent the first line of each paragraph thirteen rather than ten spaces. Use quotation marks only if they appear in the original.

In Communication for Management and Business, Norman B. Sigband and Arthur H. Bell discuss the business meeting as an important means by which companies do such things as set long-range goals, plan marketing strategies, and consider policy changes.

> An effective meeting is a forum where knowledgeable individuals come together to solve organizational problems through open and participative communication. It is a place where the will to work together is developed. It is also a group session that participants find exciting and provocative; it's one where every member who has

something to say is heard; it's one where everyone is on an equal

level; it's one where decisions are reached (2).

Poetry   You may run fewer than four lines of poetry into the text. When run in, double quotation marks should begin and end the material, and a slash mark should be placed at the end of each line.

W. H. Auden's poem, "The Unknown Citizen," has to do with the common

working man: "And all the reports on his conduct agree / That, in the

modern sense of an old-fashioned word, he was a saint, / For in everything he

did he served the Greater Community."

More than four quoted lines of poetry are treated in the same manner as lengthy prose passages.

W. H. Auden's poem, "The Unknown Citizen," has to do with the

common working man:

> He was found by the Bureau of Statistics to be
>
> One against whom there was no official complaint,
>
> And all the reports on his conduct agree
>
> That, in the modern sense of an old-fashioned word, he
>
>   was a saint,
>
> For in everything he did he served the Greater Community.

16b Use quotation marks for minor titles—short stories, short poems, essays, one-act plays, songs, articles in periodicals, and episodes of a radio or television series—and for subdivisions of books.

The article "Speak Up for Success" appeared in a recent issue of *Weekend Worker.*

Note: The title of the periodical, *Weekend Worker,* is italicized. (See also section **10**.)

16c Quotation marks are occasionally used to indicate that words are being used in a special or an ironic sense.

"Work" for him means anything that he dislikes doing.   [See also **10d**.]

Note: Either quotation marks or italics may be used in definitions such as the following: "Jargon" means anything that a nontechnical reader is likely to find unclear or confusing.

Caution: Avoid the tendency that some writers have of using quotation marks freely to call attention to clever phrasings. Many times what these writers consider to be clever ways of saying something are really only trite sayings, slang expressions, or colloquialisms that could best be stated in another way. (See also **20c.**)

> INEFFECTIVE   The sales representative thought he was a "hot shot," but the rest of us knew that, if he kept acting irresponsibly, he'd be "given the pink slip" soon.

> EFFECTIVE   The sales representative thought that he was a very successful salesman, but the rest of us knew that, if he kept acting irresponsibly, he'd be fired soon.

16d Do not overuse quotation marks.

Quotation marks are not used for titles of compositions, nor are they used to enclose a cliché or to mark a *yes* or *no* answer in direct discourse.

> NOT   "No," he didn't feel that he had a "ghost of a chance."

> BUT   No, he didn't feel that he had a ghost of a chance.

16e Follow the conventions of American printers in deciding whether various marks of punctuation belong inside or outside the quotation marks.

(1) The period and the comma are usually placed inside the quotation marks.

> "Well," he said, "I'm ready to finish writing the report."

(2) The semicolon and the colon are placed outside the quotation marks.

> The speaker pointed out that "big business is now beginning to speak out against overregulation"; indeed, it is doing more than simply speaking out.
> She looked at the folder marked "Confidential": "Not to leave the Personnel Office."

(3) The dash, the question mark, and the exclamation point are placed inside the quotation marks when they apply to the quoted matter and outside the quotation marks when they apply to the whole sentence.

> Have you read "Is Government Regulation Crippling Business?"   [The question mark applies to the quoted matter as well as to the entire sentence.]

> Have you read "Arsenic and Old Factories"?   [The question mark does not apply to the quoted matter.]

Deduct 10 for each blank incorrectly filled.

Quotation Marks   Exercise 16-1

NAME _____ SCORE _____

DIRECTIONS   In the sentences below insert all needed quotation marks. In the blanks enter the quotation marks and the first and last word of each quoted part. Include other marks of punctuation used with the quotation marks, and place them in proper position—either inside or outside the quotation marks. Do not enclose an indirect quotation. Write *C* in the blank to indicate a sentence that is correct without quotation marks.

EXAMPLE

Gray Lanier's oral report entitled "How Much Regulation Is Too Much?" was of special interest to the business majors in the audience.

"How ... Much?"

1. Gray began her report with what she termed "essential background information."

"essential ... information."
_or_
essential background information.

2. She pointed out that seventy-five years ago business was concerned about the government's stand on monopolies.

_C_

3. "Then a decade or so later," Gray explained, "the main issue that disturbed business was unionism."

"Then ... later," "the ... unionism."

4. "What is the major concern of business today?" Gray asked.

"What ... today?"

5. "Clearly, it is federal regulation," Gray responded to her rhetorical question.

"Clearly, ... regulation,"

6. For decades the public screamed, "Give us protection from big business!"

"Give ... business!"

7. "After reading an article like 'Is Government Regulation Crippling Business?' one sees how strong big business's response has been," Gray stated.

"after...'Is...Business?'...been,"

8. Gray went on to report that a bureaucracy of eighty thousand people was established to protect consumers and workers from injury.

C

9. "The many agencies created by the government to act as the public's voice have had much success, especially in the area of pollution controls," Gray said.

"The...controls,"

10. "But," Gray went on, business also has its side, as exemplified in its complaint, 'The standards set by government agencies are too confusing and costly to result in significant benefits to the American consumer.'"

"But,"..."business... 'The...consumer.'"

17

Learn to use the end marks of punctuation—the period, the question mark, and the exclamation point—and the internal marks of punctuation—the colon, the dash, parentheses, brackets, ellipsis points, and the slash, in accordance with conventional practices. (For the use of the hyphen, see section **18f.**)

Two spaces follow the period, question mark, exclamation point, and four-dot ellipsis points; one space follows the colon, the ending parenthesis and bracket, and each of the dots in three-space ellipsis points. No spaces follow the hyphen or dash.

End punctuation marks cause most writers little difficulty except when they must use these marks with direct quotations.

17a The period follows declarative and mildly imperative (command) sentences, indirect questions, and most abbreviations. (See **11a.**)

DECLARATIVE SENTENCE	Samuel Foster, head of our Communication Arts Department, decided that it would be a good idea for students to learn how to use audio-visual equipment.
MILDLY IMPERATIVE SENTENCE	Learn how to use VCRs and projectors.
INDIRECT QUESTION	Foster asked Dr. Lee if he thought it would be a worthwhile workshop.
ABBREVIATION	Dr. Lee agreed to discuss integrating the use of visual equipment into an oral report.

Note: Declarative sentences may contain direct questions.

Will the students already know this material**?** was a common question.   [No period follows the question mark and no quotation marks enclose the question.]

17b The question mark follows direct (but not indirect) questions.

What did Dr. Lee say**?**
She asked me what Dr. Lee said**.**

17c The exclamation point follows emphatic interjections and statements of strong emotion.

What an interesting presentation Dr. Lee made**!**
"Bravo**!**" some people in the audience responded.

Caution: Do not use exclamation points to make your writing sound exciting or important. Rather, use exclamation points sparingly, and only to follow those sentences that do express strong emotion.

OTHER PUNCTUATION MARKS

Of the marks that do not mark the end of a sentence (internal punctuation marks), the semicolon (see section **14**), the colon, and the dash are closely related to the period because they cause the reader to stop—rather than to pause as they would at a comma.

17d Meaning *as follows,* the colon formally introduces a word, a phrase, or a clause (but especially a list or series) that explains or identifies something mentioned in the clause preceding the colon. The colon is also used to introduce a quotation that runs for two or more sentences and to separate figures in scriptural and time references.

> Dr. Lee explained the importance of visual aids in an oral presentation: either they are absolutely necessary to save words, or they add interest and variety to the speech.   [The second main clause explains the first one.]
> Dr. Lee named the purposes of adding visual aids to a speech: clarity, variety, and reinforcement.   [The list explains purposes.]
> Dr. Lee explained: "Visual aids save many words in an oral presentation. They often show in one picture or graph what would require fifteen minutes of speaking to explain."   [The colon, rather than the comma, is used because the quotation runs for more than one sentence.]

Caution: Avoid unnecessary colons, especially between verbs and their complements, prepositions and their objects, or after *such as.*

> NOT   Three reasons for using visual aids are: clarity, variety, and reinforcement.

> BUT   Three reasons for using visual aids are clarity, variety, and reinforcement.

> OR   Visual aids add three things to an oral report: clarity, variety, and reinforcement.

The colon is also used between chapter and verse in scriptural references and between hours and minutes in time references.

> Exodus 5:23
> 6:15 P.M.

17e The dash is used to set off a parenthetical element for emphasis or clarity, to set off an introductory list or series, and to mark an interruption or break in thought.

> Clarity, variety, and reinforcement—these are three purposes of visual aids.   [The dash sets off an introductory series.]

These three purposes—clarity, variety and reinforcement—are served by visual aids. [The list sets off a parenthetical element for emphasis.]

Dr. Lee recommended—in fact, more than recommended—that we practice our oral presentations with the visual aids included.   [The dash marks an interruption or break in thought.]

Caution: Use dashes sparingly and not as lazy substitutes for commas, semicolons, or end marks.

17f Parentheses set off supplementary, incidental, or illustrative matter. They also frequently enclose figures or letters used for numbering.

Dr. Lee urged all of us to learn how to operate the various kinds of projectors (all available in our department) while we are studying oral reports.

We could use (1) opaque projectors, (2) filmstrip projectors, or (3) slide projectors.

Note: Three marks of punctuation are used to set off matter which might be called parenthetical—that is, supplementary, incidental, or illustrative. The most commonly used are commas, which cause the reader only to pause and so see the parenthetical matter as closely related to the main idea of the sentence. Less frequently used are parentheses (which diminish the importance of the matter they set off). Dashes—which create a sharp visual break in the sentences—tend to emphasize what they set off. (Dashes or parentheses rather than commas may be necessary for clarity when the parenthetical matter itself includes commas.)

The computer, unlike any other labor-saving machine, affects every aspect of modern business practice.   [Commas would be used by most writers to set off this parenthetical matter because the parenthetical material within commas is so closely related to the rest of the sentence.]

The computer (unlike any other labor-saving machine) affects every aspect of modern business practice.   [Parentheses minimize the importance of the parenthetical matter.]

The computer—unlike any other labor-saving device—affects every aspect of modern business practice.   [Dashes emphasize the parenthetical matter.]

Many factors—such as length of workday, time of shift, and occupational hazards—affect most people's attitudes toward their jobs.   [The dashes are needed for clarity to enclose the parenthetical matter that contains commas. Parentheses could also be used, but they would deemphasize the list, whereas dashes emphasize it.]

17g Brackets set off editorial comments, additions, or substitutions included within quoted matter. They may also serve as parentheses within parentheses.

When you need to insert an explanation in a quotation, enclose your explanation in brackets to show that your words are not a part of the quoted matter.

Dr. Lee explained, "They [visual aids] can cause difficulties if you have not practiced using them ahead of time."

"Many insecure managers believe that [employees] should be constantly criticized to keep them on their toes." [For clarity, the bracketed *employees* replaces the pronoun *they* which appeared in the original sentence.]

A person in the audience yelled, "I seen [sic] it with my own eyes." [*Sic* indicates something that was said or written which is not the standard word expected.]

17h The slash is used between terms to indicate that either term is applicable to mark line divisions in quoted poetry and to separate the elements in dates. (See also 16a).

Most technical writing departments have an opaque and/or overhead projector available for classroom use.

Note: No space precedes or follows the slash when indicating options.

Those who believe in the necessity of work would disagree with Ezra Pound's lines "Sing we for love and idleness, / Naught else is worth the having."

Note: One space precedes and follows the slash that marks breaks between lines of poetry.

11/24/48   MEANING   November 24, 1948

Note: No space precedes or follows the slashes in dates.

17i Ellipsis points (three spaced periods) indicate omissions from quoted passages.

Dr. Lee explained, "Visual aids . . . often show in one picture or graph what would require fifteen minutes of speaking to explain."

If ellipsis points are used to indicate that the end of a quoted sentence is being omitted, and if the part that *is* quoted forms a complete sentence itself, use the sentence period *plus* ellipsis points.

Dr. Lee asked if he would discuss ways to integrate visual equipment. . . .

Note: The ellipsis points are used in addition to the period; thus, you should leave no space after the last word in the sentence, as illustrated above.

Deduct 10 for each incorrect sentence.

End Marks of Punctuation   Exercise 17–1

NAME _____ SCORE _____

DIRECTIONS   Write a sentence to illustrate each of the following uses of an end mark of punctuation.

    EXAMPLE
    a quoted direct question

    Dr. Lee asked her, " Have you prepared your slides?"

1. an exclamation

2. a direct question

3. a declarative sentence containing dashes

4. a declarative sentence containing a colon used to introduce a list

5. a quotation that includes an ellipsis

6. an indirect question

7. a declarative sentence containing parentheses

8. a sentence containing an abbreviation

9. a mildly imperative sentence

10. a declarative sentence containing brackets

Deduct 5 for each blank incorrectly filled.

Internal Marks of Punctuation

Exercise 17–2

NAME _____ SCORE _____

DIRECTIONS   In each sentence use a caret (∧) to mark the spot where punctuation should be inserted. Then write the correct punctuation mark in the sentence at that spot and also in the blank. Some sentences will require punctuation in two places; in that case, write both marks of punctuation in the blank. This exercise includes not only the punctuation marks discussed in section **17** but also the comma (section **12**) and the semicolon (section **14**).

EXAMPLE
Clarity,∧as well as visibility,∧is important in planning visual aids for
an oral report.   ___,_,___

1. Readers of a written report can study its visual aid as long as they need to∧audiences have only a short time to understand a visual aid that is used in an oral report.   ___;___

2. Since the audience has only a short time to study it,∧the visual should be kept simple.   ___,___

3. The speaker can simplify the visual aid in several ways:∧by eliminating all but the absolutely necessary information, by using block diagrams, and by labeling graphs rather than using symbols or difficult abbreviations.   _: or —_

4. The speaker can also simplify by showing only trends,∧not exact numbers,∧in a graph.   ___,_,___

5. A clear,∧simple table is far better in an oral presentation than is a table with many columns in small print.   ___,___

6. Most visuals in books are too complex to be clear to an audience;∧therefore you should resist the temptation to make transparencies of them just as they are.   ___;___

7. To make a transparency based on a chart found in a book,∧you must eliminate a great deal of information and rewrite the remaining information in large letters.   ___,___

8. One other criterion is important in creating good visual aids:∧audience control.   _: or —_

9. Effective visual aids will help you to control an audience; on the other hand, poorly made ones distract from your speech. —— ; ——

10. Even well-planned visuals can distract from your presentation if they are in front of an audience for an entire speech; consequently, they should be removed after, or covered before and after, you have made use of them. —— ; ——

11. Visual materials that are passed around the audience can, as you might guess, be especially distracting. —— , , ——

12. You cannot control the visuals you pass around; the audience may examine them and ignore what you are saying. : or ;

13. Only a visual, then, that can be quickly removed when you are finished with it gives you audience control. —— , , ——

14. If you can change or add to the material presented in a visual, you have even more control over the visual and, consequently, over the audience. —— , ——

15. In addition to movies, slides, and transparencies, there are several simpler devices for displaying visual aids; for example, blackboards, posters, and flannel boards. : or ——

16. Blackboards—some people ignore such obvious kinds of visuals— are a readily available visual aid. —— — ——

17. Blackboards offer the speaker many advantages; they are easy to use; they do not require much preparation; and they hold the audience's attention as you write and draw on them. —— : ——

18. They do have one major drawback; they may require a great deal of your time during the oral presentation. —— : ——

19. Blackboards will present difficulties if you do not draw or write legibly, if you cannot draw and talk at the same time, or if you talk to the blackboard instead of to the audience. , , or ; ;

20. Still the blackboard, even in this technological age, is one of a speaker's best methods of presenting visual aids. —— , , ——

Deduct 5 for misplaced punctuation and 5 for each blank incorrectly filled.
Mastering Punctuation: A Review   Exercise 17–3

NAME _____ SCORE _____

DIRECTIONS   In the sentences below use a caret (**∧**) to indicate where the correct end marks *or* internal punctuation marks—periods, question marks, exclamation points, colons, dashes, parentheses, brackets, and slashes—should go. Insert the punctuation mark in the correct place in the sentence and write it in the blank. In several sentences more than one kind of punctuation mark is possible.

EXAMPLE
According to Professor James Connally, there are certain criteria for

judging the value of visuals:visibility, simplicity, and control.   : *or* —
                        ∧

1. Visibility is an obvious criterion if your audience cannot see
                        ∧
   your visual aid, they cannot gain anything from it.   ____:____

2. There are certain visuals for example, a small photograph, a
                        ∧   ̄
   typed page, and a page from a book that are too small to be
                        ∧
   seen beyond the first row.   — —

3. Transparencies and large hand-lettered posters can be seen by
   the audience if the speaker prepares his/her visuals correctly.   ____/____
                        ∧

4. There is a simple rule for lettering:letters should be at least 1
                        ∧
   inch high for each 25 feet of distance between the visual and
   the audience.   ____:____

5. No rule for the size of other elements drawings, photographs,
                        ∧
   and graphs can be given.   — —

6. The best advice that can be given is that you should set up the
        ∧
   visuals(note the list in sentence 5)and move to the back row to
   see whether they are clearly visible from that distance.   ( )
        ∧   ∧

7. "Can you see your visuals from the back row?' I was asked by
                        ∧
   my instructor after I had set them up.   ?

8. "No! I shouted back to her.   !

9. "Remember the instructions I gave you," she said;"If you can-
   ∧   ∧
   not see the visuals, then the audience can't either"   . .
                        ∧

10. In my self-evaluation I wrote, "I wonder what my audience would have thought if I had used the ones[visuals]I first pre-
    pared?"

    <u> [ ]   </u>

Deduct 10 for each incorrect sentence.

Mastering Punctuation: A Review   Exercise 17–4

NAME _____ SCORE _____

DIRECTIONS   For each of the following items, write a sentence using the punctuation that is needed to illustrate the item. If you need help punctuating your sentences, refer to the rule or rules indicated in parentheses.

EXAMPLE

a list in the middle of a sentence (**17e**)

Three main criteria—visibility, clarity, and control—determine the worth of a visual effect.

1. a declarative sentence with a quoted direct question (**16e, 17b**)

2. a quotation with an editorial comment or explanation inserted (**17g**)

3. a sentence that has a quotation within a quotation (**16a**)

4. a list or series following a main clause (**17d**)

5. a quotation of two or more sentences introduced by an expression like *she said* (**17d**)

6. a break or interruption of the thought in the middle of a sentence (**17e**)

7. an indirect quotation (**16a**)

8. a nonrestrictive clause (**12d**)

9. supplementary or illustrative information in the middle of a sentence (**17e, 17f**)

10. two main clauses not joined by a coordinating conjunction (**14a**)

SPELLING AND HYPHENATION   sp 18

18

Learn to spell and hyphenate words in accordance with the usage shown in an up-to-date dictionary.

Misspelled words abound: a sign for the "Enterance" to a shopping mall or one marking "Handicap" parking. And, unfortunately, most people label the sign painter *and* the business owner as uneducated. No other mistake is so readily picked out and ridiculed as a spelling error. Moreover, in the business world, poor spelling can severely handicap otherwise talented people by making others view them as unprofessional, inaccurate, inconsiderate, and, at the worst extreme, illiterate. Since written communications are often the only contact that a business person may have with an associate or client, correcting bad spelling habits is a must. The same holds true for the college classroom.

If you are a poor speller, one who regularly misspells enough words to have your classwork or professional work graded down, you should begin a definite program for improving your spelling skills. There are many excellent spelling manuals available today that make use of the lastest psychological studies to present words in a logical, easy-to-learn order. You may also find the following procedures helpful:

(1) Learn the rules of spelling that are presented in this section of the book.

(2) Proofread your papers carefully at least once for misspelled words only.

As you write a rough draft, it is often difficult, and always distracting, to look up a great number of words; but you can put a check or some other identifying sign above those words you have any doubts about so that you can look up their spelling when you proofread.

If spelling is a particular problem for you, you may wish to slow down your proofreading by looking at your work a word at a time, pointing to each one with your pen or pencil. Placing a ruler or sheet of paper below the line you are reading also helps to focus your attention. And reading from bottom to top or from right to left will also force you to pay attention to individual words, one by one. Finally, as you revise, be sure to write out a clean intermediate draft whenever possible since spotting spelling errors can be difficult in a text covered with corrections and cross-outs or one that is written in a hurried scrawl.

(3) Keep a list of the words you misspell.

The words that you misspell on your writing assignments should be recorded in the Individual Spelling List at the end of this *Workbook*. Since most people have a tendency to misspell certain words repeatedly, you should review the list frequently as you revise.

(4) Write by syllables the words you misspell; then write the definitions of the words; finally, use the words in sentences.

e•nig•mat•ic   puzzling or baffling

The report was *enigmatic* until I looked up words that I did not know the meanings of.

pro•pen•si•ty   a natural inclination or tendency.

My supervisor has a *propensity* for making spot-checks.

(5) Learn to spell these words, which are commonly used in business and professional writing.

absence	correspondence	influential	professional
accommodate	correspondent	initiate	prominent
accomplish	courteous	insistence	quantity
achievement	decision	interrupt	questionnaire
acquainted	defendant	judgment	receipt
address	dependent	knowledge	receive
annual	description	labeled	recognize
answer	desirable	laboratory	recommend
apparatus	development	library	reference
apparent	difference	lien	referred
appropriate	disadvantage	maintenance	repetition
argument	dissatisfied .	management	rescind
arrangement	division	maneuver	resistance
article	efficient	manual	respectfully
attach	eligible	medicine	restaurant
attendance	eliminate	mortgage	salary
attorney	envelope	necessary	schedule
balance	equipment	noticeable	secretarial
basically	especially	occasion	separate
beginning	essential	occurred	serviceable
brochure	excellent	opinion	similar
bureaucracy	experience	opportunity	sincerely
business	familiar	original	stationary
calculator	February	pamphlet	stationery
calendar	financial	parallel	strategy
catalog	foreman	possess	succeed
category	fundamental	practical	superintendent
characteristic	generally	precede	technician
college	government	prefer	technique
committee	guarantee	prepare	tendency
competition	height	presence	thorough
concede	identify	prevalent	unusual
congratulate	immediately	probably	
consensus	incessant	procedure	
convenience	indispensable	proceed	

(6) Learn the different meanings for these confusing words.

accept, except	envelop, envelope
access, excess	fair, fare
adapt, adopt	faze, phase
advice, advise	formerly, formally
affect, effect	forth, fourth
aisles, isles	forward, foreword
alley, ally	gorilla, guerrilla
allude, elude	hear, here
allusion, illusion	heard, herd
already, all ready	heroin, heroine
altar, alter	hoarse, horse
altogether, all together	hole, whole
always, all ways	holy, wholly
angel, angle	human, humane
ascent, assent	instance, instants
assistance, assistants	its, it's
baring, barring, bearing	later, latter
birth, berth	led, lead
board, bored	lessen, lesson
born, borne	lightening, lightning
break, brake	lose, loose
breath, breathe	maybe, may be
buy, by	minor, miner
canvas, canvass	moral, morale
capital, capitol	of, off
censor, censure, sensor	passed, past
choose, chose	patience, patients
cite, sight, site	peace, piece
clothes, cloths	persecute, prosecute
coarse, course	personal, personnel
complement, compliment	perspective, prospective
conscience, conscious	plain, plane
council, counsel	pray, prey
credible, creditable	precede, proceed
cursor, curser	predominant, predominate
dairy, diary	presence, presents
decent, descent, dissent	principal, principle
desert, dessert	prophecy, prophesy
detract, distract	purpose, propose
device, devise	quiet, quit
dominant, dominate	respectfully, respectively
dual, duel	right, rite, write
dyeing, dying	road, rode
elicit, illicit	sense, since

shone, shown
stationary, stationery
statue, stature, statute
straight, strait
taut, taunt
than, then
their, there, they're
thorough, through

to, too, two
track, tract
waist, waste
weak, week
weather, whether
were, where
who's, whose
your, you're

(7) Invest in a good spelling dictionary.

A spelling dictionary is a small, inexpensive book that gives only the spelling and syllable breaks for each word. It will make looking up words faster and easier.

(8) If you use a word processor, use its spelling checker.

The spell-check feature of a word processing program will help you to catch many spelling errors (except for words that are misused rather than misspelled, for example, *accept* and *except*). If your word processor does not offer a spelling check option, you can still use your computer in this way by purchasing a compatible spell-check program, a software package that can evaluate texts written in a variety of word processing programs. Your spelling checker can help you learn to be a better speller simply because it will call your attention to the mistakes you are making and because such programs require *you* to select the correct word to replace the misspelling.

Deduct 2 1/2 for each blank incorrectly filled.

Misspelling Caused by Mispronunciation

Exercise 18-1

NAME _____ SCORE _____

18a To avoid omitting, adding, transposing, or changing a letter in a word, pronounce the word carefully according to the way the dictionary divides it into syllables.

The places where common mistakes are made in pronunciation—and spelling—are indicated in **boldface**.

OMISSIONS   candidate, everything, government

ADDITIONS   athlete, laundry, drowned

TRANSPOSITIONS   perform, children, tragedy

CHANGE   accurate, prejudice, separate

DIRECTIONS   With the aid of your dictionary, write out each of the following words by syllables, indicate the position of the primary accent, and pronounce the word correctly and distinctly. (Different dictionaries vary in the way they divide words into syllables. You may find that in a few cases your word divisions differ from someone else's.) In your pronunciation avoid any careless omission, addition, transposition, or change.

EXAMPLE
similar   *sim·i·lar*

1. sophomore	*soph·o·more*	15. partner	*part·ner*
2. different	*dif·fer·ent*	16. family	*fam·i·ly*
3. represent	*rep·re·sent*	17. prepare	*pre·pare*
4. escape	*es·cape*	18. candidate	*can·di·date*
5. library	*li·brar·y*	19. interpret	*in·ter·pret*
6. recognize	*rec·og·nize*	20. professor	*pro·fes·sor*
7. hungry	*hun·gry*	21. further	*fur·ther*
8. perhaps	*per·haps*	22. prescription	*pre·scrip·tion*
9. athletic	*ath·let·ic*	23. circumstance	*cir·cum·stance*
10. environment	*en·vi·ron·ment*	24. congratulate	*con·grat·u·late*
11. mischievous	*mis·chie·vous*	25. destruction	*de·struc·tion*
12. pamphlet	*pam·phlet*	26. mirror	*mir·ror*
13. describe	*de·scribe*	27. prisoner	*pris·o·ner*
14. interest	*in·ter·est*	28. used	*used*

29. accidentally — *ac·ci·den´·tal·ly*
30. especially — *es·pe´·cial·ly*
31. temperament — *tem´·per·a·ment*
32. asked — *asked*
33. supposedly — *sup·pos´·ed·ly*
34. scissors — *scis´·sors*

35. February — *Feb´·ru·ary*
36. surprise — *sur·prise´*
37. hindrance — *hin´·drance*
38. receipt — *re·ceipt´*
39. knowledge — *knowl´·edge*
40. privilege — *priv´·i·lege*

Deduct 4 for each blank incorrectly filled.

**Confusion of Words Similar in Sound
and/or Spelling**   Exercise 18–2

NAME _____ SCORE _____

**18b Distinguish between words that have a similar sound or spelling. To be sure
of the spelling, check the word's meaning in the context of the sentence.**

affect—effect   quiet—quit—quite
loose—lose   to—too—two

(Make a note of words you misuse on the Individual Spelling List on page 412.)

DIRECTIONS   In the following sentences cross out the spelling or spellings in parentheses
that do not fit the meaning, and write the correct spelling in the blank at the right.
Consult your dictionary freely.

EXAMPLE
(Their, ~~There~~, ~~They're~~) loan did not go through.   *Their*

1. With the growth of large corporations, the success

   rate of small businesses is bound to (~~altar~~, alter).   *alter*

2. Economic ups and downs have less of an (~~affect~~,

   effect) on diversified conglomerates.   *effect*

3. People find this change hard to (accept, ~~except~~).   *accept*

4. Today, managing a successful cottage industry

   (~~presence~~, presents) many potential problems.   *presents*

5. People who think they can make a living making

   and selling crafts are often in for (~~quiet~~, ~~quit~~,

   quite) a surprise.   *quite*

6. The (principal, ~~principle~~) difficulty they encounter

   is finding a market for their goods.   *principal*

7. Many people are not (~~holey~~, wholly, ~~holy~~) con-

   vinced that individually crafted goods are worth

   the higher prices their makers charge.   *wholly*

8. A pessimist might (prophesy, ~~prophecy~~) the even-

   tual death of handmade goods.   *prophesy*

9. Others find this forecast (~~to~~, too, ~~two~~) gloomy.   *too*

10. Some theorists think that greedy consumerism

often (precedes, ~~proceeds~~) an economic recession.   *precedes*

11. Too much credit card buying can signal a (~~week~~, weak) economy.   *weak*

12. But most consumers are not (~~conscience~~, conscious) of these early warning signals.   *conscious*

13. Is there any (~~advise~~, advice) to offer the average businessperson?   *advice*

14. Traditional theories (passed, ~~past~~) over some factors that contributed to the most recent recession.   *passed*

15. This represents one (~~instants~~, instance) of the complex nature of a global economy.   *instance*

16. By the time experts could evaluate all the data, the deadline had (~~all ready~~, already) passed.   *already*

17. But an economy never becomes truly (~~stationery~~, stationary).   *stationary*

18. Even so, the reasons for its shifts continue to (elude, ~~allude~~) analysts and investors.   *elude*

19. (It's, ~~Its~~) one thing to talk about economic instability and quite another to pinpoint its causes.   *It's*

20. Some people would rather complain (~~then~~, than) try to find solutions to the problems.   *than*

21. Everyone seems to have (~~ideals~~, ideas) about how to improve the economy.   *ideas*

22. But ideas do little to lift the (morale, ~~moral~~) of people whose businesses collapse.   *morale*

23. (Whether, ~~Weather~~) one runs a cottage industry or a large corporation, profits still matter.   *Whether*

24. The desire to compete can (~~led~~, lead) people into new business ventures.   *lead*

25. Those who do not overestimate their potential for success will be the ones who do not (~~loose~~, lose).   *lose*

Deduct 3 for each blank incorrectly filled.

Addition of Prefixes

Exercise 18–3

NAME _____ SCORE _____

18c Add the prefix to the root word without dropping letters. (The root is the base word to which a prefix or a suffix is added.)

un-	+	necessary	=	unnecessary
mis-	+	spell	=	misspell
dis-	+	agree	=	disagree

DIRECTIONS   In the blank at the right enter the correct spelling of each word with the prefix added. Consult your dictionary freely. Some dictionaries may hyphenate some of the following words. (See also **18f(3)**.)

EXAMPLES

mis-	+	quote	_misquote_
pre-	+	eminent	_preeminent_
1. pre-	+	paid	_prepaid_
2. re-	+	take	_retake_
3. mis-	+	spent	_misspent_
4. dis-	+	regard	_disregard_
5. un-	+	noticed	_unnoticed_
6. mis-	+	understood	_misunderstood_
7. dis-	+	appear	_disappear_
8. re-	+	activate	_reactivate_
9. dis-	+	satisfied	_dissatisfied_
10. mis-	+	pronounce	_mispronounce_
11. un-	+	usual	_unusual_
12. dis-	+	like	_dislike_
13. mis-	+	step	_misstep_
14. re-	+	evaluate	_reevaluate_
15. dis-	+	similar	_dissimilar_
16. re-	+	activate	_reactivate_
17. over-	+	run	_overrun_
18. un-	+	necessary	_unnecessary_
19. mis-	+	management	_mismanagement_

20.	pre-	+ dominate	*predominate*
21.	un-	+ witnessed	*unwitnessed*
22.	mis-	+ shaped	*misshaped*
23.	pre-	+ caution	*precaution*
24.	dis-	+ possessed	*dispossessed*
25.	re-	+ order	*reorder*
26.	dis-	+ solve	*dissolve*
27.	pre-	+ occupation	*preoccupation*
28.	over-	+ reach	*overreach*
29.	dis-	+ appoint	*disappoint*
30.	re-	+ generate	*regenerate*
31.	dis-	+ trust	*distrust*
32.	under-	+ developed	*underdeveloped*
33.	re-	+ consider	*reconsider*
34.	un-	+ forgettable	*unforgettable*
35.	mis-	+ apply	*misapply*

Deduct 5 for each blank incorrectly filled.

Adding Suffixes—Final *e*

Exercise 18–4

NAME _____ SCORE _____

18d(1) Drop the final *e* before a suffix beginning with a vowel but not before a suffix beginning with a consonant.

bride	+	-al	=	bridal	fame	+	-ous	=	famous
care	+	-ful	=	careful	entire	+	-ly	=	entirely

Exceptions: *due, duly; awe, awful; hoe, hoeing; singe, singeing.* After *c* or *g* the final *e* is retained before suffixes beginning with *a* or *o: notice, noticeable; courage, courageous.*

DIRECTIONS   Write the correct spelling of each word with the suffix added. Consult your dictionary freely. Write (*ex*) after each answer that is an exception to rule **18d(1)**.

EXAMPLES

argue	+	-ing	*arguing*
dye	+	-ing	*dyeing (ex)*
1. become	+	-ing	*becoming*
2. outrage	+	-ous	*outrageous (ex)*
3. reverse	+	-ible	*reversible*
4. manage	+	-ment	*management*
5. advise	+	-able	*advisable*
6. extreme	+	-ly	*extremely*
7. judge	+	-ment	*judgment (ex) or judgement*
8. sincere	+	-ly	*sincerely*
9. write	+	-ing	*writing*
10. live	+	-ing	*living*
11. sure	+	-ly	*surely*
12. value	+	-able	*valuable*
13. argue	+	-ment	*argument*
14. resource	+	-ful	*resourceful*
15. like	+	-ly	*likely*
16. arrange	+	-ment	*arrangement*
17. hope	+	-ful	*hopeful*

18. excite   +   -able   *excitable*
19. use   +   -age   *usage*
20. knowledge   +   -able   *knowledgeable (ex)*

Deduct 5 for each blank incorrectly filled.

Adding Suffixes—Doubling the Consonant

Exercise 18–5

NAME _____ SCORE _____

18d(2) When the suffix begins with a vowel (*ing, ed, ence, ance, able*) double a final single consonant if it is preceded by a single vowel that is in an accented syllable. (A one-syllable word, of course, is always accented.)

mop, mopped   [Compare with *mope, moped*]
mop, mopping   [Compare with *mope, moping*]
con·fer´, con·fer´ red   [Final consonant in the accented syllable]
ben·e·fit; ben´·e·fited   [Final consonant not in the accented syllable]
need, needed   [Final consonant not preceded by a single vowel]

DIRECTIONS   In the blank at the right enter the correct spelling of each word with the suffix added. Consult your dictionary freely.

EXAMPLE			
control	+	-ed	*controlled*
1. transmit	+	-ing	*transmitting*
2. control	+	-able	*controllable*
3. stop	+	-ed	*stopped*
4. pour	+	-ing	*pouring*
5. equip	+	-ed	*equipped*
6. rot	+	-en	*rotten*
7. proceed	+	-ed	*proceeded*
8. big	+	-est	*biggest*
9. prefer	+	-ed	*preferred*
10. mirror	+	-ed	*mirrored*
11. cut	+	-er	*cutter*
12. commit	+	-ing	*committing*
13. meet	+	-ing	*meeting*
14. travel	+	-er	*traveler*
15. occur	+	-ence	*occurrence*
16. begin	+	-ing	*beginning*
17. unforget	+	-able	*unforgettable*

18. fat   +   -en   *fatten*

19. label   +   -ed   *labeled*

20. attach   +   -ed   *attached*

Deduct 10 for each blank incorrectly filled.

Adding Suffixes—Final *y*

Exercise 18-6

NAME _____ SCORE _____

18d(3) Except before *ing*, a final *ẏ* preceded by a consonant is changed to *i* before a suffix.

defy	+	-ance	=	defiance	happy	+	-ness	=	happiness
modify	+	-er	=	modifier	modify	+	-ing	=	modifying
heavy	+	-er	=	heavier	pretty	+	-er	=	prettier

To make a noun plural or a verb singular, final *y* preceded by a consonant is changed to *i* and *es* is added.

duty	+	-es	=	duties	deny	+	-es	=	denies
ally	+	-es	=	allies	copy	+	-es	=	copies

Final *y* preceded by a vowel is usually not changed before a suffix.

annoy	+	-ed	=	annoyed	turkey	+	-s	=	turkeys

Exceptions: *pay, paid; lay, laid; say, said; day, daily.*

DIRECTIONS Enter the correct spelling of each word with the suffix added. Consult your dictionary freely. Write (*ex*) after each word that is an exception to rule **18d(3)**.

EXAMPLES

boundary	+	-es	*boundaries*
pay	+	-d	*paid (ex)*
1. donkey	+	-s	*donkeys*
2. hungry	+	-ly	*hungrily*
3. lay	+	-ed	*laid (ex)*
4. chimney	+	-s	*chimneys*
5. try	+	-es	*tries*
6. monkey	+	-s	*monkeys*
7. accompany	+	-es	*accompanies*
8. bury	+	-ed	*buried*
9. fallacy	+	-es	*fallacies*
10. lonely	+	-ness	*loneliness*

Deduct 3 1/3 for each blank incorrectly filled.

Forming the Plural

Exercise 18-7

NAME _____ SCORE _____

18d(4) and 18d(5) Form the plural of most nouns by (1) adding s to the singular form of the noun, (2) adding es to singular nouns that end in s, ch, sh, or x or (3) changing a final y to i and adding es if the noun ends in a y and is preceded by a consonant (see also **18d(3)**).

boy→boys	fox→foxes	mystery→mysteries
cupful→cupfuls	Harris→Harrises	beauty→beauties
Brown→Browns	calf→calves	reply→replies
	[f changed to v]	

A few nouns change their form for the plural: *woman→women; child→children.* And a few nouns ending in *o* take the *es* plural: *potato→potatoes; hero→heroes.*

DIRECTIONS   In the blank enter the plural form of each word. Consult your dictionary freely.

EXAMPLES
day   *days*
scratch   *scratches*

1.	arbitrator	*arbitrators*	16. company	*companies*
2.	stiletto	*stilettoes*	17. woman	*women*
3.	alloy	*alloys*	18. question	*questions*
4.	wolf	*wolves*	19. Jones	*Joneses*
5.	batch	*batches*	20. stress	*stresses*
6.	contract	*contracts*	21. genius	*geniuses*
7.	leaf	*leaves*	22. industry	*industries*
8.	stitch	*stitches*	23. half	*halves*
9.	scientist	*scientists*	24. witch	*witches*
10.	stereo	*stereos*	25. tomato	*tomatoes*
11.	machine	*machines*	26. mouse	*mice*
12.	speech	*speeches*	27. business	*businesses*
13.	hero	*heroes*	28. army	*armies*
14.	policy	*policies*	29. beach	*beaches*
15.	box	*boxes*	30. elf	*elves*

Deduct 5 for each blank incorrectly filled.

Confusion of *ei* and *ie*   Exercise 18–8

NAME _____ SCORE _____

18e When the sound is *ee* (as in *see*), write *ei* after *c* (*receipt*, *ceiling*), and *ie* after any other letter (*relieve*, *priest*); when the sound is other than *ee*, usually write *ei* (*eight*, *their*, *reign*).

Exceptions: *either, neither, financier, leisure, seize, species, weird.*

Note: This rule does not apply when *ei* or *ie* is not pronounced as one simple sound (*alien, audience, fiery*) or when *cie* stands for *shə* (*conscience, ancient, efficient*).

DIRECTIONS Fill in the blanks in the following words by writing *ei* or *ie*. Consult your dictionary freely. Write (*ex*) after any word that is an exception to rule **18e**.

EXAMPLES
dec *ei* ve

ei ther (*ex*)

1. w *ei* rd (*ex*)   11. n *ei* ther (*ex*)

2. f *ie* nd   12. w *ei* ght

3. h *ei* ght   13. rel *ie* ve

4. c *ei* ling   14. spec *ie* s (*ex*)

5. gr *ie* ve   15. th *ie* f

6. sl *ei* gh   16. rec *ei* ve

7. l *ei* sure (*ex*)   17. ch *ie* f

8. gr *ie* f   18. conc *ei* ted

9. s *ie* ge   19. y *ie* ld

10. bel *ie* f   20. misch *ie* f (*ex*)

Deduct 3 1/3 for each incorrect item.

Hyphenated Words

Exercise 18–9

NAME _____ SCORE _____

18f In general, use the hyphen (1) between two or more words serving as a single adjective before a noun (except when the first word is an adverb ending in *ly*), (2) with compound numbers from twenty-one to ninety-nine and with fractions, (3) with prefixes or suffixes for clarity, (4) with the prefixes *ex-*, *self-*, *all-*, and *great-* and with the suffix *elect*, (5) between a prefix and a proper name, and (6) never before an adverb ending in *-ly*.

(1) a *know-it-all* expression
(2) *sixty-six, one-half*
(3) *re-collect* the surplus   [to distinguish from *recollect* an event]
(4) *ex-wife, self-help, all-important, great-grandmother, major-elect*
(5) *mid-July, un-American*
(6) *largely ignored* rule, *clearly expressed* ideas

DIRECTIONS   Supply hyphens where they are needed in the following list. Not all items require hyphens.

EXAMPLES
a well-spent bonus

a bonus well spent

1. ex-President Moretz

2. a commonly used adjective

3. a twenty-five-year-old building

4. He is seventy-four.

5. self-reliant

6. clumsily executed move

7. mid-July

8. a four-foot barricade

9. Senator-elect Rowe

10. a high-rise apartment

11. chocolate-covered ants

12. results that are long lasting

13. the self-paced training program

14. long-lasting results

15. a two-thirds vote of the Senate

16. the awkwardly expressed phrase

17. the all-seeing eye of the camera

18. The shop specializes in teen age fashions.

19. three-fourths of the voters said no

20. students who are career minded

21. dust-covered shelves

22. He feels all right now.

23. The officer re-searched the suspect.

24. an all-inclusive study

25. She is my great-aunt.

26. a two-part process

27. The process had two parts.

28. the up-and-down pattern of the stock exchange

29. a long-distance call

30. western-style jeans

19

Learn the ways an up-to-date dictionary can help you select the words that express your ideas exactly.

An up-to-date desk dictionary is a necessary reference tool for any student or professional person. (A desk dictionary is based on one of the unabridged—complete, unshortened—dictionaries, such as *Webster's Third New International*, usually found on a stand in the reference area of the library.) An up-to-date dictionary not only will show you how words are spelled and hyphenated, but it provides other information. For example, (1) it shows you how to pronounce a word like *harass;* (2) it gives information about a word's origin and gives the various meanings of the word as it is used today; (3) it lists the forms and possible uses of a verb like *sing;* (4) it gives the synonyms and antonyms of a word like *oppose;* and (5) it may provide usage labels for words like *poke, nowhere,* and *irregardless.* A desk dictionary may also supply you with miscellaneous information such as a brief history of the English language, the dates and identities of famous people, geographical facts, and lists of colleges and universities in the United States and Canada. A current desk dictionary is one of the best investments that you can make.

19a Learn to use an up-to-date dictionary intelligently.

Study the introductory matter to find out what your dictionary's guides to abbreviations and pronunciation are; to know what plural and tense forms your dictionary lists; to learn what attitude your dictionary takes toward usage labels (dictionaries vary in the kinds of labels they use, and some dictionaries label more words than others do); and to understand the order in which the meanings of words are listed—that is, in order of common usage or of historical development.

Most words (and most meanings of words) in dictionaries are unlabeled; that is, they are appropriate on any occasion because they are in general use in the English-speaking world.

Avoid choosing words with the labels discussed in **19b–g** unless you are certain that they are appropriate to your chosen reading audience and your purpose.

19b Use informal words only when appropriate to the audience.

There is one class of words—labeled *Informal* or sometimes *Colloquial*—that is commonly used and understood by most writers and speakers. Words in this class are appropriate in speaking and in informal writing and are usually necessary in recording dialogue, since most people speak less formally than they write. In most of your college and professional writing, however, you should generally avoid words labeled *Informal* or *Colloquial.*

INFORMAL   The writer *lifted* the passage from a report he was studying.

STANDARD OR FORMAL   The writer *plagiarized* the passage from a report he was studying.

Except in dialogue, contractions are usually not appropriate in formal writing, though they may be used (in moderation) in business letters when a conversational tone is sought.

INFORMAL   *There's* hardly anyone who *doesn't* respond to a good oral presentation.

STANDARD OR FORMAL   *There is* hardly anyone who *does not* respond to a good oral presentation.

19c Use newly coined words or slang only when appropriate to the audience.

Slang words are popular expressions that either change their meanings rapidly or pass out of use quickly. (Labeled *Slang* in the dictionary.)

SLANG   She was really *uptight* about the interview.

APPROPRIATE   She was *nervous* about the interview.

Newly coined words can be slang expressions, but they also include words created to cover new situations, concepts, and so on. Because of the newness of the concept itself, many readers may remain unfamiliar with the term used to label it. For example, until the 1988 presidential campaign, few people had heard of *spin doctors* or *sound bites*. If you are unsure whether your reader will understand the new word that you intend to use, define it or find a substitute.

NEWLY COINED WORD   Last night's news offered two *sound bites* from the candidate's speech.

APPROPRIATE   Last night's news offered two *excerpts* from the candidate's speech.

19d Use regional words only when appropriate to the audience.

These are words used by people in one section of the country; consequently, readers outside the region where a given word is current may misunderstand their meaning. (Labeled *Dialectical, Regional,* or *Colloquial* in the dictionary.)

REGIONAL   The company car is *right* nice.

APPROPRIATE   The company car is *very* nice.

19e Avoid nonstandard words and usages.

Including nonstandard words or phrases in your writing may lead your reader to think of you as uneducated. (Labeled *Nonstandard* or *Illiterate* in the dictionary or omitted entirely.)

NONSTANDARD   He *busted* the computer.

APPROPRIATE   He *broke* the computer.

19f Avoid archaic and obsolete words

These words are no longer used in ordinary writing and tend to mark the writer as being pretentious or a snob. (Labeled *Archaic, Obsolete, Obsolescent,* or *Rare* in the dictionary.)

OBSOLETE   The *eldritch* computer no longer served their purpose.

APPROPRIATE   The *ancient* computer no longer served their purpose.

19g Use technical words and jargon only when appropriate to the audience.

These words are appropriate only for a specialized audience. When the occasion demands the use of a word that is labeled as belonging to a particular profession or trade—for example, an address to a medical convention might call for technical language or even jargon—the word may be judged appropriate because the audience will understand it. But in general speaking and writing you should depend on the multitude of unlabeled words that most audiences or readers can be expected to understand.

19h Choose words and combinations of sounds that are appropriate to clear prose writing.

A poetic style is generally not appropriate in college essays or professional reports. Usually such writing seems wordy, vague, and even ridiculous.

FLOWERY   He was a *tower of power* in our community, a *blazing meteor in a prosperous enterprise.*

PLAIN BUT CLEAR   He was a *powerful* man in our community, a *remarkably successful businessman.*

Deduct 1 1/2 for every blank incorrectly filled.

Using the Dictionary

Exercise 19–1

NAME _____ SCORE _____

The full title, the edition, and the date of publication of my dictionary are as follows: _The American Heritage Dictionary, Second Collegiate edition, 1982._ *

1. Abbreviations   Where does the dictionary explain the abbreviations it uses?

In the Abbreviations section

Write out the meaning of each of the abbreviations that follow these entries:

perjure, *tr. v.*   _transitive verb_

yoeman, *n. pl.*   _plural noun_

infra-, *prep.*   _prefix_

nohow, *adv.*, Dial   _adverb, Dialect_

2. Spelling and pronunciation   Using your dictionary as a guide, write out by syllables each of the words listed below, and place the accent where it belongs. With the aid of the diacritical marks (the accent marks and symbols), the phonetic respelling of the word (in parentheses or slashes immediately after the word), and the key at the bottom of the page in the introductory matter, determine the preferred pronunciation (that is, the first pronunciation given). Then pronounce each word correctly several times.

propitiate   _pro·pi´·ti·ate_

minuscule   _min´·us·cule_

similitude   _si·mil´·i·tude_

automaton   _au·tom´·a·ton_

Write the plurals of the following nouns:

appendix   _appendices or appendixes_

ox   _oxen_

* _Answers will vary for students with different dictionaries._

potato _____*potatoes*_____

medium _____*media*_____

focus _____*foci, focuses*_____

Rewrite each of the following words that needs a hyphen:

particolored _____*parti-colored*_____

lightweight _____

selfservice _____*self-service*_____

3. Derivations The derivation, or origin, of a word (given in brackets) often furnishes a literal meaning that helps you to remember the word. For each of the following words, give (a) the source—the language from which it is derived, (b) the original word or words, and (c) the original meaning.

	Source	*Original word(s) and meaning*
pronounce	*Latin*	*pro + nuntiare = to announce forth*
antidote	*Greek*	*anti + didonai = to give against*
neighbor	*Old English*	*neāh + gebūr = near dweller*

4. Meanings Usually words develop several different meanings. How many meanings are listed in your dictionary for the following words?

catch, *n.* _*11*_   run, *v. tr.* _*27*_   out, *adv.* _*13*_

round, *adj.* _*17*_   with, *prep.* _*28*_   home, *n.* _*10*_

Does your dictionary list meanings in order of historical development or in order of common usage? _____*common usage*_____

5. Special labels Some words have technical, or field, labels. These words are likely to be understood by people involved in a particular field of study or occupation, but their definitions may be unknown to people outside the field. Based on your dictionary's label of the word, what field would be likely to use each of

Using the Dictionary   Exercise 19-1 (continued)

the following words? (If the label is abbreviated and you are unfamiliar with
it, consult your dictionary's list of abbreviations.)

googol　　　_mathematics_

porphyry　　_geology_

epineurium　_medicine_

trochee　　　_poetry_

hydroponics　_agriculture_

6. Usage labels   For each italicized word in the items below, consult your dictionary to see if the meaning of the word as it is used here has a usage label
(such as *Slang* or *Informal*). If it does, enter the label in the blank and rewrite
the entire expression in standard English. If it does not, leave the blanks empty.

	Usage label	*Standard English usage*
most everyone	_Informal_	_almost everyone_
suspicion nothing	_Nonstandard (as verb)_	_suspect nothing_
speaker *don't* see	_Nonstandard_	_speaker doesn't see_
he *reckons* so	_Dialect_	_he thinks so_
tardiness *bugs* me	_Slang_	_tardiness bothers me_
bust the window	_Informal_	_break the window_
a *bad* looking man	_Slang_	_a good looking man_
finalized the contract		
tough luck	_Slang_	_bad luck_

7. Synonyms   Even among words with essentially the same meaning (synonyms), one word usually fits a given context more exactly than any other. To
differentiate precise shades of meaning, some dictionaries include special para-

graphs showing groups of closely related words. What synonyms are specially differentiated in your dictionary for the following words?

yearn, v. _long, pine, hanker, hunger, thirst_

enormous, adj. _immense, huge, gigantic, colossal, mammoth, tremendous, stupendous, gargantuan, vast_

8. Capitalization Check your dictionary; then rewrite any of the following words that may be capitalized.

achilles _Achilles_ sociology _____

feminism _____ misogynist _____

el salvador _El Salvador_ korean _Korean_

9. Grammatical information Note that many words may serve as two or more parts of speech. List the parts of speech—*vt., vi., n., adj., adv., prep., conj., interj.*—that each of the following words may be.

mission _n., vt._

in _prep., adv., adj., n._

clear _adj., vt., vi._

low _adj., adv., n., vi._

what _pro., adj., adv., interj., conj._

10. Miscellaneous information Answer the following questions by referring to your dictionary, and be prepared to tell in what part of the dictionary the information is located.

Who was Sojourner Truth? _American abolitionist_

Where is Annapurna? _Nepal_

What is a CPU? _Central Processing Unit_

Does your dictionary give a history of the English language? _Yes_

20

Choose words that are precise, appropriate, and specific.

To communicate clearly, you must choose your words carefully, using words that express your ideas and feelings *exactly*.

As you learned in **18b** and in section **19**, there is a great difference in meaning between two words like *accept* and *except*, even though they sound nearly the same. There is also a great difference in meaning between *famous* and *notorious*—two words that suggest fame but in very different senses. Imagine how few products your company would sell if you used *notorious* for *famous* in your advertising copy.

> Our styling spray is *notorious* the world over for its effects on men's hair.

Obviously, the audience for your advertisement would envision undesirable results from using your company's product.

To be exact requires more than choosing words that are correct. You must also choose words that are specific enough to be clear and that are appropriate for the audience you are addressing. If you say that your company's styling spray makes hair "look nice," you may know what you mean, but such a general description is not likely to give your audience a clear picture of your product's effect. And if you say that the styling spray "imparts aesthetic enhancements to one's coiffure," you will probably lose your audience midway through your first sentence. Exactness, then, means that your words are correct, specific, and appropriate for your audience and purpose.

20a(1) Choose words that express your ideas precisely.

Inexact words can confuse readers or cause them to make associations that you had not intended. Often these problems arise because a writer has neglected to take into account a word's denotation (its explicit, dictionary meaning) or has ignored its connotation (what the word can suggest or imply). Practiced writers make sure that they choose the words they use with care to avoid unintentionally offending, alienating, or confusing their readers.

DENOTATION PROBLEM	I urge you to *adapt* my proposal in its *entity*.
CORRECT DENOTATION	I urge you to *adopt* my proposal in its *entirety*.
CONNOTATION PROBLEM	I *beseech* you to adopt my proposal.
CORRECT CONNOTATION	I *urge* you to adopt my proposal.

Remember that a wrong word is very noticeable to your reader and may, like a misspelled word, discredit your entire letter, report, or essay.

20a(2) Choose appropriate words.

Technical terminology that is appropriate for a reader familiar with your field may be meaningless to others. Technical jargon, or field talk, should be confined to presentations made to people within your own specialized area. When writing or speaking to a general audience, always clearly define any technical terms that you use, and use only those technical terms for which no ordinary word or explanation is available.

TECHNICAL   Our word processor uses diskettes that can *store 130,000 bytes of information.*

CLEAR   Our word processor uses diskettes that can *contain 75 typed pages of information.*

Appropriate words, then, are words that your audience is likely to be familiar with. Never use a fancy term like "ocular enhancers" when you simply mean *glasses.* Avoid other heavy, ornate language unless you want to be considered snobbish and pretentious. In short, choose the simple and familiar word or phrase whenever possible.

20a(3) Choose specific words.

Words like *big, interesting, exciting, wonderful,* and *good* are too general to communicate an idea clearly to your reader. Giving exact details is essential in technical-report and business-letter writing—think how disastrous it would be if a doctor told a patient to take a *couple* of sleeping pills *every now and then.* Whenever possible, choose the specific word or phrase that communicates the exact quality you have in mind.

GENERAL   Mr. Chomsky's report was *interesting.*

SPECIFIC   Mr. Chomsky's report *explained the government regulations that apply to the labeling of drugs.*

GENERAL   Learning to be a sales representative requires *a lot of things.*

SPECIFIC   Learning to be a sales representative requires that you *get to know the product well, to understand its main selling points,* and *to determine the specific needs of your customers.*

20b Use idiomatic expressions correctly.

Exactness also includes the choice of idiomatic language. Idioms are expressions whose meaning differs from what the meanings of the individual words would lead you to expect. Native speakers are able to use idioms without thinking, but for someone unfamiliar with an expression such as *kick the bucket,* idioms can be confusing.

You use many idiomatic expressions every day without considering their meaning, especially phrasal verbs—for example, "I ran *into* an old friend" and "She *played down* the importance of money." In these examples and in other such expressions, the choice of the particle (*into*, *down*) accounts for the expression's being idiomatic. While most of us would not make the error of writing "I *ran over* an old friend" when we mean that we *met* an old friend, we might slip and use the unidiomatic *comply to* rather than the idiomatic *comply with*.

UNIDIOMATIC   The product did not *comply to* the company's standards.

IDIOMATIC   The product did not *comply with* the company's standards.

20c Choose fresh expressions instead of trite, worn-out ones.

Trite expressions, or clichés, are idiomatic expressions that have been used so often that they have become meaningless. At one time readers would have thought the expression "tried and true" was effective, a fresh and exact choice of words. Today, readers have seen and heard the expression so often that they hardly notice it, except perhaps to be bored or amused by it. In your reader's eyes, clichés can also mark you as a lazy, uncaring writer, one who will not make the effort to find a fresh way of saying something. Although clichés are common in most people's speech and may even occur at times in the work of professional writers, such words and phrases should generally be avoided because they no longer convey ideas exactly.

TRITE   *Last but not least*, our sales people will have to *put their shoulders to the wheel* or our competitors will *blow us away* in the next quarter.

EXACT   *Last*, our sales people will have to *work hard* or our competitors will *outdistance us* in the next quarter.

Deduct 5 for each blank incorrectly filled.

Exactness

Exercise 20-1

NAME _____ SCORE _____

DIRECTIONS   In the following sentences cross out the word choice in parentheses that would be incorrect, trite, or inappropriate in an essay written for a general audience. Write the exact or appropriate word choice in the blank. Consult your dictionary freely.

EXAMPLE

Most business persons dress (appropriately for, ~~apropos of~~) the occasion.

appropriately for

1. It is (~~for sure,~~ clear) that first impressions *do* make a difference.

clear.

2. If your clothes look too trendy, they (~~deflect,~~ distract) your customers and may even offend them.

distract

3. Our skills, not our wardrobe, are the (predominant, ~~predominate~~) thing we want business associates to remember.

predominant

4. While jeans and a sweatshirt may not be out of place at a service station, they would (~~turn off,~~ alienate) the clients of a real estate agent.

alienate

5. Inappropriate dress can be a (~~principle,~~ principal) reason that a customer reacts negatively to a salesperson.

principal

6. Looking professional is the (~~sine qua non,~~ essential element) in winning a customer's confidence.

essential element

7. Furthermore, a neat, well-groomed appearance (~~attributes,~~ contributes) to your own confidence.

contributes

8. The way you talk can also (~~infer,~~ imply) things to your customer.

imply

9. And, in some (~~instants,~~ instances), you can offend your customer if you use inappropriate language.

instances

10. You should be (conscious, ~~conscience~~) of the impact
    that your way of speaking has on your clients.   *conscious*

11. You should not appear to be excessively (enthusias-
    tic, ~~enthused~~), or your customer may think you are
    insincere.   *enthusiastic*

12. You should also be (aware, ~~cognizant~~) that slang
    makes some people think you do not take them seri-
    ously.   *aware*

13. Like slang, too many jargon terms can (~~blow~~, un-
    dermine) your chance of making a good impres-
    sion.   *undermine*

14. (~~Obfuscating~~, Clouding) the issue with big words
    impresses few people, even experts.   *Clouding*

15. People often feel talked down to when someone
    uses (too many, ~~a bunch of~~) technical terms.   *too many*

16. Taking your customers' needs into account is actu-
    ally a way of paying them a (~~complement~~, compli-
    ment).   *compliment*

17. Mannerisms such as gum chewing and nail biting
    can also (irritate, ~~tick off~~) customers.   *irritate*

18. The (~~less~~, fewer) distractions you give your cus-
    tomers, the more successful you will be in your job.   *fewer*

19. Of course, being considerate should also (affect, ~~ef-
    fect~~) your customers' good opinion of you.   *affect*

20. The truly (~~great~~, effective) business person is the
    one who puts the customers' needs first.   *effective*

21

Avoid wordiness in your essays, reports, and letters.

Wordiness results from inexact word choice (see also section **20**). Few writers, in their first drafts, are likely to make the best choices in phrasing. Therefore, to insure exactness and to eliminate wordiness, writers must carefully proofread and then revise their first drafts.

Today

~~In today's society~~ workers are concerned not only with protection from hazardous

working conditions ~~and situations~~ but ~~they are~~ also ~~concerned~~ with the quality

of the workplace. They ~~ask and~~ demand that work be more than safe; they also

it
want ~~work~~ to be interesting.

21a Use only those words or phrases that add meaning to your writing.

Most wordiness in composition results from a writer's attempt to achieve an elevated style, to write sentences that sound impressive. Many unnecessary phrases inevitably show up in the compositions of writers who never use one exact word when they can instead write a long, impressive-sounding phrase. The temptation to use impressive words leads to monster sentences. Readers, however, are likely to spot the pretentiousness and may dismiss the content of the writing as foolish even when it is not.

No one wants her or his ideas to be laughed at, but the quickest way to get that response is to write something like "Immediately if not sooner it would be prudent when in the presence of combusting materials for all employees and staff to exit and leave the nearby premises by the most expeditious means possible as soon as they are physically able to do so." What did the writer want to say? "In case of fire, immediately leave the building by the nearest exit." By the time the reader finishes the first sentence, the paper (and the reader) might well be ashes. In other words, be direct.

Here is a sampling of verbose phrases and pretentious words, along with their briefer, more straightforward counterparts.

Wordy	*Concise*
to be desirous of	want OR desire
to have a preference for	prefer
to be in agreement with	agree
due to the fact that	because OR since

Wordy	*Concise*
in view of the fact that	because OR since
in order to	to
at this point in time	now
in this day and age	today
with reference to	about
prior to	before
in the event of	if
subsequent	after
substantial	big, large
inadvertency	error
promulgate	issue
domicile	home, house
remuneration	pay
disclose	show, uncover
utilize	use
circa	about
sequent	following
i.e.	that is
e.g.	for example
along the line of	about
consensus of opinion	consensus
during the time that	while
for the purpose of	for
have the need for	need
in due course	soon
in many cases	often, frequently
few and far between	seldom
under the circumstances	because
in some cases	sometimes
in most cases	usually
in spite of the fact that	although

Another source of wordiness, particularly in student compositions, is the writer's lack of confidence in his or her opinions. Expressions such as "I think," "it seems to me," "in my opinion," and "would be" (for *is*) may be appropriate in writing about issues that are genuinely controversial, but more often they can be omitted. If you do not express your ideas confidently, your reader's confidence in them will be diminished, too.

WORDY   *It seems to me that* one reason for boredom among workers *would be* their mistaken belief that a job, to be satisfying, must be free of routine tasks.

CONCISE   One reason for boredom among workers *is* their mistaken belief that a job, to be satisfying, must be free of routine tasks.

Finally, you should work to eliminate unnecessary expletive constructions from your writing. This type of sentence uses *there* plus a form of *to be* and places the subject after the verb. An expletive construction generally weakens a sentence by removing the subject from the position of strong emphasis—the beginning.

WORDY   *There are* many causes of worker dissatisfaction.

CONCISE   Worker dissatisfaction has many causes.

It is also an expletive when it lacks an antecedent and is followed by a form of *to be.*

WORDY   *It was* tedious listening to the report.

CONCISE   Listening to the report was tedious.

Note: In a few cases, no logical subject exists and the *it* expletive construction is necessary: *It is* going to rain.

21b Restructure sentences whenever necessary to avoid wordiness.

Often you can combine two main clauses through subordination (see **1e** and **24a**) to avoid wordiness.

WORDY   Many people feel that everyone except them has escaped routine chores, and as a result of this feeling they become dissatisfied with their work.

CONCISE   Many people become dissatisfied with their work because they feel that everyone except them has escaped routine chores.

21c Avoid needless repetition of words and ideas.

Repetition of the same word in several sentences, unless for emphasis (see section **29**), results in monotonous writing. The use of pronouns and synonyms helps to avoid excessive repetition.

REPETITIOUS   Even creative *writers* face a number of routine chores. *Writers* must sit down at their desks each day and work a certain number of hours at their *writing. Writers* must revise the same piece of *writing* again and again.

BETTER   Even creative *writers* face a number of routine chores. *They* must sit down at their desks each day and work a certain number of hours at their *writing. They* must revise the same piece of *text* again and again.

Combining sentences, using a colon if appropriate, can also eliminate needless repetition.

REPETITIOUS   There are two major causes of wordiness in writing. *These two causes are* needless repetition and the use of meaningless words and phrases.

CONCISE   There are two major causes of wordiness in writing: needless repetition and the use of meaningless words and phrases.

OR

The two major causes of wordiness in writing are needless repetition and the use of meaningless words and phrases.

Several popular expressions are always repetitious: "each and every," "any and all," "various and sundry," "if and when," "combine together," "return back," "red in color," "triangular in shape," "city of Cleveland," and "a total of two."

REPETITIOUS   *Each and every* job involves a certain amount of routine.

CONCISE   *Every* [OR *Each*] job involves a certain amount of routine.

REPETITIOUS   *A total of three people* complained about boredom.

CONCISE   *Three people* complained about boredom.

In introducing quotations, many inexperienced writers tend to overwork forms of the verb *say*. Remember that verbs besides *say* can introduce quotations effectively—for example, *explain, point out, note, describe, observe, believe, feel,* and *think.*

REPETITIOUS   Albert S. Glickman, a researcher on work and leisure, *says,* "Work and leisure are part of one life." Glickman also *says* that "we need to improve the net quality of life." He *says* we are inexperienced in handling our leisure time by *saying:* "So far we haven't had much experience in the use of free time."

BETTER   Albert S. Glickman, a researcher on work and leisure, *believes* that "work and leisure are part of one life." Glickman *says,* "We need to improve the net quality of life." He *feels* that we are inexperienced in handling the leisure part of our lives: "So far," Glickman *points out,* "we haven't had much experience in the use of free time."

Deduct 4 for each incorrect revision and 2 2/3 for each blank incorrectly filled.

Avoiding Wordiness and Needless Repetition   Exercise 21-1

NAME _____ SCORE _____

DIRECTIONS   Cross out needless words in each of the following sentences. For each sentence that requires no further revision other than capitalization, punctuation, or deletion only, write *1* in the blank; for sentences that require additional changes in wording, write *2* in the blank and make the needed revision.⁕

EXAMPLE
~~Due to the fact~~ *Because* that the speaker appeared to be calm and confident,

the audience paid attention.   __2__

1. ~~The reason why~~ /the audience listened carefully ~~was~~ because

   the speaker kept his anxieties hidden.   __1__

2. ~~The person giving the~~ *a* successful ~~speech~~ *speaker* has learned ways to

   deal with the jitters.   __2__

3. Taking your time ~~and not~~ walking toward the podium ~~too~~

   ~~quickly~~ can help you stay calm ~~and remain collected.~~   __1__

4. ~~In the event that~~ *If* you are still nervous, pause ~~and take time~~ to

   arrange your note cards or manuscript.   __2__

5. You can also look out at your audience ~~as well as survey the~~

   ~~people there.~~   __1__

6. ~~It is obvious that~~ *Obviously* you should establish eye contact with your

   audience before you begin to speak.   __2__

7. Greet your audience in an appropriate way ~~and manner,~~ then

   open your speech on a positive note.   __1__

8. ~~There is~~ *O* one thing you should not do in your opening sentence,

   ~~and this~~ is ~~to~~ apologize to your audience.   __1__

⁕ *Students may find ways to eliminate wordiness other than those shown here, in which case they should be given credit.*

9. ~~In the event that~~ *If* you have had delays in getting to the speak-

   ing engagement, do not tell the audience about your hard-

   ships.   2

10. ~~It is recommended that an audience~~ *Your audience should* be at ease in your pres-

    ence, not concerned with inconveniences you experienced.   2

11. *Because* Many people feel that all speeches should have a humorous

    introduction, ~~and because of this~~ they always begin their pre-

    sentations with a joke.   2

12. If you begin with a joke, ~~it is important to~~ remember that a

    joke should be not only funny but ~~it should~~ also be appropriate

    to the topic of the speech.   1

13. A joke that the audience ~~listening to the speech~~ does not find

    funny ~~in quality~~ is a poor way to begin a speech.   1

14. Most speech textbooks say to begin with a joke only if it has

    been tested. They also ~~say that~~ *advise* you ~~should~~ *to* avoid a humorous

    beginning if you do not tell jokes well. And they ~~say~~ *point out or suggest* that you

    should be prepared to continue your speech immediately if the

    audience does not find your joke funny. ~~and fails to laugh at~~

    ~~it.~~   2

15. If the point of your joke is not appropriate to the purpose of

    your speech ~~and is off the topic,~~ your audience may spend the

    next few minutes trying to figure out ~~and understand the rea-~~

    ~~son~~ why you included it ~~in your speech.~~   1

22

Include all words necessary for clarity or emphasis.

Note: Since writers often omit words that are needed to complete a parallel construction, section **22** may profitably be studied together with section **26**.

22a Include all necessary articles, pronouns, conjunctions, and prepositions.

Note: Use a caret (**Λ**) to mark the place *below* the line where an omitted word, phrase, or mark of punctuation is to be inserted. Write the insertion *above* the line.

DIRECT QUOTATION   My speech teacher pointed out, "Your body language often communicates as much as your words do."

INDIRECT QUOTATION   My speech teacher pointed out *that* body language often communicates as much as words do. [The word *that* generally introduces an indirect quotation; without *that*, *body language*, rather than the entire clause, seems to be the object of *pointed out*.]

Avoid using intensifiers like **so** and **such** without a completing *that* clause; do not write *The speaker was* **so** *tense* or *The speaker was* **such** *an interesting person*. Either omit the *so* or *such* or explain the meaning of the intensifier with a *that* clause.

The speaker was so tense/ *that he made his audience uncomfortable.*

Note: The word *that* may be omitted when the meaning of the sentence would be clear at first reading without it.

The speaker was so tense he made his audience uncomfortable.

Omitting a preposition can result in unidiomatic phrasing.

The speaker believed *in* and made use of gestures during oral presentations. [*Believed in* (an idiom) means something quite different from *believed*. Without *in*, the sentence says that the speaker *believed gestures*—not what the writer intended.]

The type *of* gestures used by the speaker emphasized certain points. [Without *of*, *type* seems to be an adjective modifying *gestures*.]

Do not omit an article from a list of items that requires both *a*'s and *an*'s in order for it to make sense.

Effective body language includes *a* use of gestures, *a* movement on stage whenever

appropriate, and *an* expressive face.

22b Include necessary verbs and helping verbs.

Speakers have always *used* and will continue to use gestures during their presentations.   [Without the *used* the sentence would mean "Speakers *have* always *continue* and *will continue* to use gestures during their presentations." *Have continue* is an error in tense form.]

22c Include all words necessary to complete a comparison.

The speaker's gestures were as good *as* if not better than *those of* any other speaker I had observed.

Body language is as important as any *other* part of the speech.

Deduct 10 for each blank incorrectly filled.

Avoiding Omissions   Exercise 22–1

NAME _____ SCORE _____

DIRECTIONS   In the following sentences insert the words that are needed to complete the sense; then write those words in the blanks.

EXAMPLE

Many people do not understand that oral reports ^*are* something

they will present frequently.   *are*

1. Giving an oral report makes most people more nervous

   than preparing a written ^*report*   *report*

2. Accomplished speakers may be nervous, ^*but* they never let

   their uneasiness show.   *but*

3. Good speakers understand the importance ^*of* and know

   how to use gestures to keep their audience's attention.   *of*

4. An outline and ^*a* list of visual aids will help you keep your

   speech well organized.   *a*

5. People often ask what type ^*of* outline is best for presenta-

   tions.   *of*

6. You will find ^*that* the gestures you use in ordinary conversa-

   tion will be the most convincing.   *that*

7. Remember, too, *that* speaking too fast and not pausing for

    breath will make your report hard to understand. _____*that*_____

8. Voice coaches counsel their students *that* deep breathing will

    help them relax and speak distinctly. _____*that*_____

9. Eye contact, however, has *been* and always will be the best

    way for you to let your audience know you are sincere. _____*been*_____

10. If you cannot look at your audience, they will feel left

    out, and *you* will not know how they are reacting. _____*you*_____

SENTENCE UNITY   su 23

23

Make sure that all parts of a sentence are clearly related and that the subject, or central focus, of the sentence is clear.

Errors in unity are so common and so varied that it is impossible to show more than a sampling of them. (Often the instructor marks this type of mistake with a *K*, indicating that the sentence is awkward and needs to be entirely rewritten.) Most mistakes of this type stem from (1) a failure to establish a clear relationship between clauses in a sentence or (2) a tendency to overcrowd a sentence with adjectives and adverbs, thereby losing focus and confusing the reader.

23a Establish a clear relationship between main clauses in a sentence: develop unrelated ideas in separate sentences. (See also section **24**.)

UNCLEAR   Creighton Alexander lost his audience after only three minutes of speaking, and his face never showed a change of expression.

CLEAR   Because his face never showed a change of expression, Creighton Alexander lost his audience after only three minutes of speaking.
          OR
          Creighton Alexander's face never showed a change of expression even though he lost his audience after only three minutes of speaking.
          OR
          Creighton Alexander lost his audience after only three minutes of speaking. His face never showed a change of expression.

23b Keep the central focus of a sentence clear.

Adding too many phrases or clauses to the base sentence (*subject–verb–complement*)—even when they are relevant additions—will make the focus of the sentence unclear.

UNCLEAR   Creighton Alexander, with his shifting eyes and rigid body, which showed his nervousness all too clearly, while he stood as if planted behind the lectern, failed to establish any rapport with his audience. [The focus of the sentence—*Creighton Alexander*—has been lost.]

CLEAR   Creighton Alexander, with his shifting eyes and rigid body, failed to establish any rapport with his audience.

23c Do not mix constructions.

MIXED   When speakers ramble and stumble causes their audience to lose the thread of the argument.   [adverb clause + predicate]

REVISED   When speakers ramble and stumble, they cause their audience to lose the thread of the argument.   [adverb clause, main clause]

MIXED   It was a long speech but which was quite interesting.

REVISED   It was a long speech, but it was quite interesting.

OR

It was a long speech which was quite interesting.   [noun + adjective clause]

Note: Sometimes a sentence is flawed by the use of a singular noun instead of a plural one: "Many who attended the sales meeting brought their own cars." [NOT car]

23d Avoid faulty predication.

Faulty predication occurs when the subject and predicate do not fit each other logically.

ILLOGICAL   Because the speaker was enthusiastic kept the audience interested. [A *because* clause is not a noun or a pronoun and thus cannot function as a subject.]

LOGICAL   The speaker's enthusiasm kept the audience interested.   [*Enthusiasm* is a noun and can serve as the subject.]

OR

Because the speaker was enthusiastic, the audience stayed interested.

23e Avoid faulty *is-when* or *is-where* definitions.

ILLOGICAL   Gesturing is when a speaker uses his hands to clarify or emphasize certain points.   [*Gesturing* is an act, not a time.]

LOGICAL   Gesturing is the speaker's use of his hands to explain or emphasize certain points.

Deduct 7 for each incorrect revision and 3 for each blank incorrectly filled.
Unity of Sentence Structure Exercise 23–1

NAME _____ SCORE _____

DIRECTIONS   In the blanks enter *1* or *2* to indicate whether the chief difficulty in each sentence is (1) the linking of unrelated ideas or (2) unnecessary or excessive additions to the base sentence. Then revise the sentences to make them unified.⁂

EXAMPLE

~~When you take the time to look,~~ *I*f people are not paying attention

to your talk, you should, ~~and probably would want to,~~ change

your manner of presentation.   __2__

1. Look closely at the people you are addressing, and the pitch,

   rate of speech, and volume of your voice *also* help to establish rap-

   port with your audience.   __1__

2. If your audience seems not to be listening to you, the problem

   may be that you are speaking too softly *so* or that the audience

   cannot hear you.   __1__

3. Sometimes, besides talking too softly, another reason *p* people

   also cannot follow you is when you are speaking indistinctly.   __2__

4. Sometimes people have trouble understanding you if you talk

   too rapidly and *s* sometimes a high-pitched voice can also irri-

   tate the audience.   __1__

5. The audience's attention drifted, and *because* the speaker's voice was

   so low that what he had to say appeared boring.   __1__

⁂ *Students may find ways to achieve unity other than those shown here, in which case they should be given credit.*

6. ~~One of the least excusable errors in oral presentation,~~ *S*lurred

speech, which can be described as a lazy way of talking that

suggests ~~to your audience that~~ you are not really concerned

about ~~them,~~ *your audience* can make it very difficult for your listeners to

understand what you have to say.   _2_

7. Many speakers ruin the conclusion of their speeches by bela-

boring the issue, making their listeners think that they are fin-

ished when they are not, *a* ~~so all~~ speakers should keep their con-

cluding remarks concise and relevant.   _2_

8. One of the most common problems in speeches *occurs* ~~is~~ when the

speaker continues for many minutes after he has indicated that

his speech is about to end.   _2_

9. Finally, a speaker should not hurry from the rostrum once the

speech is completed, *since* ~~and~~ the audience may want to applaud.   _1_

10. Applause, ~~which is not expected in certain situations, such as~~

~~a company briefing, and~~ which usually follows a few seconds

of silent eye contact with the audience, should be accepted

from the rostrum, not from your seat.   _2_

24

Use subordination to show exact relationships between ideas. Use coordination to give ideas equal emphasis.

In section **1** you learned that short, choppy sentences may often be combined. When one of the short sentences is made into a sentence addition or modifier, the writer is using subordination. A writer uses subordination, or sentence combining, not only to improve style but also to show more clearly the relationships between ideas.

24a Instead of writing a series of short, choppy sentences, combine the sentences by expressing the main idea in the main or base clause and the less important ideas in subordinate clause or phrase additions.

CHOPPY	A question-and-answer period may follow your speech. Be sure to be courteous and correct in your responses.
SUBORDINATION	*If a question-and-answer period follows your speech,* be sure to be courteous and correct in your responses.
CHOPPY	Repeat the question. Answer it concisely and carefully.
SUBORDINATION	*After repeating the question,* answer it concisely and carefully.
CHOPPY	Andrea Joseph accepted questions from many people. The people were seated in various parts of the room.
SUBORDINATION	Andrea Joseph accepted questions from many people *who were seated in various parts of the room.*

24b Instead of writing loose, strung-out compound sentences, express the main idea in a main clause and make the less important ideas subordinate. Use coordination to give ideas equal emphasis.

STRUNG-OUT	A hostile person in the audience tried to harass Andrea with questions she was not qualified to answer, so Andrea replied simply, "I do not have the information to answer your questions at this time."
SUBORDINATED	When a hostile person in the audience tried to harass her with questions she was not qualified to answer, Andrea replied simply, "I do not have information to answer your questions at this time." [The writer emphasizes Andrea's reply.]
COORDINATED	A hostile person in the audience tried to harass Andrea with questions she was not qualified to answer, and she replied simply, "I do not have the information to answer your questions at this time." [The writer gives equal emphasis to the harassment of Andrea and her reply.]

24c Avoid excessive subordination.

Too many subordinate clauses in a sentence can make the focus of the sentence unclear. (See also **23b**.)

UNCLEAR   Andrea, who had never had to deal with a hostile member of an audience before, showed composure, particularly considering the circumstances, which included an overheated room and inadequate lighting, when she answered the person's question quickly but politely and then went on to respond to other questions.

CLEAR   Andrea, who had never had to deal with a hostile member of an audience before, showed composure when she answered the person's question quickly but politely and then went on to respond to other questions.

Subordination and Coordination   Exercise 24-1

NAME _____ SCORE _____

DIRECTIONS   Combine each of the following groups of choppy sentences by using either subordination or coordination. *

EXAMPLE

Most speakers will be given time to answer questions from the audience. People in

the audience often want to have certain points clarified.

Most speakers will be given time to answer questions from the audience since people often want to have certain points clarified.

1. Some of the questions people ask may sound silly. A good speaker never

makes the person asking the question feel foolish.

Although some of the questions people ask may sound silly, a good speaker never makes the person asking the question feel foolish.

2. Often a question may require a lengthy answer. In order to respond to as

many people as possible, a speaker should keep track of the time.

Often a question may require a lengthy answer, so, in order to respond to as many people as possible, a speaker should keep track of the time.

3. Speakers are sometimes asked a question outside their field. Careful speakers

do not pretend to be experts in all areas. They acknowledge their inability

to answer those questions.

If asked a question outside of their field, careful speakers do not pretend to be experts in all areas but acknowledge their inability to answer those questions.

* *Students may combine sentences effectively in ways other than those shown, in which case they should be given credit.*

285

4. Some people in an audience ask questions in an attempt to badger the speaker. A practiced speaker replies courteously and does not engage in pointless arguing.

Some people in an audience ask questions in an attempt to badger the speaker, but a practiced speaker replies courteously and does not engage in pointless arguing.

5. Other questioners give miniature speeches. These people may be trying to teach the speaker and the audience something. They may have a hidden agenda.

When other questioners give miniature speeches, they may have a hidden agenda, and they may be trying to teach the speaker and the audience something.

6. A person may ask about material already covered. It may have been in the speech itself or in an answer to another question. The speaker's reply should be brief and courteous.

The speaker's reply to a person asking about material already covered in the speech or in an answer to another question should be brief and courteous.

7. Some people ask for additional information. Conscientious speakers do what they promise to do. They mail it promptly to them.

As they promise to, conscientious speakers promptly mail additional information to those who ask for it.

8. Some speakers may use the question-and-answer period to expand on their original material. This additional information was perhaps too technical to include in the speech itself.

   Some speakers may use the question-and-answer period to expand on their original material with additional information that was perhaps too technical to include in the speech itself.

9. Well-prepared speakers anticipate many of the questions they are asked. They bring additional explanatory materials. These materials will help them answer such questions clearly.

   Well-prepared speakers anticipate many of the questions they are asked, and they bring additional explanatory materials which will help them answer such questions clearly.

10. Good speakers prepare for the question-and-answer period as well as for the speech itself. They enjoy this part of their presentation.

    Because good speakers prepare for the question-and-answer period as well as for the speech itself, they enjoy this part of their presentation.

25

Place modifiers carefully to indicate clearly their relationships with the words they modify.

While most adverbial modifiers may be moved to various places in a sentence without affecting the clarity of the sentence, adjectival modifiers usually must be placed either just before or just after the words they modify. (See also **1d**.)

ADVERBIAL   *When you think about the number of hours you will spend working,* you realize how important a choice of careers is. [Notice that the *when* clause may be moved to the end of the sentence or to the middle, after the main verb *realize*, without affecting clarity.]

ADJECTIVAL   Most people *who hold full-time jobs* can expect to spend ten thousand days of their lives working. [Notice that the *who* clause cannot be moved anywhere else in the sentence without affecting clarity.]

ADJECTIVAL   *Optimistic about the future,* most high-school and college students expect to achieve recognition and status in their occupations. [Notice that the verbal phrase may be placed either before or after the word it modifies—*students*—but nowhere else in the sentence without affecting clarity.]

25a Avoid needless separation of related parts of the sentence.

MISPLACED   Fifty percent of all college seniors expect to become wealthy *who were interviewed in 1988.*

CLEAR   Fifty percent of all college seniors *who were interviewed in 1988* expect to become wealthy.

AWKWARD   You will find that most students are, *when you analyze their expectations,* determined to have successful careers. [Even an adverbial modifier should not be placed so that it awkwardly splits parts of the verb.]

CLEAR   *When you analyze their expectations,* you will find that most college students are determined to have successful careers.

INFORMAL   Perhaps students *almost* expect too much from their careers.

CLEAR   Perhaps students expect *almost* too much from their careers.

25b Avoid dangling modifiers.

Dangling modifiers do not refer clearly and logically to another word or phrase in the sentence. (Most dangling modifiers are misplaced verbal phrases.) To correct a dangling modifier, either rearrange and reword the sentence base so that the modifier clearly refers to the right word or add words to the sentence to make the modifier clear by itself.

DANGLING   *Not wanting to waste forty years of their lives,* students' concern about their careers is not surprising.   [The verbal phrase illogically modifies *concern.*]

CLEAR   *Not wanting to waste forty years of their lives,* students, not surprisingly, are concerned about their careers.   [The verbal phrase logically modifies *students.*]

OR

Since most students do not want to waste forty years of their lives, their concern about their careers is not surprising.   [The verbal phrase is made into a clear subordinate clause with *students* as its subject.]

DANGLING   *Once unheard of,* many people today change their careers.   [The verbal phrase illogically modifies *people.*]

CLEAR   *Although the practice was once unheard of,* many people today change their careers.   [The verbal phrase is made into a clear subordinate clause.]

OR

Once unheard of, changing careers is common today.   [The verbal phrase logically modifies *changing.*]

Note: A dangling modifier usually cannot be corrected by simply moving it to the end of the sentence.

DANGLING   *Having mastered one job or skill,* another one may be tried.   [The verbal phrase illogically modifies *one.*]

DANGLING   Another one may be tried, *having mastered one job or skill.*   [The verbal phrase still illogically modifies the subject, *one.*]

CLEAR   *Having mastered one job or skill,* a person may try another.   [A subject, *person,* is supplied for the verbal phrase to modify.]

**Avoiding Misplaced Parts
and Dangling Modifiers**

Exercise 25-1

NAME _____ SCORE _____

DIRECTIONS   In each of the following sentences either a misplaced part or a dangling modifier is in italics. Rewrite the sentence or add the words needed so that the reference is clear and logical. ✳

EXAMPLE
Some things have changed during the last few years *about the job market.*

*Some things about the job market have changed
in the last fifteen years.*

1. Liberal arts majors *almost* were certain to have a difficult time finding a job during the early 1970s.

   *Liberal arts majors were almost certain to have
   a difficult time finding a job during the early 1970s.*

2. Graduates with a general education were, *during the late 1960s and early 1970s,* considered to be too plentiful.

   *During the late 1960s and early 1970s, graduates with
   a general education were considered to be too
   plentiful.*

3. *Not specifically trained for any one job,* many businesses refused to hire these graduates.

   *Many businesses refused to hire these graduates
   since they were not specifically trained for
   any one job.*

4. Today many businesses are seeking liberal arts majors *that did not hire them during the early 1970s.*

   *Today many businesses that did not hire liberal
   arts majors during the early 1970s are seeking
   them.*

   ✳ *Students may find various ways to eliminate the problems
   other than those shown, in which case they should be given credit.*

5. *Offering something valuable to the job market,* the late 1970s began to appreciate graduates with a general education.

   Offering something valuable to the job market, graduates with a general education began to be appreciated during the late 1970s.

6. Liberal arts majors can be molded for particular jobs *who have received a general education* by the companies that hire them.

   Liberal arts majors who have received a general education can be molded for particular jobs by the companies that hire them.

7. *Able to adapt themselves to different kinds of jobs,* many companies now appreciate graduates with a general education.

   Because graduates with a general education are able to adapt themselves to different kinds of jobs, many companies now appreciate them.

8. Many career planning offices are, *so that students will have greater job flexibility,* advising them to train for more than one limited area of work.

   So that students will have greater job flexibility, many career planning offices are advising them to train for more than one limited area of work.

9. A field may be overcrowded by the time a student graduates *that seems promising at the moment.*

   A field that seems promising at the moment may be overcrowded by the time a student graduates.

10. Persons who *only* can do one thing may not be able to find a job in their area of specialization.

    Persons who can only do one thing may not be able to find a job in their area of specialization.

26

Use parallel structure to give grammatically balanced treatment to items in a list or series and to parts of a compound construction.

Parallel structure means that a grammatical form is repeated—an adjective is balanced by another adjective, a verb phrase is balanced by another verb phrase, a subordinate clause is balanced by another subordinate clause, and so on. Parallel structure can emphasize ideas (see section **29**), make relationships clear, and contribute to coherence within and between paragraphs (see also section **32**).

There are several connectives that frequently call for parallel structure: *and, but, or, nor,* and especially *not only . . . but also, either . . . or, neither . . . nor,* and *as well as.* These words and phrases—and sometimes *rather than* or *not*—can be used to give a balanced treatment to items in a list or series or to parts of a compound construction.

Examples in this section are given in outline form to show the parallel structure (printed in italics) and the connectives (printed in boldface).

> Each year more and more women enter traditionally "male" professions:
>> *they become* civil or electrical engineers;
>> *they become* attorneys, public defenders, and judges;
>> **and**
>> *they become* professors of physics and computer science.

26a To achieve parallel structure, balance a verb with a verb, a prepositional phrase with a prepositional phrase, a subordinate clause with a subordinate clause, and so on.

> People no longer believe
>> *that it takes* brawn to design a skyscraper
>> **or**
>> *that one needs* muscle to perform open-heart surgery.   [balanced subordinate clauses]

> *Gaining equal recognition for equal responsibilities*
>> **as well as**
> *earning equal pay for equal work* concerns women in the work force. [balanced verbal phrases]

26b Whenever necessary to make the parallelism clear, repeat a preposition, an article, the sign of the infinitive (*to*), or the introductory word of a long phrase or clause.

The number of women demanding equal opportunity is not likely
> *to* decrease in the future
>> **but**
>
> *to* increase during the next decade.

A woman who enters a career wants to be seen
> *as* a competent worker first
>> **and**
>
> *as* a woman second.

Deduct 7 points for each incorrect revision and 3 for each incorrect underlining.

Parallel Structure

Exercise 26–1

NAME _____ SCORE _____

DIRECTIONS   In the following sentences underline the connective(s) that call for parallel structure; then make the structure(s) parallel.

EXAMPLE

want

Today women <u>not only</u> want challenging careers <u>but also</u> ~~to have~~ equal pay and

esteem for what they do.

holding

1. In the 1970s the number of women attending college <u>and</u> ~~who held~~ jobs

increased noticeably.

2. Since the early 1900s women's rights have expanded to include voting, edu-

ownership of

cation, <u>and</u> ~~that they could own~~ property.

gaining

3. Three major problems facing women are ~~to gain~~ access to education, finding

suitable employment after graduation, <u>and</u> being paid equal salaries for

equal work.

enrolling

4. In the past women had difficulty ~~to enroll~~ in certain educational curricu-

lums <u>and</u> finding employment in certain professions.

5. Many women explored career paths that were very nontraditional; these

wanted

women ~~want~~ to be hired for their skills rather than as tokens.

6. Many people believed that women were physically unable to do such things

cut

as work in law enforcement, ~~cutting~~ trees, <u>or</u> fly commercial airplanes.

7. Current studies indicate that many women now start their own businesses,

   work

   ~~working~~ out of their homes, ~~or~~ freelance for a number of companies rather

   than follow more customary career paths.

8. Unlike women entering the job market in the 1970s <u>or</u> those ~~who looked~~ for

   looking

   work in even earlier times, young women today have many role models in

   almost all walks of life to look to for inspiration.

9. Women have flown in space, hold elective office at all levels of federal,

   administer

   state, and local government, and ~~administering~~ many large corporations.

10. Ratification of the equal rights amendment would assure that all people

    that   *has*

    have equal rights under the law and ~~for~~ no one ~~to have~~ his or her rights

    denied.

Parallel Structure   Exercise 26–2

NAME _____ SCORE _____

DIRECTIONS   To make a topic outline easily readable, a writer should use parallel structure for Roman-numeral and capital-letter headings. The following outline fails to use
parallel structure in five places. Revise these five parts so that all divisions of the outline
will be immediately clear to the reader.

Thesis: The American worker is likely to experience at least three major kinds of

change in his or her job during the next twenty years.

I. Changes in the work schedule

    A. Fewer hours

    B. ~~Working~~ *f*lexible schedules

    C. ~~Companies will use~~ *j*ob sharing

II. Changes in the workplace

    A. Less stressful environments

    B. Recreational facilities

    C. *Elimination of routine chores*
        ~~Many routine chores will be handled by robots and computers.~~

III. *Changes in*
      ~~There will be many new~~ fringe benefits.

    A. Educational opportunities

    B. Sabbaticals

    C. ~~Providing~~ *O*n-site day-care centers

27

Avoid needless shifts in tense, mood, voice, number, and person. Also avoid needless shifts from indirect to direct discourse.

27a Avoid needless shifts in tense, mood, and voice.

SHIFT IN TENSE
: During the 1970s women all over the world *became* concerned about their status and *establish* organizations to work for improvements. [The verbs shift from past to present tense.]

CONSISTENT
: During the 1970s women all over the world *became* concerned about their status and *established* organizations to work for improvements.

SHIFT IN MOOD
: To understand the recent history of the women's movement, first *read* Betty Friedan's *The Feminine Mystique*, and then you *should examine* what feminists in the 1970s and 1980s have said about women's rights. [*Should examine* is a shift to the indicative mood from the imperative (command) mood, *read*.]

CONSISTENT
: To understand the recent history of the women's movement, first *read* Betty Friedan's *The Feminine Mystique*, and then *examine* what feminists in the 1970s and 1980s have said about women's rights.

SHIFT IN VOICE
: First we *will read The Feminine Mystique;* then the writings of contemporary feminists *will be examined.* [The verbs shift from the active to the passive voice.]

CONSISTENT
: First we *will read The Feminine Mystique;* then we *will examine* the writings of contemporary feminists.

Shifts in tense are especially troublesome. The tendency to shift tenses is particularly strong when you are referring to what others have written, since the customary correct practice is to speak of written observations in the present tense even though they were written in the past.

SHIFT
: In *The Feminine Mystique* (1963) Betty Friedan *discusses* the lack of fulfillment modern women feel and *showed* that their sense of loss results from their inability to find meaningful occupations outside the home.

CONSISTENT
: In *The Feminine Mystique* (1963) Betty Friedan discusses the lack of fulfillment modern women feel and *shows* that their sense of loss results from their inability to find meaningful occupations outside the home.

27b Avoid needless shifts in person and in number. (See also section **6**.)

SHIFT IN PERSON   *If you* study the history of the women's rights movement, *one* cannot help being startled by the changes that have occurred. [The pronouns shift from second to third person.]

CONSISTENT   *If you* study the history of the women's rights movement, *you* cannot help being startled by the changes that have occurred.

SHIFT IN NUMBER   *Each* woman fighting for equality in the working world feels that *they* have a valid cause.   [The pronouns shift from singular to plural.]

CONSISTENT   *Each* woman fighting for equality in the working world feels that *she* has a valid cause.

27c Avoid needless shifts between indirect and direct discourse.

SHIFT   Women are now saying, "Give us the opportunity to enter the same professions men do" and that they want to be paid the same salaries as men.   [The sentence shifts from direct to indirect discourse.]

CONSISTENT   Women are now saying that they want the opportunity to enter the same professions men do and that they want to be paid the same salaries as men.

OR

Women are now saying, "Pay us the same salaries as men, and give us the same opportunity to enter the same professions."

Deduct 7 for each incorrect revision and 3 for each blank incorrectly filled.

Avoiding Needless Shifts   Exercise 27–1

NAME _____ SCORE _____

DIRECTIONS   In each of the following sentences, indicate the kind of shift by writing *1* if the shift is in tense, mood, or voice; *2* if it is in person or number; or *3* if it is from indirect to direct discourse. Then revise the sentence to eliminate the needless shifts.

EXAMPLE
we
When ~~one~~ look*s* back over history, we realize how much the role of

women in society has changed.   ___2___

they received
1. In most ancient societies women remained at home, and no

   formal education. ~~was received by them.~~   ___1___

2. Roman women had more legal rights and social freedom than

   d
   other European women did, but their status decrease*s* with

   the spread of Christianity.   ___1___

3. Examine Old Testament tradition, and ~~you should~~ see why

   the Church affirmed the dominant role of men.   ___1___

4. Indeed, most of the world's religions questioned the equality

   their ability to
   of women, and ~~could they~~ do any useful work other than

   housework and child rearing.   ___1___

5. Before the 1800s very few women in the United States worked

   did
   outside the home, and those who did often ~~do~~ so out of neces-

   sity.   ___1___

6. When we examine the course of the Industrial Revolution,

   we
   ~~you~~ find that one of its results was the emergence of women
   ∧

   as a significant part of the work force.   _2_

7. At first the working conditions in textile mills and in other

   factories that employed women were reasonably good, but, as

   went   *worsened*   *ped.*
   time ~~goes~~ by, conditions ~~worsen~~ and salaries drop;   _1_
        ∧   ∧   ∧

8. The women's rights movement, which began during the first

   made
   half of the 1800s, ~~makes~~ progress with the introduction of a
                         ∧

   constitutional amendment granting women the right to vote.   _1_

9. Beginning in 1873 the amendment was brought before Con-

   passed
   gress every year until it finally ~~passes~~ in 1920.   _1_
                                        ∧

10. Each of the major wars fought by our country has also had

   its
   ~~their~~ effect on the role of women outside the home.   _2_
   ∧

28

Make each pronoun refer unmistakably to its antecedent.

A pronoun usually depends on an antecedent—a word it refers to—for its meaning. If the antecedent is not immediately clear so that the reader can understand without difficulty, we say that the *reference* of the pronoun is vague. Reference can be vague because *two* possible antecedents appear, or because no specific antecedent has been provided, or because the pronoun refers to the general idea of the preceding sentence or sentences rather than to something more specific.

> *They* claimed that the standard work week would be only thirty-five hours by the middle of the 1980s. *They* said *this* because it had decreased continually since 1900.

There are three main ways to correct an unclear reference of a pronoun: (1) rewrite the sentence to eliminate the pronoun; (2) provide a clear antecedent for the pronoun to refer to; and (3) substitute a noun for the pronoun or, in the case of *this*, add a noun, making the pronoun an adjective.

> *A report produced by the American Institute for Research* claimed that the standard work week would be only thirty-five hours by the middle of the 1980s. *The researchers who worked on the report* made *this claim* because the *work week* had decreased continually since 1900.

28a Avoid ambiguous references.

Recast the sentence to make the antecedent clear, or replace the pronoun with a noun.

> AMBIGUOUS   John wrote to Oliver when *he* got *his* new job.
>
> CLEAR   When John got his new job, he wrote to Oliver.
>   OR
>   When Oliver got his new job, John wrote to him.

28b Avoid remote or obscure references.

Recast the sentence to bring a pronoun and its antecedent closer together or substitute a noun for the obscure pronoun.

> REMOTE   Oliver studied the job description. A variety of skills and a considerable amount of work experience were required. *It* convinced Oliver that he was not qualified for the position.
>
> CLEAR   Oliver studied the job description. A variety of skills and a considerable amount of work experience were required. The *job description* convinced Oliver that he was not qualified for the position.

OBSCURE   When *Mrs. Mazaki's* company was founded, *she* asked Oliver to join her staff. [A reference to an antecedent in the possessive case is unclear.]

CLEAR   When *Mrs. Mazaki* founded her company, *she* asked Oliver to join her staff.

28c In general, avoid broad references—that is, the use of pronouns like *which, it,* and *this*—to refer to the general idea of a preceding sentence or clause.

BROAD   Oliver was a skillful writer, and he used *it* to get ahead in the new company.

CLEAR   Oliver used his *writing skill* to get ahead in the new company.

BROAD   The new company sent out many proposals. *This* was Oliver's specialty.

CLEAR   The new company sent out many proposals. *This type of writing* was Oliver's specialty. [One way to correct a vague *this* is to add a noun for the pronoun to modify.]

OR

The new company's need to submit many proposals made use of Oliver's specialty. [The vague *this* is eliminated by rewriting the two sentences as one.]

28d Avoid the awkward or superfluous use of pronouns.

(1) Avoid the awkward placement of the pronoun *it* near the expletive *it*.

AWKWARD   Although *it* was difficult for Oliver to get a new job, he decided to do *it*. [The use of the first *it*—an expletive—makes the meaning of the second *it*—a pronoun—unclear.]

CLEAR   Although *it* was difficult for Oliver to get a new job, he decided to do so.

(2) Avoid the use of a meaningless *it* or *they* in a construction like the following.

AWKWARD   In the yellow pages *it lists* the names of all insurance companies in the area. [This construction is wordy as well as awkward.]

CLEAR   The *yellow pages list* the names of all insurance companies in the area.

OR

In the yellow pages are the names of all insurance companies in the area.

AWKWARD   In my business-writing textbook *they* name two kinds of proposals.

CLEAR   My business-writing textbook names two kinds of proposals.

OR

The author of my business-writing textbook names two kinds of proposals.

Deduct 7 for each incorrect revision and 3 for each blank incorrectly filled.

Reference of Pronouns   Exercise 28–1

NAME _____ SCORE _____

DIRECTIONS   In the following discussion of leisure time, mark a capital *V* through each pronoun whose reference is vague and write the pronoun in the blank. Then revise the sentence or sentences to clarify the meaning.*

EXAMPLE

t
The number of hours spent at work may lessen during
Because

the coming decade, ~~which will cause~~ people ~~to~~ reeval-
will

uate their idea of leisure time.   *which*

1. The four-day work week, is used by some compa-

    nies, ~~This~~ gives employees more leisure time.   *This*

2. Increased automation is bound to give employees

    more leisure time. It is hard to say what employees
    their additional leisure time.
    will do with ~~it~~.   *it*

3. In (Sebastian de Grazia's) *Of Time, Work, and Lei-*

    sure, ~~he~~ explains the ancient and modern attitudes

    toward leisure.   *he*

4. The ancient Greeks had a different notion of lei-

    sure from ours. We think of using our leisure time

    to accomplish to definite task, like painting our
    the Greeks, leisure time
    house or washing our car. To ~~them~~ ~~it~~ meant time

    to do something enjoyable for its own sake.   *them; it*

* *Give credit for correct revisions not shown here.*

5. Many Americans ~~are totally dedicated~~ to the work
   total dedication

   ethic. ~~This~~ causes them to take a second job if they

   have very much spare time.   *This*

6. When Americans retire from their careers, they

   often do not know what to do with ~~it~~   *it*
   their time.

7. Although it has been a tradition in our country to

   retire at the age of sixty-five, we are now unsure

   that ~~it~~ is a good thing.   *it*
   retirement

8. ~~Many~~ people find nothing to give them a sense of   *which*
   Because

   fulfillment outside their work, ~~which leads to per-~~
   they become

   ~~sonal unhappiness.~~
   unhappy.

9. Perhaps we need to adopt the ancient Greek atti-

   tude toward leisure. ~~They~~ thought that just think-   *They*
   The Greeks

   ing, or even doing nothing, could be worthwhile.

10. Automation may well allow us to have three days

    off during each week and to have twenty or more

    years of retirement living. We must educate our-

    selves to use ~~this~~ creatively.   *this*
    our time

29

Arrange the parts of a sentence, and the sentences in a paragraph, to emphasize important ideas.

The following suggestions will help you stress the main ideas in your sentences and paragraphs.

29a Place important words at the beginning or at the end of the sentence—especially at the end—and unimportant words in the middle.

UNEMPHATIC   *Leisure time can be a problem*, sociologists tell us.

EMPHATIC   *Leisure time*, sociologists tell us, *can be a problem*. [Note how *problem* gains emphasis.]

29b Occasionally use a periodic instead of a loose sentence.

In a loose sentence the main idea comes first; periodic sentences place the main idea last, just before the period.

LOOSE   Some people find leisure time troublesome, causing them problems such as boredom, anxiety, and stress.

PERIODIC   Problems such as boredom, anxiety, and stress trouble some people faced with leisure time.

Caution: Do not overuse periodic sentences; if you do, they will lose their effectiveness.

29c Occasionally arrange ideas in an ascending order of climax—that is, by building from the least to the most important.

UNORDERED   Some people regard leisure time as wasteful, as unhealthy, or as a nuisance.

ORDERED   Some people regard leisure time as wasteful, as a nuisance, or even as unhealthy.

29d Rely on the active voice.

Sentences in which the grammatical subject and the doer of the action are the same usually present your ideas strongly and directly.

PASSIVE   Most people's leisure time *is spent* watching television.

ACTIVE   Most people *spend* their leisure time watching television.

29e Gain emphasis by repeating words or structures. (See also section **26**.)

UNEMPHATIC   The prospect of retirement has many unpleasant associations for people who have no interests outside work. It makes them think of boredom. And it may also bring to mind uselessness and loss of self-respect.

EMPHATIC   The prospect of retirement has many unpleasant *associations* for people who have no interests outside their work—*associations* such as boredom, uselessness, and loss of self-respect.

29f Gain emphasis by occasionally inverting the word order of a sentence. (See also **30b**.)

NORMAL ORDER   Most people need to feel that they contribute to their community in a productive way.

INVERTED ORDER   Feeling that they contribute to their community in a productive way is what most people need.

Caution: If overused, this method of gaining emphasis will make your style seem stilted and contrived.

29g Gain emphasis by using balanced sentence construction.

A balanced sentence uses grammatically equal structures—usually main clauses with parallel elements—to express contrasted (or similar) ideas. The balance emphasizes the contrast (or similarity).

To use leisure time well is to feel productive; to use leisure time ineffectively is to feel aimless.

29h Gain emphasis by writing the main ideas in sentences that are noticeably shorter than the other sentences.

[1]"Stopping out," or taking a temporary leave from college, is not a new phenomenon, but it is a practice that is gaining popularity among college students. [2]One national survey shows that 95 percent of all college students have seriously considered stopping out during their undergraduate years. [3]Many students would like to leave school temporarily to travel, to work, or just to find themselves. [4]They feel that what they learn during their absence from college will introduce them to the real world, will motivate them to become better students, and will enable them to set realistic goals for their futures. [5]*Certainly stopping out can do all of these things.*

[6]College administrators and many students who have unsuccessfully tried stopping out warn about the disadvantages: getting permanently sidetracked from one's education, finding that travel plans and jobs do not always work out, being tempted to do nothing during the absence from college. [7]*Thus, stopping out is not to be tried on impulse.* [8]It requires careful planning so that a student will not waste

a semester or a year, and it requires informing advisors and filling out forms so that the college will know what the student will be doing during the leave and when he or she will return.

Note: These two paragraphs also illustrate the use of the active voice—in all sentences—and parallel structure—in sentences 3, 4, and 6—to achieve emphasis.

Deduct 10 for each unemphatic sentence.

Emphasis Exercise 29-1

NAME _____ SCORE _____

DIRECTIONS   In each of the following, write a sentence that achieves emphasis by means of the pattern given. Then underline the part of the sentence that you wished to emphasize.

EXAMPLE
Place important words at the beginning of a sentence.

How many people, one wonders, look forward to retirement?

1. Use balanced sentence construction to emphasize the similarities between two ideas.

2. Emphasize your idea by repeating structures.

3. Use balanced sentence construction to emphasize the differences between two ideas.

4. Emphasize your ideas by repeating key words.

5. Write a series of sentences in which the most important idea is contained in a sentence that is noticeably shorter than the others.

6. Place important words at the end of the sentence.

7. Emphasize ideas by arranging them in the order of climax, from the least to the most important.

8. Emphasize your idea by inverting the usual word order of the sentence.

9. Use the active voice.

10. Emphasize ideas by means of a periodic sentence.

•

30

Vary the length, structure, and beginnings of sentences to create a pleasing style.

A writer of essays is usually more concerned about variety than a writer of business letters and reports is. In occupational writing, quite understandably, the emphasis is on clarity and simplicity rather than on style. But even the occupational writer, to hold the reader's attention, must avoid too many short, choppy sentences, strung-out compound sentences, or sentences that begin in the same way. In short, business and technical writers, as well as general writers, need to know how to vary their sentence structure to produce writing that is not only clear but also pleasing to read.

30a Vary the length of sentences, using short sentences primarily for emphasis (see **29h**); **also vary the structure of sentences** (see also **1d** and section **24**).

SIMPLE   A few companies have set up retirement clinics. These clinics help workers prepare for their retirement years.

COMPOUND   A few companies have set up retirement clinics, and these clinics help workers prepare for their retirement years.

COMPLEX   A few companies have set up retirement clinics that help workers prepare for their retirement years.

30b Vary the beginnings of sentences.

(1) Begin with a modifier.

Gradually, workers learn to cope with retirement.

(2) Begin with a phrase.

Through courses and counseling, the clinics help people discover the talents they would like to develop.

(3) Begin with a subordinate clause.

Because more and more people are reaching retirement age, these clinics may become commonplace in the future.

(4) Begin with a coordinating conjunction or a transitional expression when the word or phrase can be used to show the proper relationship between sentences.

More people are reaching retirement age in our country than ever before. *And* [or *In addition*,]   many employees are retiring at the age of fifty-five or earlier.

30c Avoid loose, stringy compound sentences. (See also **24b**.)

To revise a loose, stringy compound sentence, try one of the following methods.

(1) Make a compound sentence complex.

COMPOUND   Many older executives have achieved high salaries, and so they are expensive to keep on the payroll, and so their companies force them to retire early.

COMPLEX   Many highly paid older executives, who are expensive to keep on the payroll, are forced by their companies to retire early.

(2) Use a compound predicate in a simple sentence.

COMPOUND   Often people plan ahead, and they save money, and they retire much earlier than the "standard" age of sixty-five.

SIMPLE   Often people plan ahead, save money, and retire much earlier than the "standard" age of sixty-five.

(3) Use an appositive in a simple sentence.

COMPOUND   Many people plan ahead, and they are prudent, and they invest wisely the money they are saving for retirement.

SIMPLE   Many people, prudent individuals, plan ahead and invest wisely the money they are saving for retirement.

(4) Use a prepositional or verbal phrase in a simple sentence.

COMPOUND   The economy is unpredictable, and people saving for retirement know they must take inflation into account.

SIMPLE   In an unpredictable economy, people saving for retirement know they must take inflation into account.

30d Vary the conventional subject-verb sequence by occasionally separating subject and verb with words or phrases.

S-V-C   Some employees are retiring from their present jobs at the age of fifty-five to start a new career.

VARIED   Some employees, *at the age of fifty-five*, are retiring from their present jobs to start a new career.

OR

Many employees, eager to start a new career, are retiring from their present jobs at the age of fifty-five.

Note: This kind of variety must be used with discretion because separating sentence parts too frequently makes the writer's style unnatural and even difficult to follow. (See also **25a**.)

30e Occasionally use an interrogative, imperative, or exclamatory sentence to vary from the more common declarative sentence.

Retirement clinics are not commonplace today. In fact, only a very few companies supply them. *But who can say how popular they may become in the next twenty years when the greatest percentage of workers in our history will be reaching retirement age?*

Variety   Exercise 30–1

NAME _____ SCORE _____

DIRECTIONS   Analyze the ways in which the writer has achieved variety in the paragraphs below by answering the questions that follow. When the question asks, "*Which
sentence . . .?*" use the sentence's number to identify your answer.

[1]Until recently, most people believed that once they chose a profession as
young adults they had to stick with it until they retired. [2]Now some of them are
challenging this assumption. [3]Unlike their co-workers who never change fields,
these people are abandoning the security of a known routine to explore a new
occupation.

[4]Why do professionals such as lawyers, teachers, administrators, and business
executives "quit"? [5]Because they have decided that their comfortable salary and
relatively secure position are less important than their desire to feel satisfied with
their work. [6]In their professional occupations they feel bored. [7]They admit that
they are unhappy. [8]So why not change? [9]In some respects they are only doing
what all of us dream about: following our secret ambitions. [10]However, these
people—without any guarantee of success—have had the courage to put their
dreams into action. [11]What finally has convinced them to risk the change is the
thought that if they do not at least try, they will never know if they *could* have
succeeded. [12]That is the best challenge of all. [13]They want and need to test themselves.

[14]These days there are even counselors who help professionals as they make
this difficult decision to change their lives. [15]A switch from banking to weaving
blankets is dramatic. [16]But if a banker is tired of three-piece suits and has always
wanted to move to a mountain resort and restore antique furniture, a career
counselor can help determine whether or not the change is likely to be for the
best. [17]Of course, not everyone who considers changing careers will actually do
so. [18]But for those who take the risk, a happier life may be waiting.

[19]I know how difficult it is to make the switch, but it can be done. [20]I live in
a resort area where many people come to try out their secret ambitions. [21]My

317

next-door neighbor used to be a social worker in Miami; now he weaves baskets. [22]A couple down the road taught school for years, until they decided that they would rather run a country store. [23]And a former geological consultant raises Christmas trees and rhododendrons. [24]When I ask these people if the expense and the uncertainty of the change have been worth it, I always get the same answer. [25]"Yes!"

ANALYSIS

1. Which sentences are shortest? *2,6,7,8,12,13,15,19,and 25*

   Why do you think the writer used them? *for emphasis*

2. How many simple sentences are there? *5*

   How many compound sentences? *2*

   How many complex sentences? *17*

3. How many sentences begin with something other than the subject? *12*

   Which sentences begin with an adverb or an adverb phrase? *1,2,5,9,14,and 24*

   Which begin with an adverb clause? *3, 16, and 24*

   Which begin with a coordinating conjunction or transitional expression?

   2, 8, 10, and 23

4. In which sentence is the usual subject-verb sequence interrupted by a word or phrase? *10*

5. Which sentences are not declarative sentences? *4, 8, and 25*

   What kind are they? *interrogative (4,8) and exclamatory (25)*

Variety   Exercise 30–2

NAME _____ SCORE _____

DIRECTIONS   Write sentences to illustrate the techniques for achieving variety listed below. You may want to continue this book's theme of the world of work.

1. a sentence beginning with an adverb clause

2. a sentence beginning with a single-word modifier

3. a sentence beginning with an adverb or an adverb phrase

4. a sentence in which the subject and verb are separated by an intervening
   word or words

5. a complex sentence

6. a sentence beginning with a subordinate clause

7. a simple sentence containing a compound predicate

8. a sentence beginning with a verbal phrase

9. a simple sentence containing at least one prepositional phrase

10. two sentences, the second beginning with a coordinating conjunction

Mastering Variety: A Review

NAME _____ SCORE _____

DIRECTIONS   Rewrite each of the following paragraphs so that the sentences flow more smoothly and the style is more varied. Use a transitional expression or two, vary the beginnings of some of the sentences, combine sentences, and omit or add words if you wish.

¹In the last decade more and more people started their own businesses. ²They grew tired of working for someone else. ³These independent businesspersons frequently work out of their homes. ⁴This trend is sometimes referred to as cottage industry. ⁵It has its roots in the traditional arts and crafts practiced by people in remote rural areas. ⁶The types of contemporary cottage industries operating today include much more than the production of handicrafts. ⁷People working at home do such diverse things as develop computer software, make specialty products, and act as freelance consultants. ⁸People working out of their homes like the freedom gained from being their own boss. ⁹They gain satisfaction from creating and running their own businesses.

REVISION *(Sample revision)*

In the last decade more and more people started their own businesses because they grew tired of working for someone else. These independent businesspersons frequently work out of their homes, a trend sometimes referred to as cottage industry. It has its roots in the traditional arts and crafts practiced by people in remote rural areas. But the types of contemporary cottage industries operating today include much more than the production of handicrafts. For example, people working at home develop computer software, make specialty products, and act as freelance consultants. People working out of their homes like the freedom gained from being their own boss and the satisfaction of creating and running their own businesses.

[1]We can find plenty of examples of the worthwhile use of leisure time in our society. [2]The arts are attracting many new participants and fans. [3]People are painting, writing, dancing, and making music as never before. [4]Small rural communities are being visited by symphony orchestras and art exhibitions. [5]Handicrafts are flourishing everywhere. [6]A majority of the citizens in some towns are involved in making things. [7]They are making things like pottery, furniture, and macramé items. [8]People are buying the works that are produced. [9]Artists of all types are able to make a living from their crafts.

REVISION *(Sample revision)*

We can find plenty of examples of the worthwhile use of leisure time in our society. For example, the arts are attracting many new participants and fans. People are painting, writing, dancing, and making music as never before. And small rural communities are being visited by symphony orchestras and art exhibitions. Handicrafts, especially, are flourishing everywhere. In some towns, a majority of the citizens are involved in making things like pottery, furniture, and macramé items. Because people are buying the works that are produced, artists of all types are able to make a living from their crafts.

31

Base what you say and write on clear, logical thinking. Avoid common fallacies.

Most readers are reasonable people who will listen to what you have to say. How readily they will be persuaded to look at an issue from your point of view, however, depends on how well you present your case. In many respects, informing your reader about an issue is similar to a lawyer's presenting a case to a jury. The more logical the presentation—that is, the more clearly stated and reasonably argued—the more likely your reader will be to listen to your ideas. The more sense a piece of writing makes, the more confidence your reader will have that you know what you are talking about.

31a Learn how to use inductive reasoning in your writing.

When you reason inductively, you reach a conclusion based on the available evidence. For example, if you were writing a memorandum to argue that one of your company's customers should be refused further credit (your conclusion), you would base your recommendation on the customer's poor record of past payment (the evidence). You are reasoning that because the customer has repeatedly failed to meet his obligations in the past, he will probably fail in the future. Note that there is an element of probability, rather than certainty, in inductive reasoning. This requires that you present as much evidence as possible to support the conclusion you want the reader to accept. But, because successful inductive arguments rest on convincing evidence, the conclusions that they reach strike the reader as possible and believable.

Using evidence as the basis of its argument, inductive reasoning can be a powerful persuasive tool, lending strength and authority to any material you present. The evidence you present to your readers helps to convince them that the conclusions you reach are valid ones. It is, therefore, essential that you select with care the material that you present; insufficient evidence will make your conclusions look weak, while evidence clearly expressing exceptional cases or bias will cause readers to doubt your conclusions.

When you use induction, you can arrange your material in one of three ways: (1) present the evidence first and then draw the conclusions, (2) let the reader draw the conclusions, or (3) state the conclusion first and then develop the evidence that led you to form that conclusion. The first two methods are effective if you are writing for a reader who is likely to disagree with you; it is best to let this reader evaluate the evidence and then draw the conclusion along with you as you sum up or reach the conclusion that you, the writer, leave unstated. The third method, presenting the conclusion first and then discussing the evidence that supports it, works well for a reader who is likely to be receptive. Which strategy you select will depend on your audience and the effect you wish to produce.

31b Learn how to use deductive reasoning in your writing.

While inductive reasoning uses examples and draws a conclusion based on those instances, deduction usually starts with a generalization and reaches a conclusion about a particular instance based on the generalization. For a deductive argument to be successful, your reader must accept as true the generalizations (premises) you use. In deductive reasoning the writer argues logically from principles (assertions of truths) rather than from evidence; if A is true and B is true, then it follows that this C *must* be true. This basic logical structure is called a syllogism. Syllogisms contain three parts: a major premise (usually a generalization), a minor premise (usually a specific fact), and a conclusion that fits both the major and the minor premises. In a deductive argument, you must carefully examine your premises to make sure that they are both true, for even if you reason logically you may reach a wrong conclusion if one of your premises is false. Finally, for your argument to be effective, you must be certain that your premises are ones that your reader can accept.

MAJOR PREMISE   People doing the same job should be paid the same salary.

MINOR PREMISE   Both men and women work at this job.

CONCLUSION   Men and women doing this job should be paid the same salary.

31c Avoid fallacies in your reasoning.

Fallacies are errors in arguments that have to do with false premises, faulty reasoning, insufficient or biased evidence, or other factors that distort or misrepresent the issues.

(1) *Non Sequitur:*

A conclusion that does not follow from the premise.

This product outperforms its competitors; therefore it will sell well.   [Many superior products do not sell well.]

(2) Hasty Generalization:

A generalization based on too little, or on exceptional or biased, information.

People dislike changing to new products.   [This may be true of some people, but certainly not all.]

(3) *Ad Hominem:*

Attacking the person who presents an issue rather than dealing with the issue itself.

It may be true that my competitor makes a superior product, but what has he done for our community? [The competitor's contribution to the community has no bearing on the quality of the product.]

(4) Bandwagon:

An argument that says in effect, "Everyone else is doing (or thinking or saying) this, so you should."

Everyone likes this make of computer, and you will too. [You will not necessarily *respond* in the same way as the majority.]

(5) Red Herring:

Bringing up an irrelevant issue in order to avoid the real issue.

Never mind the workers' demands for better benefits; what we really need is an improved customer service department. [Improving customer relations has nothing to do with meeting workers' demands.]

(6) *Either. . . or* Fallacy:

Asserting that there are only two options when other options exist.

Our drop in profit last year leaves us with only two options: freeze wages or lay off 25 percent of our employees in order to give raises to the other 75 percent. [In fact, other options exist.]

(7) False Analogy:

Assuming that because two things are similar in certain ways they must be similar in other ways.

Since this computer costs the same as the other model, it will perform all the functions the other does. [Equal price does not necessarily indicate that the two products will be of equal value to the company.]

(8) Equivocation:

An assertion that illogically relies on the use of a term in two different senses.

You have a right to complain, so do what is right and complain. [The word *right* means both "a just claim" and "correct."]

(9) Slippery Slope:

Assuming that if one thing is allowed it will only be the first step in a downward spiral.

Using computers in college classrooms will ultimately lead to the replacement of teachers with machines. [Assumes that the machines can do everything that a human teacher can.]

(10) Oversimplification:

A statement or argument that leaves out relevant considerations about an issue.

> Because he is over sixty he cannot possibly be an effective administrator.   [Assumes that all older persons are ineffective.]

(11) Begging the question:

An assertion that restates the point just made. Such a statement is circular in that it draws as its conclusion a point stated in the premise.

> He habitually is late because he finds it impossible to be on time.   [Being late and finding it impossible to be on time mean the same thing.]

(12) False Cause:

Assuming that because one event followed another, the second was caused by the first. Sometimes called *post hoc, ergo propter hoc* ("after this, so because of this").

> Last week we redecorated our showroom, and already the number of customers has increased by 25 percent.   [The assumption that the redecoration *caused* the increase is not warranted.]

Deduct 5 for each incorrectly filled blank and 5 for each incorrect reason given.

Arguing Logically

Exercise 31–1

NAME _____ SCORE _____

DIRECTIONS   Identify the logical fallacy that weakens each statement, and explain why it is fallacious. Refer to the list of fallacies in this section.

EXAMPLE

John has been an accountant for six years; therefore he is better at his job than the new man we hired last month.   *Non Sequitur*

Reason: *Being in a job longer does not necessarily mean that a person is more skilled than someone hired more recently.*

1. Only two courses of action are possible: we can accept the added overtime assignments or go on strike.   *Either . . . or*

Reason: *More opinions are possible: for example, negotiating, or resigning to find another job.*

2. In a free enterprise system we should be free to do whatever we want.   *Equivocation*

Reason: *The free in free enterprise has a limited meaning that the second free greatly exceeds.*

3. We installed this new record-keeping system in October, and already fifteen files have disappeared.   *False Cause*

Reason: *The disappearance of the files needs not be a result of the new system.*

4. Every other homeowner in your neighborhood has one of our insurance policies; you should too.   *Bandwagon*

Reason: *What is right for some may be wrong for others.*

5. Why should I accept your criticism of my work
   when you can't even get your own work done on
   time? _Ad Hominem_

   Reason: *That you cannot get your own work done
   has no bearing on the quality of another person's work.*

6. We're sorry you found our salesperson rude, but
   we're sure you understand that this is an extremely
   busy time of the year for us. _Red Herring_

   Reason: *Being busy is no excuse for rudeness.*

7. Since these two vacuum cleaners are about the
   same size and weight, either one will do the job. _False Analogy_

   Reason: *That the two machines are similar in size
   and weight does not mean that they will work
   equally well.*

8. Our company offers higher starting salaries, so the
   people we hire are better employees. _Non Sequitur_

   Reason: *People paid high salaries are not
   necessarily better employees.*

9. Customers are gullible. _Hasty Generalization_

   Reason: *Some customers may be gullible, but not
   all.*

10. It is impossible to give our secretaries additional
    pay increases because we cannot raise salaries at
    this time. _Begging the Question_

    Reason: *Pay increases and raising salaries mean the
    same thing.*

THE PARAGRAPH

32

Write unified, coherent, and adequately developed paragraphs.

We recognize the beginning of a new paragraph in a composition by the indention—about an inch when handwritten and five spaces when typewritten. Although a paragraph may be only one sentence long, most paragraphs require several sentences to adequately develop the central, or controlling, idea. We expect, by the time we finish reading the paragraph, to know what the writer's controlling idea is and to be able to recognize the relationship that each of the other sentences has to the sentence that states or suggests this controlling idea. And, finally, we expect the sentences to flow along smoothly so we do not have to mentally fill in any words or phrases or stop reading after every sentence or two to refocus our attention.

32a Make each sentence in the paragraph contribute to the controlling idea (central thought).

The controlling idea is printed in italics in the following paragraph. Notice that the key word, *flextime*, is echoed in each of the other sentences in the paragraph. (The words that echo *flextime* are printed in boldface.)

> [1]*Flextime is here to stay.* [2]Surveys, like one conducted by *Psychology Today* in 1978, suggest that the American worker strongly approves of **flextime**; fully 78 percent of those questioned by *Psychology Today* wanted to have some say in the time they started and finished their workday. [3]Employers, while they acknowledge some problems with **individualized work schedules**, seem equally satisfied with the system; as proof, only two percent of the companies that have tried **flextime** have returned to eight- or nine-to-five schedules. [4]Based, then, on present trends, **flextime** seems certain to replace the rigid work schedules that people have followed since the outset of the Industrial Revolution. [5]Looking ahead to the kind of workplace we will have in the year 2001, William Abbott, editor of the World Future Society's newsletter, *Careers Tomorrow*, says quite confidently, "Workers will schedule their own hours under **flextime**."

The unity of this paragraph would be destroyed by inserting a sentence that is not a part of the plan called for by the controlling idea. Try reading the paragraph with these sentences inserted between sentences 2 and 3: "People obviously have different biological rhythms. Some people go to bed early and awaken at 6:00 or 7:00 ready for a full day's work. Others cannot fall alseep before 12:00 or 1:00 a.m. and are not really prepared to face the workplace before 10:00 a.m." Although pertinent to the general subject of convenient work schedules, these three sentences, or even one of them, would shift the focus of the paragraph away from the specific controlling idea: *Flextime is here to stay.*

To maintain unity in a paragraph, then, you must be conscious of your controlling idea each time you add a sentence.

The sentence that states the controlling idea of a paragraph is called the *topic sentence*. Although a paragraph may have unity without an expressly stated topic sentence, inexperienced writers will find that a clear, specific topic sentence in each paragraph helps them keep their writing well organized. Since the controlling idea gives direction to the other sentences in the paragraph, the topic sentence usually appears early in the paragraph—as the first or second sentence. But it may be placed elsewhere—for example, at the end if the writer wishes to build up to a dramatic closing.

32b Link the sentences in the paragraph so that the thought flows smoothly from one sentence to the next.

A coherent paragraph is one in which the relationship of any given sentence to the ones before it is clear and the transitions between the sentences are smooth. A coherent paragraph is easy to read because there are no jarring breaks—the sentences are arranged in a clear, logical order (for example: by time, from general to specific, from least important to most important, or by location of items being described) and there are smooth transitions between sentences: (1) pronouns are used to refer to antecedents in preceding sentences; (2) key words or ideas are repeated; (3) transitional expressions are used; and (4) parallel structures are used where appropriate.

The following paragraph illustrates the four methods of achieving coherence. The sentences are arranged in order of climax (from least important to most important); the methods of making smooth transitions between sentences are indicated by numbers—1 through 4—that correspond to those cited above.

> There is much evidence that the roles of the sexes are changing. [3] First, and most noticeable, is the change in dress and appearance. Today many young men and women look much alike. [1] Their hair may be similar in style. [1, 4] They may wear the same shirts and pants. [1, 4] They may in fact go to the same unisex hair stylists and boutiques. [3, 2] But more significant evidence of the shift in sex roles is apparent in the job market. While a generation ago no more than one out of ten women with young children was employed outside the home, today one out of three is so employed. [3] And positions that were once considered appropriate only for men are now being filled by women. [3, 2] Conversely, many men today are training to be nurses, secretaries, and flight attendants—positions once considered unmistakably feminine.

32c Develop the argument adequately so that it presents enough information about its central idea to satisfy the reader.

The length of a paragraph varies with its purpose. Thus a one-sentence paragraph or even a one-word paragraph ("Yes" or "No") may say emphatically all that the writer needs to say. Paragraphs that report dialogue are usually short because a new paragraph must begin each time the speaker changes. Most paragraphs in expository writing tend to vary in length from about seventy-five to two hundred fifty words, the average length being about one hundred words. (And remember that when you write in longhand your paragraph looks much longer than it would if it were typed or set in print.)

(1) Use relevant, specific details.

The use of details is the most common method of developing a controlling idea, and almost every paragraph makes some use of it. Pertinent facts and details about the changing roles of the sexes are used to develop the controlling idea of the paragraph illustrating coherence. Notice that the most significant fact is discussed last, a common type of arrangement for this method of development.

(2) Use one striking example or several closely related examples.

A paragraph developed by examples is almost certain to hold the reader's attention. The success of one of the most popular books ever printed, Dale Carnegie's *How to Win Friends and Influence People*, depends primarily on the author's use of hundreds of examples. Because of the interest generated by a well-chosen example, many essays and speeches begin with this type of development. In his book *Megatrends*, John Naisbitt discusses what it takes for a company to be labeled "successful" and offers the following illustration:

> [1]But even among the most successful [companies], Tandem is remarkable. [2]The founder of the fast-growing $100-million-a-year conpany, James Treybig, emphatically states that the human side of the company is the most critical factor in reaching his goal—the $1 billion mark in annual sales. [3]Treybig frees up 100 percent of his personal time to spend on "people projects." [4]Tandem's people-oriented management style includes Friday-afternoon beer parties, employee stock options, flexible work hours (unlike Intel, where everyone is expected to show up promptly at 8:15 A.M.), a company swimming pool that is open from 6:00 A.M. to 8 P.M., and sabbatical leave every four years—which all employees are *required* to take. [5]Reviews and meetings occur spontaneously with no formal procedures.
>
> —JOHN NAISBITT, *Megatrends*

Examples may be fully developed, like the one above, or simply listed in passing, like the series of examples in the following paragraph used to illustrate the characteristics of workaholics during childhood.

> [1]Marilyn Machlowitz, a psychologist for New York Life Insurance Co., has spent the past eight years studying the obsessive worker—first for her doctoral dissertation at Yale, more recently for her book *Workaholics: Living With Them, Working With Them*. [2]From interviews with 165 apparent workaholics, she has found that most exhibit identical characteristics early in their lives. [3]They turn games into imitations of work and go about them with intensity. [4]They set up lemonade stands, run sidewalk carnivals and cash in returnable soda bottles. [5]Later, they sell more Girl Scout cookies, Christmas cards and magazine subscriptions than anyone else on the block. [6]And their teachers love them because they are such hard-working, attentive students.—"Thank God, It's Monday," *Dun's Review*

32d Learn to use various methods of paragraph development.

The controlling idea of a paragraph may be developed in a number of ways. Most experienced writers use several methods of development in each paragraph without having to think about what they are doing. But as an inexperienced writer, you may need to practice consciously the methods discussed below until you are able to use them automatically and naturally. A study of these methods will help you not only to think of things to say but also to organize your thoughts, since the method of development usually suggests a pattern of arrangements for the sentences in the paragraph. Keep in mind that the subject matter will also determine which method or methods of paragraph development will be most effective.

(1) Narrate a series of events.

Strong paragraphs are internally consistent—their ideas relate to each other logically. If you are describing an event or a sequence of events, one good way to ensure that your paragraph is strongly unified is to discuss those events in the order in which they occurred. The following paragraph describes the method one businessman employs to make his company successful. Note that the ideas are arranged in chronological order, that is, in the order in which they take place.

> [1]When it comes to choosing between business and social activities, Howard Bronson knows where his priorities lie: with his job. [2]Bronson, who heads his own financial public relations firm, is up by four a.m. and has mapped out his day by the time he gets to his Manhattan office at 6:45. [3]He works at a furious pace, often skipping lunch, until about 6:30 in the evening. [4]Then, after dinner, he puts in another hour and a half of reading before turning in at 12:15.
> —"Thank God, It's Monday," *Dun's Review*

(2) Use description to make a point.

The use of well-chosen descriptive details will help your reader to visualize what you are talking about and to share the experience more fully. Carefully chosen, concrete details strengthen a paragraph, and you will want to be sure that the ones you use are relevant to the main purpose of the paragraph.

> [1]The fault ran straight through Culligan's ranch house, and had split its levels, raising the back twelve feet. [2]The tornado sound had been made by eighty million tons of Precambrian mountainside . . . half the mountain came falling down in one of the largest rapid landslides produced by an earthquake in North America in historical time. [3]People were camped under it and near it. [4]Among the dead were some who died of the air blast, after flapping like flags as they clung to trees. [5]Automobiles rolled overland like tumbleweeds. [6]They were inundated as the river pooled up against the rockslide, and they are still at the bottom of Earthquake Lake, as it is called—a hundred and eighty feet deep.   —JOHN MCPHEE, *In Suspect Terrain*

Present details in a clear order—from general to specific, from top to bottom, from near to far, from right to left. By doing so you provide a logical and orderly scheme for your reader to follow and help prevent confusion. Use appropriate descriptive details that appeal to all of the senses, not just sight.

(3) Explain a process.

Paragraphs that are organized around a process explain how something is done or made. Like the narrative paragraph, this type of paragraph follows a series of events as they occur through time and thus employs a chronological arrangement. In fact, a reader would likely be confused by a process paragraph that violated the ordinary chronological sequence of a group of events as it described them.

In the following instructions for repairing faucets, the reader would more than likely become confused if the chronological order were jumbled.

> [1]Turn the handle [of the pipe cutter] to the right until there is no resistance. [2]Then separate the two wheels. [3]Hold the lower one fast and give the handle a fraction of a turn into the work. [4]Tighten the upper wheel against the lower. [5]Again turn the handle to the right. [6]In this way, the cutter removes a layer of metal.
>
> —MAX ALTH, *Do-It-Yourself Plumbing*

(4) Show cause and effect.

A cause and effect paragraph explains why a particular outcome has occurred. To use this method effectively, you must supply enough evidence to convince your reader that you understand the cause or causes for a particular effect. The following two paragraphs rely primarily on comments from interviews to persuade us that the editors of *Newsweek* have correctly identified two causes for the American worker's lack of commitment to the work ethic.

> [1]The problem traces to two main factors: a younger work force—25 per cent of which is under 25 years old—and the nature of work itself in a highly industrialized society. [2]"It's mainly a problem of this younger worker," said Benjamin Aaron, director of the Institute of Industrial Relations at UCLA. [3]"He doesn't want to work to get ahead; he wants to work to get enough money for a while and then he wants to drop out." [4]Or, as Jerry Wurf, president of the American Federation of State, County and Municipal Employees, put it: "The Depression is something they learned about in a history class."
>
> [5]Once on the job, workers all too often find that, however good their wages and working conditions, work is a totally unsatisfying experience. [6]"People my age don't take much pride in this work," says Victoria Bowker, a 27-year-old blueprinter at Lockheed Aircraft. [7]"In the old days, you used to start a job and you used to finish it. [8]Now things have become so diversified you can't see your product; you start something and it goes through 50 million other hands before it's completed." [9]Mike Eckert, a longtime Lockheed employee twice Miss Bowker's age, agrees that things have changed. [10]"Today's management doesn't have any compassion for the person that's down the line," he says. [11]"They treat you like a machine . . . and you can't treat human nature that way." [12]And when a worker begins feeling like a machine, he'll probably resort to one of two alternatives: goldbrick, or start looking for another job. [13]"I'll tell you how attitudes are," UAW vice president Ken Bannon summed up last week. [14]"You will find people who say they would rather work in

cleanup and take a cut of 15 cents an hour than work the assembly line. [15]At least on cleanup you have the choice of sweeping the pile in the corner or sweeping the pile by the post."

—"Too Many U.S. Workers No Longer Give a Damn," *Newsweek*

(5) Use comparison and contrast.

In everyday conversation you often explain or evaluate something by comparing or contrasting it with something else. In compositions, too, comparison or contrast is often useful. In general, the people, ideas, or objects to be compared or contrasted should belong to the same class (one type of roommate is compared or contrasted with another type of roommate, not with some other type of person).

The following paragraph compares the importance of three values—work, family, and leisure.

[1]Along with family life, work and leisure always compete for people's time and allegiance. [2]One or the other is usually the center of gravity, rarely does the individual strike an equal balance among all three. [3]For the New Breed, family and work have grown less important and leisure more important. [4]When work and leisure are compared as sources of satisfaction in our surveys, only one out of five people (21 percent) states that work means more to them than leisure. [5]The majority (60 percent) say that while they enjoy their work, it is not their major source of satisfaction. [6](The other 19 percent are so exhausted by the demands work makes of them that they cannot conceive of it as even a minor source of satisfaction.)

DANIEL YANKELOVICH, "The New Psychological Contracts at Work"

(6) Use classification and division.

Classification organizes things and ideas by placing them in larger groups that share certain common characteristics. Division, on the other hand, separates objects and ideas into smaller subclasses according to some dividing principle. For example, the following paragraph on "alternate work schedules" breaks its subjects down into the four categories of compressed time, flextime, part-time, and shared time.

[1]Alternate work schedules are rapidly replacing the rigid eight- or nine-to-five workdays of the past. [2]For example, the 10-hour, four-day workweek has been used in industry for many years. [3]This type of compressed-time job schedule allows the worker to enjoy a regular three-day weekend. [4]But surpassing compressed-time scheduling in popularity with workers is flextime, which lets them choose their own hours to begin and end their workdays so long as they work a certain number of hours a week and so long as they are on the job during a mid-day core period. [5]Also, part-time work, which involves one out of every six workers in this country, continues to gain in popularity as people, especially the young, begin to value leisure as much as they do money. [6]And shared-time work schedules, whereby two employees share one full-time position, are saving employers as well as employees from massive lay-offs in an increasingly automated society.

Classification and division often work together in the same paragraph or set of paragraphs.

(7) Use an extended definition.

Sometimes you may need to compose a paragraph or even an entire essay to define a difficult term or a term that you want the reader to understand in a special way. The essayist Jon Stewart uses two paragraphs to define a silicon chip for a general audience of readers who may be unfamiliar with the workings of microprocessors and computers.

> [1]The revolution, of course, is that wrought by the silicon chip, that virtually invisible, spiderlike network of tiny electronic circuits etched on a flake of silicon (sand) less than half the size of the fingertip. [2]In the form of microprocessors, or miniature computers, it is invading every aspect of American life—the way we play, work, even think.
>
> [3]This computer-on-a-chip, with amazing powers of memory and computation, has immediate applications almost everywhere from universities to automobile engines, from corporate offices to farms, from hospitals to satellites. [4]Virtually any routine work can be taken over by the devices, which have shrunk to less than 1/30,000 the size of their original predecessors, those giant room-size computers of yesterday. [5]And they grow smaller and more versatile almost daily. [6]IBM recently announced that it can now produce a chip containing 256,000 bits of information, four times as many as are crammed onto the most highly integrated chip today.
>
> —JON STEWART, "Computer Shock: The Inhuman Office of the Future"

(8) Use a combination of strategies.

The various methods of developing a controlling idea have been listed and illustrated separately, but almost every paragraph makes use of more than one method. For example, the paragraph developed by cause and effect (see **(4)** above) also uses details, and the paragraph developed by classification (see **(6)**) also uses definition and examples to explain the types of alternate work schedules given.

Note: Since paragraphs do not often include more than twelve sentences, you do not need a detailed or complicated outline to follow. But you may find it useful to jot down the controlling idea and the main points of development before you begin to write a paragraph.

Deduct 7 1/2 for each incorrect answer.

Analyzing Paragraphs   Exercise 32–1

NAME _____ SCORE _____

DIRECTIONS   Analyze the unity, coherence, and development of the following paragraph by answering the questions that follow it. When the question asks, "*Which sentence . . .?*" use the sentence's number to identify your answer.

¹During the 1970s and 1980s both men and women have registered complaints about the role of women in the work force. ²Obviously, a possible reason for women's unhappiness with their jobs relates to their salaries: women generally earn far less than men for the same kind of work. ³Employers who pay women less than men offer many excuses for doing so. ⁴They assert that women are less dependable at work than men. ⁵And they claim that women are absent from work more frequently than men. ⁶Yet many employers have found these prejudices to be untrue. ⁷When placed in positions of responsibility women are as capable of handling the work as their male counterparts. ⁸Furthermore, women supervisors seem to be able to handle uncooperative workers more easily than male authority figures do. ⁹Finally, employers have found that female administrators are capable problem solvers. ¹⁰Although the job market is more open to women than it was one hundred years ago, many working women still find it difficult to advance as rapidly as men holding the same job, despite the increased opportunities.

ANALYSIS

1. Which sentence states the controlling idea of the paragraph? __*1*__

2. What is the major method of development used in the paragraph?

   _____*Use of relevant details*_____

3. Which sentences show the use of comparison or contrast? __*4, 5, 7 and 8*__

4. What is the key term that is repeated throughout the paragraph?

   _____*women*_____

337

5. Which sentences use transitional expressions? ___*2, 5, 6, 8, and 9*___

6. Which two sentences are linked by parallel structure? ___*4 and 5*___

7. Which sentence is the shortest one in the paragraph? ___*4*___

   What is its purpose? ___*It introduces the main point of the second half of the paragraph.*___

8. Which sentence is the clincher, the one that repeats the controlling idea? (Not all paragraphs have this kind of sentence.) ___*10*___

9. What is the basis for the arrangement of the sentences in the paragraph: is it by time, from general to specific, by order of climax, or by location of what is being described? ___*general to specific*___

10. Which two sentences use an introductory phrase to vary from the usual word order of placing the subject first? ___*1, 7, 9, and 10*___

    Which sentence begins with a single adverb? ___*2 (or 8 or 9)*___

    Which sentence uses an introductory subordinate clause? ___*10*___

Deduct 8 1/2 for each blank incorrectly filled.

**The Controlling Idea
and the Methods of Development**   Exercise 32–2

NAME _____ SCORE _____

DIRECTIONS   For each of the following four paragraphs list (1) the number of the sentence that states the controlling idea; (2) the main method of development used to support the controlling idea; and (3) an additional method of development used in the paragraph.

PARAGRAPH ONE

[1]Many people mistakenly think that creativity is the ability to think thoughts that no one else has ever thought. [2]In fact, creativity is just a way of looking at the ordinary in a different way. [3]Alex Osborn, one of the pioneers in the study of creativity and imagination, discovered that almost everyone is more creative than he thinks. [4]We usually don't recognize our good ideas as creativity in action. [5]For example, in a large midwestern city a gang of thieves had worked out a coordinated routine that was so smooth and fast that they could break into a clothing store, sweep the clothes off the racks, and be gone before the police could answer the alarm. [6]Then a young detective got an idea. [7]He asked all the clothing merchants in the area to alternate the way they placed the hangers on the rack. [8]He told the store owners: "Turn one hook toward the wall and the next one toward the aisle. [9]Do it that way throughout the store." [10]When police answered the next alarm they found the frustrated thieves removing the garments one at a time. [11]Everyday "shirtsleeve creativity" is simply the adaptation of existing ideas—taking another look at all of the pieces of the situation from a new perspective.   —DALE O. FERRIER, "Shirtsleeve Creativity."

1. Controlling idea __2__

2. Main method of development __definition or example__

3. Additional method of development __example or definition__

PARAGRAPH TWO

[1]Even in the past decade, the average U.S. farm worker's productivity has increased 185 percent, while the manufacturing worker has upped productivity by 90 percent. [2]Those figures may not be as high as in the past, or in other parts of the world today, but they certainly compare favorably with the performance of U.S. office workers. [3]In the past 10 years, according to studies done by the Massachusetts Institute of Technology and others, the white-collar worker's productivity has increased a mere four percent. [4]This figure is reached by measuring time spent on work tasks, as well as by counting units (letters typed, reports written, cases handled) where possible. [5]Four percent is the total for the whole past 10 years, not an annual rate of productivity increase.

—RAYMOND P. KURSHAN, "White-collar Productivity"

1. Controlling idea __2__

2. Main method of development __comparison/contrast__

3. Additional method of development __details__

PARAGRAPH THREE

[1]Psychologists are also starting to unravel the mystery of why some people turn out to be workaholics while others do not. [2]It is becoming increasingly apparent that the process begins in early childhood. [3]Psychiatrist Lawrence Susser, who treats workaholics on his yacht in New Rochelle, New York, claims that workaholics are the products of "controlling parents"; that is, parents who, rather than simply supporting or setting guidelines for their children, are constantly pushing them to excel. [4]The children fear that unless they live up to these expectations, love will be withheld. [5]Eventually they develop a sort of "inner voice" that prods them in the same manner as their parents did. [6]This voice can be very demanding, Dr. Susser says. [7]It does not let them relax.

—"Thank God, It's Monday," *Dun's Review*

1. Controlling idea ___2___

2. Main method of development ___*cause/effect*___

3. Additional method of development ___*details*___

PARAGRAPH FOUR

[1]Of course, not everyone who works long hours is a workaholic. [2]Many people simply have more work than they can handle on a normal schedule. [3]Others work for companies where long hours are part of the job. [4]Some Wall Street law firms, for example, are notorious for expecting associates to work late into the night; and young lawyers, even when they have no work to do, frequently remain at their desks until their superiors have left the office. [5]There are also a number of people who reluctantly moonlight because they need the money.

—"Thank God, It's Monday," *Dun's Review*

1. Controlling idea ___1___

2. Main method of development ___*classification*___

3. Additional method of development ___*comparison/contrast or example*___

Mastering Paragraphs: A Review   Exercise 32–3

NAME _____ SCORE _____

DIRECTIONS   A paragraph requires planning if it is to have unity and if it is to develop the controlling idea fully. For a paragraph about work, make notes for a controlling idea and the supporting development. (You may find the facts and ideas presented in the exercises of this workbook useful in planning your paragraph.) Think about your paragraph as specifically as possible. Once you have made your list, look it over carefully to make sure that all the points of development clearly support your controlling idea. Then arrange the points in a logical order. Finally, write your paragraph, using your controlling idea in the first or second sentence.

SUGGESTED TOPICS

1. new types of job openings in your major field

2. the best (or worst) way to prepare for your chosen career

3. possible internships available in your major field

4. the reasons why people work (or why *you* work)

5. proof that people in our society value work too much (or too little)

6. the types of jobs available in your major field

7. the reasons why you chose your major or your potential career

8. the types of writing demanded by your chosen profession

9. the advantages and/or disadvantages of early retirement or "stopping out"

10. the effects of automation or computerization on the job market or on your chosen profession

CONTROLLING IDEA

DEVELOPMENT

PARAGRAPH

33

Learn to plan, draft, and revise your compositions effectively.

33a Consider the purpose, audience, and occasion of your composition.

No matter what type of writing you do, you engage in a process of developing a subject for presentation to a specific audience. As you focus on your subject, you develop a thesis statement which will help you determine what material to include in your essay and the order in which you will present your ideas. This writing process is not a "straight line" that runs from the initial conception of a topic to a final draft. Rather, most writers find they must revise their original draft many times to make it a clear, well-unified piece of writing.

As you write, you process ideas, explore and answer questions, rethink strategies, stop in the middle of discussing one idea to take up another that has just occurred to you and so on. You may decide that your original thesis is not specific enough—or that it is not appropriate for your audience. The writing process is a dialogue between you (the writer) and your ideas; having new ideas grow out of the ones that you are currently working on is not a sign that you are a poor writer or that you do not know what you want to talk about. Rather, it indicates that you are working toward an understanding of exactly what you want to say. For this reason your first draft will probably need reorganizing and polishing before all the ideas can work together in a unified way.

Purpose   The first question you will need to ask yourself is, "What do I want to accomplish in what I am about to write?" The purpose of your composition will determine how you organize your material, the tone you adopt, even the length of sentences and the complexity of the vocabulary you use. All compositions have a purpose—for example, to inform or to persuade the reader. Be sure you have your purpose firmly in mind before you begin planning and writing.

Audience   You will also need to ask yourself what sort of readers you are writing for. Will they be familiar with the topic you have selected? What areas of the topic may need explaining? What level of technicality will your readers be able to understand? Are there aspects of your audience that you need to keep in mind, such as age or attitude toward the subject? What tone will best appeal to your audience? Will your readers "be on your side" or will you need to convince them to think about your topic from your point of view? Will you be writing for one or multiple audiences?

Occasion   You will also need to take into account the occasion for which you are writing. For example, an essay would be structured differently than a letter to the editor of a newspaper or a talk to a group.

Tone The purpose, audience, and occasion will determine the tone that you use in your essay. Tone reflects your attitude about the subject and varies in level of formality depending on the particular writing situation. For example, the tone you would adopt in a letter thanking a company for an interview would be quite different from the tone you would use in writing to a friend about your experiences in that same interview. The tone of the first letter would be formal and perhaps reserved; the tone of the letter to your friend, however, would be more relaxed and candid.

33b Choose an appropriate topic.

The appropriateness of a topic depends on the writer, the reader, and the occasion. You must know and care enough about the topic to have something interesting to say. But you must also be sure that the topic is acceptable to your intended reader or readers and suitable to the occasion on which it will be read.

If your subject is already assigned, or if your situation controls what you will write about, you will be able to begin your work with a consideration of your audience. However, in college writing your instructors may often ask you to select the subject you will write about, which is for some people the most difficult aspect of the writing process.

One way to find a subject to write about is to draw on your own experience, attitudes, or knowledge. What do you like to do with your time? What issues interest you? What has happened recently that made you stop and examine your own attitudes about the subject? Is there a particular event, place, or person you could share with a reader? Being able to select your own topic usually means you can write a more interesting paper because it will deal with something that you care about.

Often, however, the subject you are asked to write about will be one that is unfamiliar to you. For example, you may be required to write a paper for a European history class; the purpose of the paper will be to demonstrate your command of the subject to your instructor. In few papers of this kind will it be appropriate for you to write an essay which focuses on your personal opinions. However, writing about an aspect of the subject that interests you will help you write a stronger essay. To select such a topic, review your notes and the chapters in your textbook for issues that catch your attention, look in the subject catalog, or browse through books and articles on the topic in the library. If you are still unable to settle on a topic, discuss the assignment with other students or talk it over with our instructor.

Many times you will be required to write a paper bound by other constraints as well. For example, although you may be allowed to select your topic, your instructor may give you a length limit of six to eight pages. In this case, you would need to make certain that the topic you choose provides you with enough material to satisfy that requirement. Whatever the restrictions, it will be up to you to choose a topic that meets the requirements.

33c Explore and focus the subject.

How well you limit the topic depends on your ability to focus on an aspect that you can cover adequately in the time allotted to the writing of the paper. For example, "occupational writing" is a topic that might be covered in a book; it is clearly not limited enough to be discussed adequately in the hour or two most students have for writing an in-class paper. There are several methods of limiting a general topic.

(1) Explore your subject.

Listing   Often when you begin working on an essay, you will have so many ideas that they will become disorganized if you try to review them all in your mind. Put this surplus information to work for you: make a list of everything that occurs to you about your topic. At this stage of the writing process you should not worry about imposing any order on your ideas. Just jot them down as rapidly as they come to mind and in whatever order they occur. What matters at this point is that you record the ideas themselves; grammar, spelling, and organization are all things you can concern yourself with after you have some material to work with.

As you write your list, one idea will often lead naturally to another. Jot it down. Interrupt your current train of thought if you suddenly think of an important, new aspect of your topic. Experiment until you learn how the listing method can work most effectively for you.

Questioning   Another way to explore your topic is to ask yourself the journalist's questions "*who? what? when? where? why?* and *how?*" Investigating your topic by answering these questions may help you to see your topic more clearly as well as to consider its various aspects. You will force yourself to consider *who* is concerned about the material you are developing, *how* something works the way it does, *why* an event happened as it did, and so forth.

Strategies for Development   Finally, consider which development strategies can best help you explore your topic (discussed fully in **32d**). These strategies parallel the ways in which we think about almost any subject: narration (retelling an event); process (how to do something or how something works); cause and effect (why something happened); description (what something is like); definition; classification and division (placing things into larger categories or breaking something down into its component parts); analysis (why something happened or is the way that it is); example; and comparison and contrast (how things differ from and resemble each other). These strategies can serve as prompts to help you think about the various aspects of your topic.

(2) Limit and focus your subject.

Once you have explored your topic you must decide which aspects of it to discuss; that is, you must limit and focus your topic. The following analogy will help you understand the importance of this step. When you use a microscope, you first decide what you want to view under the lens, select the appropriate slide, and place it in the viewing field. Next, you use the rough focusing wheel to bring the object into view, turn the light up or down to sharpen or soften the contrasts in the image, and move the slide around on the viewing stage until the segment you wish to concentrate on is under the lens. Finally, you use the fine focusing wheel to bring this segment into sharp focus.

Focusing and limiting your subject works in much the same way. You must find those parts of the topic that meet the requirements of your reading audience. If, for example, you are writing an essay for your history class about the ways in which medieval monasteries preserved manuscripts, you will not want to include information about the architecture of a typical cloister or about the rivalries among the different monastic orders. Such material might be interesting, but it has little bearing on the subject you have chosen.

The particular focus you employ will be determined by your purpose, your audience, the length of your essay, and the amount of time you have in which to write it.

33d Construct a focused, specific thesis statement containing a single main idea.

A thesis statement can make the focus of your essay clear to your reader. It will help you to think more exactly about your topic and to avoid straying from the topic as you write. The thesis statement is to the essay what the controlling idea is to the paragraph. As you discuss the various aspects of your topic, refer to your thesis statement from time to time to make sure that what you are saying relates to your main idea. Furthermore, if you have difficulty developing specific material that relates to your topic, a clear thesis statement can often help you organize your thoughts and explore new aspects of the topic. Finally, once you have formulated a thesis statement you should not think that you cannot change it. As you write you may find that you wish to explore a different or modified version of your topic, in which case you will need to rethink and revise your thesis statement.

Most frequently, thesis statements appear in the beginning paragraph; however, they may appear at whatever point in your essay best suits your purpose. For example, if the conclusion is one which you must prepare your reader to accept, your thesis will appear in the conclusion. Or, if you first need to give your reader background information about the broad aspects of your subject, your thesis statement could appear several paragraphs into your paper. In other types of essays—such as narrative or descriptive writing—a thesis statement is often omitted; in still others, it is only implied. Yet no matter what tactic you choose, a thesis statement can help you give direction to your writing—even if it never appears in the finished essay. Use your thesis statement to help you select the information you will include in your essay.

33e Choose an appropriate method or combination of methods of development for arranging ideas, and prepare a working plan.

A working plan can help you write your first draft more efficiently. The strategies for organizing paragraphs (see **32d**) and exploring ideas (see **33c**) are the same as those you will use to organize and develop your essay. The methods you finally use will be determined by your purpose, audience, occasion, subject, and focus; and you may find that a combination of methods will be most useful for organizing your material. But, no matter what method or methods you choose, you will probably want to create a written guide to follow as you work on your first draft. Some writers like to create a highly structured, formal outline and use it almost like a map; other writers feel that such a detailed outline inhibits them, that it stifles the development of their ideas. For these writers, jottings or informal lists work better. The formal outline or the formal arrangement are helpful, however, if you are working on a long or a complex project. Try all three ways; then use whichever one works best for you.

Informal Working Plans   Your informal working plan can be simply an organized list of the topics you plan to discuss. This list may resemble the one you generated as you initially explored your subject (see **33c**) with one important difference—in this new list you will arrange the topics in the order you wish to discuss them. As you generate your working plan, your ideas may overlap; arrange and refine the entries on the list until you have a good picture of the general structure of your essay. Like the other methods for arranging ideas, a working plan can be changed at any time—before or as you write.

Outlines   Roman numerals mark the headings that set forth the main points used to develop the thesis statement. The subheadings (signaled by capital letters) present the specific proof for the main headings. If the composition is very long—ten pages or more—further subheadings (signaled by Arabic numbers and then by lower-case letters) may come under the capital letter divisions.

The outline may or may not have an introduction and a conclusion. If during the planning stage you have in mind a way to introduce your thesis statement, write it down as a part of the outline. Likewise, if an idea for a conclusion or a concluding sentence occurs to you while planning the outline, record it at the time.

TOPIC OUTLINE

How Not to Choose a Career

Thesis: Students have four major misconceptions about how to choose a career.

I. That the decision must be made alone, without the help of others
   A. Qualified friends and family members
   B. High-school and college counselors
   C. Employment agencies

II. That the decision must be based entirely on reason
   A. The importance of emotions in decision making
   B. Examples of unhappy workers in occupations that seemed to be logical choices
III. That the decisions must never be changed
   A. Changing job market
   B. Realization of a wrong choice
IV. That the decision must make a person constantly happy
   A. The good and the bad side of all decisions
   B. The importance of other aspects of life
   C. The likelihood of emotional setbacks

SENTENCE OUTLINE

How Not to Choose a Career

Introduction: The choice of a career is one of the most important decisions a person makes in life. Yet many people are poorly prepared for this decision.

Thesis: Students have four major misconceptions about how to choose a career.

   I. They think they must make the decision unaided.
   A. Qualified friends and family members can be helpful.
   B. High-school and college counselors have special training to guide students in selecting their careers.
   C. Employment agencies can help students find the jobs that fit their skills and talents.
   II. They think that their decisions must be based entirely on reason.
   A. Emotions are important in career planning.
   B. There are many examples of unhappy workers in occupations that seemed to be logical choices.
   III. They think that their decisions must never be changed.
   A. The changing job market often necessitates a change in career plans.
   B. Actual work experience often reveals a wrong decision.
   IV. They think that their decision must make them constantly happy.
   A. There is a good and a bad side to all decisions.
   B. Other aspects of life also influence happiness.
   C. In any job there is the likelihood of an emotional setback.

Conclusion: If students are aware of these common misconceptions about how to choose a career, they will be better prepared to make one of life's most important decisions.

Note these points about sentence and topic outlines:

(1) The thesis is stated as a sentence regardless of the type of outline.
(2) The introduction and the conclusion may or may not be included in the outline.
(3) In both the sentence and the topic outlines, there must be at least two headings at each level (two Roman numerals, two capital letters) for the development to be adequate.
(4) In the sentence outline, only sentences are used; in the topic outline, parallel structure is used.
(5) In any outline, proper indention is maintained to make the outline easy to read.

Avoid making these four errors in outlines:

(1) *Overlapping headings.* If information in one heading (for example, in II.B.) overlaps information in another (for example, in I.A.) or restates it in different words, then the essay will be repetitious.
(2) *Misarranged headings.* The headings show the order of presentation. If the arrangement is not logical, the paper cannot be coherent. (See also **32b.**)
(3) *Inadequately developed headings.* Usually three main headings (Roman numerals) and at least two subheadings (capital letters) are necessary to supply adequate development.
(4) *Needless shifts in tense or number.* This weakness is more noticeable in the sentence outline than in the topic outline. Usually a needless shift in the outline is carried over to the composition.

FORMAL (OR CLASSICAL) ARRANGEMENT

You may follow a formal arrangement pattern when your main purpose is expository or persuasive:

Introduction   Announce the subject, set the tone, and gain the reader's attention.

Background   Provide any background information that the reader may need.

Definition of Terms and Issues   Define technical terms and stipulate meanings for ambiguous ones.

Development or Proof   Develop thesis.

Refutation   Answer disagreements or questions that your reader might have.

Conclusion Summarize the main points. You may repeat the thesis considered in a wider context or ask the reader to take action or reconsider an accepted point of view.

Depending on the type of essay that you are writing, you may not need to include all of these parts, and you may emphasize certain parts more than others.

33f Write the first draft.

Once you have created your informal working plan or formal outline, let it guide you as you write the first draft of your essay. Your most important goal is to get all of your material down on paper; do not worry if the sentences are not as polished as you would like them to be or if you misspell words or make grammatical mistakes. You will concentrate on eliminating the weak spots later on as you revise. Write as rapidly as you can; refer periodically to your working plan or outline to check your progress: Have you strayed from the main focus? Are you covering all the points you wished to consider? Your working plan or outline can also serve as a prompting tool when you cannot think of what to say next. You may want to stop occasionally to look over what you have already written; doing so will help you to gain a better perspective on the overall progress of your essay as well as to reassess the points you plan to cover next. Once you have completed your draft, set it aside for a time—preferably for a couple of days—so that you will be able to look at it from a less biased perspective when you begin to revise.

A composing process that works well for one writer may be a disaster for another. There is no one right way to generate a working draft. Some writers like to "blurt out" the entire essay at one sitting, while others work best when they write their compositions a portion at a time and wait till the revision stages to piece the parts together in a logical sequence. Become familiar with your own writing process so that you can use whatever method enables you to produce the best results most efficiently.

The following is an example of the first page of a rough draft for a composition on "How Not to Choose a Career."

How Not to Choose a Career

As, children most of us, find our careers in a row of buttons: doctor, lawyer, teacher, police officer, fire fighter, astronaut, dancer. Ten years or so later, when what we want to be in life is a real question, many of us continue to be arbitrary in our choice of careers. We may ~~be certain that we want~~ decide to be accountants even though we have never been good at mathematics, or we may choose to be nurses even though we cannot tolerate the sight of an open wound or an infected eye. ~~We sometimes make the most important decision of our lives without any reasonable guidelines.~~ It is not surprising, ~~then~~ to learn that many of us, ~~are~~ will be unhappy with our work, for we, ~~have approached~~ approach the choice of a career with a variety of misconceptions.

The first and perhaps most serious misconception ~~that many of us have~~ think about career choices is that, we must make the decision alone, unaided. Actually there are many people who ~~not only want to help us make the decision but who can also~~ help us make the right decision: friends, family members, teachers, and guidance counselors.

33f(1) Write an effective introduction.

In the average-length student paper—three hundred to five hundred words—the introduction and the conclusion need not be long. The introduction gets the reader interested in the body of the paper and may need to be no more than the thesis statement or a sentence that suggests the thesis statement. Students may use as an introduction a striking example, a shocking statement that is later explained, or a question that leads into the thesis.

33f(2) Write an effective conclusion.

The conclusion of your essay should wrap up the points you have made. It may be no more than a restatement, in different words, of the thesis; or, if the thesis is only suggested in the introduction, the conclusion may be the first forthright statement of the thesis. A writer strengthens the conclusion by suggesting a solution to a problem presented in the essay. In the conclusion the writer should avoid raising a new point that is not to be explored, nor should the writer apologize for reaching the conclusion that he or she has stated.

33f(3) Choose an appropriate title.

Usually a title will occur to you during the planning or the writing of the essay. Certainly you should not spend the time you need for writing your paper sitting and thinking about a title. If you have not thought of a title by the time that you finish the composition, however, use the topic or some form of it—for example, "Common Misconceptions About Career Choices." Rereading your introduction and conclusion and examining key words and phrases in the essay will also help you to identify possible titles.

When time permits, though, give attention to the title. Choose one that is provocative, that will make a reader want to read your essay. But never sacrifice appropriateness for cleverness; above all else, the title should suit the content of the essay. In general, it is best to avoid long, wordy titles or declarative-sentence titles that tell the reader too much about the essay.

Many instructors prefer the title on a separate page, along with your name, the course name and section number, the date, and the paper number. Remember that the title should not be punctuated with quotation marks or italics (underlining) unless you are referring to a literary or artistic work and that the title should be followed by an end mark of punctuation only if it is a question or an exclamation.

33g Revise and edit the composition.

Many inexperienced writers make the mistake of thinking that revising is the same thing as proofreading, which it is not. Very few people can produce a well-written essay in only one draft. In fact, most writers will find that they revise in one way or another throughout all the stages of the writing process: they reorganize their writing plan as they jot down ideas; they consider and discard ideas and topics even before they begin to write; they rephrase or refocus their thesis statement, and so forth. But the majority of your revisions will be made once you have completed the first draft of your essay; in fact, some writers will tell you that they spend more of their time revising than creating a working draft.

After you have let your draft cool off (at least overnight if not longer), look at it first for overall concerns, since you would be wasting your time to correct mechanics, word choice, sentence structure, spelling, and the like in material that may very well be changed as you reorganize your composition. Have you established the focus of your essay early on? Are the sections of the essay organized in the most logical order? Have you strayed at times from your main point or raised issues that do not pertain to your thesis? As you work on these global revisions, check also to see that you have kept your audience in mind.

Next, apply the same perspective to your paragraphs. Are they well focused? Do they use transitions to move smoothly from one idea to the next and from one paragraph to the next? Have you varied sentence structure and length to provide variety, eliminate choppiness, and improve clarity? Look to see if you have maintained a consistent tone, style, level of diction, and point of view.

After you are satisfied with the order in which your paragraphs appear and with their general content, turn your attention to the sentences themselves. Are they clear? If not, examine the structure of each, the words you have used, and the relationship of the ideas to the other sentences in the paragraph. Identify those sentences that use the passive voice and make them active. Look for weak repetitions of words and phrases, for clichés, for redundancy; strengthen these weak spots with more effective words and phrases. Make certain that the words you use are appropriate for your audience and occasion and that you have defined technical and unfamiliar words. Finally, edit each of your sentences for errors in punctuation, mechanics, and spelling, and proofread for typographical errors. Make certain that your manuscript has a neat, professional appearance.

Approached in this manner, revision will be a powerful tool that can help you make your writing forceful and persuasive. In fact, many writers feel that revision is the most important part of the writing process, the part where they clarify, sharpen, and strengthen their writing—deleting, adding, and reorganizing again and again until their composition communicates their ideas clearly to a specific audience. The following suggestions for proofreading may help you to revise your composition.

(1) Wait at least one day, if possible, before you revise and edit your first draft. Then you will be more likely to spot weaknesses and mistakes.

(2) Proofread at least three times: once for organization; a second time, out loud, for style; and a third time for grammar, punctuation, and spelling. If you have serious problems with grammar, punctuation, or spelling, proofread still another time for the error or errors you most frequently make.

(3) When proofreading for errors, slow your reading down. To make yourself go more slowly, actually point to each word with your pencil as you read. If you have real difficulties with spelling, try reading each line from right

to left instead of the usual left to right so that you will notice words individually.

(4) Read your writing assignment to someone else and ask your listener to stop you when something does not make sense or does not sound right.

(5) Type your written work. Even if you do not type well enough to make the final copy, type at least one draft of your work. Typing the manuscript forces you to take a close look at what you have written. (Many writers do most of their editing while they are typing.)

You may wish to use a word processor instead of a typewriter, both to create or to work on your rough drafts and to produce the final copy of your essay. A word processor will allow you to draft, revise, and edit your work in a variety of sophisticated ways. Before using one, however, be sure to check with your instructor to see if it is all right to do so, particularly to see if the type style of your printer is acceptable. If possible, use a printer that will allow you to select a near-letter-quality mode, a setting that produces print closely resembling that of a typewriter.

The Essay   Exercise 33–1

NAME _____ SCORE _____

DIRECTIONS   Choose a topic from the list of suggested subjects in Exercise 32–3 (p. 343) or a topic of your own for an essay of three hundred to five hundred words. (If you choose to write about work, you may find the facts and ideas presented in this workbook useful in planning your essay.) You may use the following page for a working plan or outline as your instructor directs. Then write a first draft of the composition. Revise it carefully according to the suggestions in **33g**. (Save your rough draft for future reference.) Follow your instructor's directions with regard to the placement of your title, and number the pages of the paper, using Arabic numerals, beginning in the upper right-hand corner of page 2.

TOPIC

WORKING PLAN OR OUTLINE

35

Write effective letters and résumés, memos, and reports.

Success in business depends a great deal on good communication skills, both person-to-person and written. Many times the only way that a business associate or client will know you will be on paper, so it is essential that what you write communicates clearly and sounds professional. Misunderstandings resulting from poorly written business documents cost money and lose clients. In addition, many business documents are legally binding, and for this reason it is essential that they say clearly and precisely what you mean. Finally, effective business communication eliminates extra work; no one who is busy wants to spend extra time trying to figure out what the writer of a letter, memo, or report "really meant." In the world of work, effective writing pays off: it fosters goodwill; it creates a favorable impression of the company; and, ultimately, it results in increased profits.

35a(1) Use acceptable format for the letters you write.

Format   Business letters are usually typed on only one side of white, unlined, $8\frac{1}{2} \times 11$ inch paper. Standard business envelopes measure about $3\frac{1}{2} \times 6\frac{1}{2}$ inches or 4×10 inches. (Letterhead stationery and envelopes vary both in size and color.)

Check to see if your company or organization has a policy about letter format. Most companies use either full block (see p. 362) or modified block (see p. 364) for regular correspondence, though an indented format is often used for personal business correspondence such as thank-you notes, congratulations, and the like.

A business letter has six parts: (1) heading, (2) inside address, (3) salutation, (4) body, (5) closing, which consists of the complimentary close and signature, and (6) added notations.

The *heading* gives the writer's full address and the date. If letterhead stationery is used, the date is typed beneath it flush left, flush right, or centered, depending on your format. If plain stationery is used, the address of the writer followed by the date is placed toward the top of the page—the distance from the top arranged so that the body of the letter will be attractively centered on the page—flush with the left- or right-hand margin, as in the letters on pages 362 and 364. Notice that the heading has no end punctuation.

The *inside address*, typed two to six lines below the heading, gives the name and full address of the recipient.

The *salutation* (or greeting) is written flush with the left margin, two spaces below the inside address, and is followed by a colon.

* The numbering in section 35 does not correspond to that of the handbook.

When the surname of the addressee is known, it is used in the salutation of a business letter, as in the following examples.

Dear Dr. Davis: Dear Mayor Rodriguez:
Dear Mrs. Greissman: Dear Ms. Joseph:

Note: Use *Miss* or *Mrs.* if the woman you are addressing has indicated a preference. Otherwise, use *Ms.*, which is always appropriate and which is preferred by many businesswomen, whatever their marital status.

In letters to organizations, or to persons whose name and sex are unknown, such salutations as the following are customary:

Dear Sir or Madam: Dear Mobil Oil:
Dear Subscription Manager: Dear Registrar:

For the appropriate forms of salutations and addresses in letters to government officials, military personnel, and so on, check an etiquette book or the front or back of your college dictionary.

The *body* of the letter should follow the principles of good writing. Typewritten letters are usually single-spaced, with double spacing between paragraphs. The first sentence of each paragraph should begin flush with the left margin (in full block or modified block) or should be indented five to ten spaces (in indented format). The subject matter should be organized so that the reader can grasp immediately what is wanted, and the style should be clear and direct. Do not use stilted or abbreviated phrasing:

NOT	The aforementioned letter	BUT	Your letter
NOT	Please send it to me ASAP.	BUT	Please send it to me as soon as possible.

The *closing* is typed flush with the left-hand margin in full-block style. In modified block and indented style, it is typed to the right of the letter, in alignment with the heading. Here are the parts of the closing:

Complimentary close: This conventional ending is typed, after a double space, below the last paragraph of the body of the letter. Among the endings commonly used in business letters are the following:

FORMAL	LESS FORMAL
Very truly yours,	Sincerely,
Sincerely yours,	Cordially,

Typed name: The writer's full name is typed four lines below the closing.

Title of sender: This line, following the typed name, indicates the sender's position, if he or she is acting in an official capacity.

Manager, Employee Relations
Chairperson, Search Committee

Signature: The letter is signed between the complimentary close and the typed name.

Notations are typed below the closing, flush with the left margin. They indicate, among other things, whether anything is enclosed with or attached to the letter (*enclosure* or *enc.*, *attachment* or *att.*); to whom copies of the letter have been sent (*cc: AAW, PTN*); and the initials of the sender and the typist (*DM/cll*).

MODEL BUSINESS LETTER: full block format (all parts flush with the left margin)

LETTERHEAD CONTAINING **Rowe's Nursery**
RETURN ADDRESS Route 1 Box 156 } HEADING
Brewster, WA 98865

January 25, 1990

Customer Service Representative
Interface Computing Service
2001 Halvorsen Drive } INSIDE ADDRESS
Diablo, TX 75643

Dear Customer Service Representative: } SALUTATION

I run a small nursery business with a fairly complicated inventory. For years
I have kept track of my nursery stock on paper; now I would like to use a
microcomputer and inventory software program to simplify my operations.
Could you please tell me more about your Invent inventory software package,
which I saw advertised in last month's issue of Seeds magazine?

I would appreciate it if you could answer the following questions:

1. What is the price of this software package?
2. Can you customize it for a nursery business, and, if so, how much more
   would that cost?

BODY

3. Will the Invent program run on a Computec 2000 computer?
4. Can you give me the name, address, and phone number of your nearest sales
   representative?
5. I would like to keep track of the different varieties of nursery stock I sell
   (seeds, trees, bushes and shrubs, vegetables, roses, and so on). Will I be
   able to subdivide the inventory categories by both variety and Latin name?

Because I will be placing my spring stock orders within the next month, I
would like to have an inventory software package set up and running before the
end of March so that I can work out all of the bugs before the spring rush
begins. I would be grateful if you could send me the information I have
requested within the next two weeks so that I can place my order soon.

Sincerely yours,
COMPLIMENTARY CLOSE

Mathew Rowe
SIGNATURE } CLOSING

TYPED NAME
Matthew Rowe
TITLE
Owner

MPR/ff } NOTATION

MODEL BUSINESS ENVELOPE

Rowe's Nursery
Route 1 Box 156
Brewster, WA 98865

> Customer Service Representative
> Interface Computing Service
> 2001 Halvorsen Drive
> Diablo, TX 75643

35a(2) Write effective application letters and résumés.

The first real business writing that you do may be the letter and résumé you prepare when you look for a job. Obviously, you will want to take particular care that these documents represent you well; a future employer will judge you on the basis of how professionally you present yourself in these samples of your written communication skills.

Both your application letter and your résumé should show the reader that you are suited to fill the job for which you are applying. The letter first identifies the exact job for which you wish to be considered, then discusses your skills *as they relate to* the requirements of the job itself, and finally requests an interview. Your letter should refer to the company by name several times in the body and should call your reader's attention to the résumé that you will have enclosed.

Never send an application letter without an accompanying résumé or a résumé without an application letter. These two documents work together to persuade the reader to ask you to come for an interview. Be especially careful to make your letter and accompanying résumé look professional; do not send out material that contains corrected typographical errors or that looks poorly arranged on the page. Neither your résumé nor your application letter should exceed one page in length (unless you have been working for a long time and have a great deal of experience related to the job for which you are applying).

Note: It is thoughtful to send a thank-you letter after an interview (see p. 379).

MODEL APPLICATION LETTER: modified block format (heading and closing may be placed in the center or near the right margin)

Box 743 Wellborn Hall
Washington State University
Pullman, WA 99163
November 9, 1990

Mr. Thomas McLaughlin
Personnel Manager
Laser Corporation
2183 Davis Drive
Seattle, WA 98250

Dear Mr. McLaughlin:

IDENTIFY POSITION
SOUGHT AND HOW
LEARNED ABOUT

I believe that my background—a degree in Marketing and Management, experience in retail sales, and familiarity with computer software—qualifies me to be a productive member of the Laser Corporation's sales department. Please consider my application for the position of field representative trainee which you advertised in the February 1990 issue of On-Line.

INDICATE MAJOR
QUALIFICATIONS
FOR JOB

Double majors in Marketing and Management, along with a minor in Computer Science, have provided me with a strong and diverse background for sales work. In particular, I have learned to apply theory to the practical use of computer technology in small business management. My training will enable me to show my clients how to make the best use of Laser's software packages such as FastCalc and Ready Ledger.

REFER TO RÉSUMÉ
INDICATE FURTHER
QUALIFICATIONS
FOR JOB

My activities and work experience show that I enjoy working with people and can handle responsibility effectively. From my résumé you can see that I have learned to adapt to and work effectively in different situations: counseling marketing majors, designing efficiency surveys, and working as a waitress. That I worked to pay all of my college expenses demonstrates my initiative and determination to meet the goals that I set for myself. I will bring this same hardworking attitude to the Laser Corporation.

REQUEST
INTERVIEW

I would appreciate the opportunity to meet with you and discuss the ways I can fill Laser's needs. Since you will be on the Washington State University campus the week of March 25, could you please contact me at the above address or phone me at (505) 342-9817 after 3 p.m. to schedule an interview?

Sincerely yours,

Cheryl Claassen

Cheryl Claassen

Enclosure: Résumé

Business Letters

NAME _____ SCORE _____

DIRECTIONS   Using the full or the modified block style, write a letter of application for a job in your field, a letter of complaint about a product you bought that is not performing satisfactorily, and a letter ordering a product that you would like to purchase by mail (use a catalog advertisement or the "For Sale" column of a newspaper or magazine for the product information). Do your planning of the letters in the space provided below, but type or neatly handwrite your letters on white bond paper.

PLANNING SPACE

PLANNING SPACE (CONTINUED)

Your résumé gives a brief overall picture of your qualifications for the job you are seeking. It provides more specifics than you can, or should, discuss in your application letter. Although a résumé may be organized in a number of ways depending on which material you wish to emphasize, it should cover the following categories:

1. Personal Data: name, mailing address, and phone number (with area code)
2. Educational Background
3. Work Experience
4. Honors and Activities
5. References

The material you include in your résumé should illustrate the ways in which you are qualified to fill the position you are applying for. Do not try to list everything about yourself; pick and choose carefully. Consider designing a résumé specifically aimed at the particular job you are applying for. A customized résumé stands out when it is reviewed because it addresses the employer's particular needs. It shows that you have thought carefully about the job and the company.

An excellent way to put together an effective résumé is to make lists of all your qualifications using a separate sheet of paper for each category. Write down everything you can think of about yourself—jobs held, classes taken, honors, activities, and so forth. Then go back and fill in details: dates, supervisors' names, job responsibilities. After you complete your brainstorming, *then* go back and mark those items that you want to include in the résumé you are developing for this particular job. Within each category, arrange information in order with the most recent first: May 1989–present, December 1988–May 1989, and so forth.

Type a neat first draft of your résumé to see how it looks on the page. Do not crowd material too closely together; let information stand out surrounded by some blank space so the reader will easily notice each important aspect of your background. Finally, type a clean copy; if you make an error, do not correct it but retype the page until everything is perfect. Errors and corrections make a résumé look sloppy and unprofessional. Especially if you are not an excellent typist, you may want to have your résumé professionally printed. Choose good stationery—white or a dignified off-white shade such as beige or light gray—and consider buying matching blank paper and envelopes for your application letter.

The following tips will help you prepare a well-organized résumé.

TIPS ON RÉSUMÉ WRITING

1. Don't forget to include your name, address, and telephone number; unless relevant to the job, personal data such as age and marital status are better left out.

2. Mention your degree, college or university, and pertinent areas of special training.
3. Think about career goals but generally reserve mention of them for the application letter or interview (and even then make sure they enhance your appeal as a candidate). Your interest should be to match your qualifications to the employer's goals.
4. Even if an advertisement asks you to state a salary requirement, any mention of salary should usually be deferred until the interview.
5. Whenever possible, make evident any relationship between jobs you have had and the job you are seeking.
6. Use an acceptable format and make sure the résumé is neat, orderly, and correct to show that you are an efficient, well-organized, thoughtful person.
7. Be sure to ask people's permission before listing their names as references.

MODEL RÉSUMÉ

CHERYL CLAASSEN

College Address
Box 743 Rankin Hall
Washington State University
Pullman, WA 99163
Phone (505) 342-9817
Before May 14, 1990

Permanent Address
Route 1 Box 966
Davis, CA 91304
Phone (916) 659-1954
After May 14, 1990

Position Sought

    Entry-level position as sales representative with a computer firm.

Education

    Bachelor of Science Degree in Marketing and Management, Washington
        State University, expected May 1990.

Grade Point:	3.53/4.00 scale
Major Courses:	Consumer Behavior, Managerial Strategies, Business Law, Accounting
Minor Courses:	COBOL, PASCAL, FORTRAN
Related Courses:	Business Communications, Technical Writing

Employment (provided 100% of college expenses)

    Programming Intern, ReadyWare Software, Davis, CA
        Debugged specialized accounting packages
        Developed application recordkeeping package for dentists
        Advised clients
        May–August 1989

    Sales Representative, Brandes ComputerWorld, Sacramento, CA
        Demonstrated various software packages to the public
        Developed efficiency evaluation survey
        October 1987–May 1988

Honors and Activities

    Phi Kappa Phi Scholastic Honorary
    Alpha Lambda Delta Freshman Honorary
    TRW Scholarship, 1987
    Team leader, College of Business orientation, 1988–present
    District Five Representative, Faculty-Student Senate, Washington State
        University, 1988–1989

References

    Placement Bureau
    Bryan Hall
    Washington State University
    Pullman, WA 99163

The Résumé

Exercise 35–2

NAME _____ SCORE _____

DIRECTIONS   Write a résumé for a summer job, a permanent job, or an internship. Tailor your résumé to meet the specific requirements of the job for which you are applying. Use the space below to list your qualifications, to list the job requirements, and to write a rough draft of your résumé. Type a final copy of your résumé on white bond paper.

JOB REQUIREMENTS

MY QUALIFICATIONS

ROUGH DRAFT OF RÉSUMÉ

35a(3) Write effective business letters.

Letter of Inquiry   Many business letters are requests for information. Such letters should be direct and should give sufficient background so that the person you write to can answer your questions fully. If you need the information by a certain date, be sure to say so (and, in any case, a date will help motivate your reader to get back in touch with you promptly). A stamped, self-addressed envelope can also speed up the reply.

The first paragraph of a letter of inquiry should begin with the most important question. It should also give any background information necessary for the reader to understand why you are asking for the information and to focus the answers accordingly. For example, if you were inquiring about stereo systems for your home, you would probably want to mention the price range you have in mind and the options that you want in the system. Otherwise, the reader might not tell you about the right sort of equipment.

The middle section of your letter contains any questions of a specific kind. Arranging them in a numbered list may make them easier for your reader to answer.

Use the final section of the letter to express appreciation (but avoid the phrase "thank you in advance," which is wordy and might strike your reader as presumptuous). This final paragraph is also the place to mention the date by which you need to receive the information.

MODEL INQUIRY: full block format

5602 King Street
Bangor, ME 17895
December 21, 1990

Ms. Loretta Katz
Shady Brook Kennels
2886 Laurel Lane
Cincinnati, OH 65432

Dear Ms. Katz:

ASK YOUR MOST
IMPORTANT
QUESTION FIRST
GIVE SOME
BACKGROUND
INFORMATION

Will it be possible for me to board my Welsh Corgi from January 28 to 31? Your kennel was recommended to me by my brother-in-law, Paul Klinghammer, who has boarded his retriever with you many times.

I will be visiting the Cincinnati area and will be unable to keep my dog with me while there. Tigger is a five-year-old male who is very docile; however, he is an active dog and it is important that he have an outdoor run where he can exercise.

Could you please tell me

ASK THE REST
OF YOUR
QUESTIONS

1. If you have room for my dog
2. What your kennel facilities are like
3. The cost for the four days
4. If you have a groomer and how much it would cost to have my dog bathed

REQUEST A
REPLY AND GIVE
A DATE

Because I will be leaving Bangor on my trip on January 15, I would appreciate hearing from you as soon as possible so that I can complete my plans.

Sincerely yours,

Edwin T. Arnold

Edwin T. Arnold

Claim and Adjustment Letters   Claim and adjustment letters are letters that you write to ask someone to resolve a problem for you. These letters are similar to inquiries in that you must explain what you want done and must use specific details so your reader will understand exactly what you want. However, the claim letter requires special diplomacy: remember that even though you may be annoyed by the problem you are writing about, you must not offend or anger your reader. A calm reader is more likely to do what you ask. If you must "blow off steam," do it in your rough draft; then edit out all impolite or accusatory tone as you revise. Appealing to your reader's sense of business integrity and fair play will gain a better response than calling names.

The claim or adjustment letter briefly states the problem in the first paragraph, uses the middle paragraphs to give supporting details, and concludes by outlining what you wish the reader to do. As in the inquiry letter, asking that the problem be resolved by a particular date may speed up the reply process.

In writing a letter of this type details are important. For instance, if a jacket that you ordered prepaid has not yet arrived, send a copy of the cancelled check, give the date on which you placed your order, and list the item number, size, color, and price. Or, if the manufacturer refuses to fix a tape deck still under warranty, provide the model name and number and the date of purchase, and send copies of your receipts and warranty registration cards (keep the originals for your records). Be sure to mention each enclosure in the text of your letter so that your reader will know what to look for.

MODEL CLAIM LETTER

Rt. 5, Box 87
Charlotte, NC 27654
May 5, 1990

Customer Service Manager
Efficient Electrix, Inc.
P.O. Box 765
Manhattan, KS 57744

Dear Customer Service Manager:

STATE THE PROBLEM	I have always found your appliances to be reliable; that's why I purchased your model 543 pop-up toaster last December. But recently the bread will not come out of the toaster the way that it should.
DESCRIBE WHAT HAPPENED	Starting a week ago, whenever I put a piece of bread in the slot and pushed down the handle one of two things happened: the bread stuck to the wires, refused to pop up, and burned; or the bread flew about 18 inches out of the toaster and landed on the floor. Needless to say, I'm unhappy about the mess and the waste.
STATE WHAT YOU WOULD LIKE DONE	Because I followed your "Care and Maintenance Suggestions" that came with my 543, I believe the problems stem from a mechanical malfunction rather than from neglect on my part. For this reason, I believe that my toaster should be repaired at no expense to me, especially since it is still covered by warranty. The enclosed copy of my receipt indicates that I have owned this appliance for less than six months.
ASK FOR A RESPONSE; GIVE A DATE AND A REASON FOR NEEDING IT BY THAT DATE.	Would you please tell me where to send my toaster to be repaired and how to make sure that I am not charged for the service? Since I use this appliance every day, I would appreciate hearing from you within the next two weeks so that I can have my 543 back in working order soon.

Sincerely yours,

Thelma M. Baker

Thelma M. Braker

Enclosure: sales slip   SEND ALONG COPIES OF NECESSARY
                        INFORMATION

Thank-you Letter   Frequently in business it will be appropriate for you to write a thank-you letter; these types of letters make the reader see you as a considerate person and build goodwill for your company or organization. When someone has done you a favor, has been more than ordinarily helpful or generous, or has entertained you as a guest, a letter of thanks is in order.

In addition, it is always a good idea to write a thank-you letter to someone who has interviewed you for a job. Not only will such a letter remind the reader who you are, but it will also convey your sincerity and good business sense. It is appropriate to reiterate briefly some important point you made in your interview, but do not belabor the issue. Keep a thank-you letter brief.

MODEL THANK-YOU LETTER

534 Valley Crucis Road
Fargo, SD 44678
April 15, 1990

Ms. Edelma Huntley
Oakley Inc.
P. O. Box 12543
Lafayette, LA 75902

Dear Ms. Huntley:

Thank you for taking the time to talk to me about my qualifications for the position of sales representative with Oakley Inc. I enjoyed learning more about the job and about the new product line that Oakley will be marketing this fall.

During our meeting you said that you were looking for a person with at least two years' sales experience after college. Although I recognize that such experience can be valuable, I would like you to consider as equivalent training my two years as advisor for the local Junior Achievement Club and my volunteer work as a fund raiser and coordinator of sales for the campus-wide Fight Hunger Drive.

The extensive travel that the job requires is anything but a discouragement to me; on the contrary, I would welcome the opportunity. I enjoy meeting new people and seeing new places and would be glad to have the chance to do both as a field representative for Oakley Inc.

I look forward to hearing from you soon about your decision.

Sincerely yours,

Eugene Miller

Eugene Miller

35b Write effective memos.

While business letters generally go to people outside your company, a memo is the standard way to share information within the firm. Clear, effective writing is just as important for people within your firm as for people outside it. Not only is clear communication essential to the company's operation, but what you write will be evaluated by people who are in a position to affect your future.

Often the tone of a memo can be less formal than that of a letter sent to someone outside your company; let the situation itself govern the level of formality you use. When in doubt, it is generally best to be slightly more formal since familiarity can offend some readers, even though they may be people whom you see every day at the office. This is particularly true if you are relatively new in your job or are a trainee.

Memos can be short or lengthy, depending on their purpose, but the basic format remains the same; most companies have printed forms for memos. The heading of a memo lists the names (and usually the titles) of the recipient and the writer, the subject, and the date.

TO: Henry W. Wills, Vice President

FROM: Sarah O. Jenkins, Quality Control Supervisor

DATE: November 24, 1990

SUBJECT: Product Endurance Test Results

If a memo is long, headings should be used to label the sections. In fact, some reports may be written in memo form; these begin with a general statement of purpose followed by a summary section outlining what will follow. The remaining sections discuss various aspects of the topic in greater detail. If the content warrants it, a memo report concludes with a recommendation or conclusion section which states what should be done, by whom, and when. The fairly standard structure of most reports is designed to help busy readers grasp the purpose and important points as easily as possible.

MODEL MEMO

INTEROFFICE MEMORANDUM

Reliable Plastics
.

TO: M. Andrew Simons, Sales Manager

FROM: Jacob Lenz, Production Manager *J.L.*

DATE: June 10, 1990

SUBJECT: The Missing Pipe Insulators

Thank you for forwarding Mr. John Rollins's letter about the Rollins Company's incomplete order #234987. I have investigated the problem of the 5,000 missing 3/4″ × 8′ styrofoam pipe insulators, stock no. 45612. As I understand it, Rollins received the lengths of PVC pipe but not the insulators.

We have experienced production delays this month caused by a malfunctioning foam extruding tube in our Gary plant. We are currently three weeks behind schedule on filling standing orders for all varieties of pipe insulators. Apparently Shipping and Receiving ran the standing orders for July through the computer, sent out what was available, and neglected to inform some of our customers, including the Rollins Company, about the current delay.

The remainder of the order can be shipped on August 15 in time for the deadline the Rollins Company specified in their order last December. Because we plan to run overtime until we are caught up, we can guarantee that Rollins will receive the pipe insulators by the middle of August.

Please tell Mr. Rollins when he can expect his shipment.

JML/mb

Copies to:
Shipping and Receiving:	Carmean
Production:	Wellborn
Sales:	Durham

35c Write effective reports.

Businesses require reports for a variety of purposes: to describe mechanisms and processes; to provide instructions; to relate progress on the development of products or procedures; to analyze systems and procedures; to present proposals; and to record trips, minutes of meetings, and accidents.

35c(1) Learn to write a process analysis.

Process analyses are step-by-step explanations of how something is made, how it works, or how it is done. Reports of this type often include diagrams to help the reader grasp the concepts being discussed. In a process analysis it is very important to consider for whom you are writing; your audience will dictate what level of complexity you will use in your discussion. What follows is a process analysis of how a thermometer works, written for an eighth-grade science class.

HOW A THERMOMETER MEASURES THE TEMPERATURE

A thermometer is usually a glass tube with a small bulb at the bottom end. The bulb contains a liquid, either mercury or alcohol, that rises or falls inside the glass tube. As the illustration shows, the tube is divided into marked segments of equal size called degree markings; these marks are used to show how much the liquid has risen or fallen. The higher the liquid rises in the tube, the hotter the temperature of the solid, liquid, or gas which is being measured is said to be; the lower the liquid falls, the colder the temperature of the solid, liquid, or gas. The temperature is determined by noting the degree marking with which the top of the liquid in the tube aligns.

A COMMON THERMOMETER USING THE FAHRENHEIT SCALE

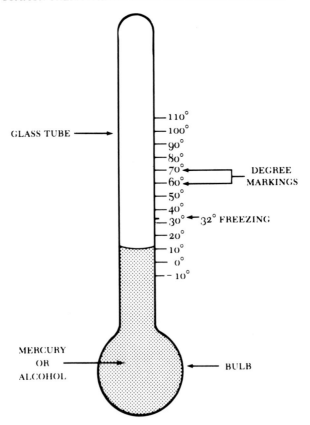

The process by which the thermometer works is quite simple. When what is being measured is hotter than the liquid inside the tube, the liquid expands. Since there is not enough room inside the bulb of the thermometer to contain all of the expanding liquid, some of it rises up the glass tube. The liquid stops rising when its temperature becomes the same as that of the solid, liquid, or gas being measured. The process is reversed when something colder than the liquid in the thermometer's bulb is being measured. A colder temperature of a substance surrounding the bulb of the thermometer causes the liquid inside the bulb to contract. Consequently, the liquid level in the tube falls, and continues to fall until the liquid is at the same temperature as the solid, liquid, or gas being measured.

The Process Analysis Report

Exercise 35–3

NAME _____ SCORE _____

DIRECTIONS   Write a process analysis in which you explain clearly and fully how something is made (for example, a contact lens, soap, or pipe tobacco), how something is done (for example, registering at your college, tuning up an automobile engine, or grafting roses); or how something works (for example, the human heart, a single lens reflex camera, or a solar heating system). Specify the kind of audience for whom you are writing and decide how much or how little your audience knows about the topic you have selected.

In the first paragraph, identify the process. In the remaining paragraphs, describe each of the steps in the process.

Consider including a diagram with labels to help clarify the process for your reader. If you use a diagram, make certain that you refer your reader to it in the text of the report.

AUDIENCE

PLANNING SPACE

35c(2) Learn to write a documented report.

Many reports that you will be asked to write may be based on research—on various expected findings or on speculations about a given topic. The use of facts and ideas gathered from sources requires an ability to do three things in addition to the usual planning, writing, and reviewing needed for any composition: (1) paraphrase material taken from sources—that is, report clearly and accurately *in your own words* the ideas and facts that someone else has presented, (2) quote correctly any material that you use exactly as it is stated in the source, and (3) provide documentation for the facts and ideas that you take from sources (the form of documentation varies depending on what guide you are using; the important thing is to follow exactly the format your instructor or supervisor requests in documenting your research).

Formal reports are generally longer than informal reports, and they usually include additional sections not found in shorter, less complex documents: a letter of transmittal, title page, abstract, executive summary, table of contents, glossary, appendix, notes, and list of works cited.

Note: Not all reports will make use of all of these elements.

The first page of a long report is the *title page*, which gives the full title of the report, the name and title (and sometimes the address) of the person for whom the report was prepared, the name and title (and sometimes the address) of the person who prepared the report, and the date on which the report was completed or is due.

The next page is the *letter of transmittal*. Generally addressed to the person who requested the report, this letter (or memo) introduces the report and sometimes gives the report's conclusions and recommendations.

The *abstract* provides a short summary of the contents of the report. By reading this abstract, a person is able to tell if the report will be useful and which parts of the report he or she needs to read. A report intended primarily for a technical audience often includes an *executive summary* written in nontechnical language for administrators.

The *table of contents* outlines the report's structure so that readers may easily find those sections of the report that they need to read. The simplest way to create a table of contents is to go through the report and list all major headings with their page numbers.

If a report contains illustrations, charts, or tables, these are often listed on a separate page immediately after the table of contents.

If you are writing for an audience who may not understand all of the technical terms that you use in your report, you should include a *glossary*, an alphabetical list that defines the terms. If you include a glossary, you will not need to interrupt your discussion to define terms. You may place the glossary either at the end of the report or after the table of contents.

Supplementary information may be placed in an *appendix*, which would be listed in the table of contents and mentioned in the body of the report. Appendixes are given individual titles and are placed immediately after the last section of the body.

Notes and a bibliography (a list of sources used in the report) appear at the end of the report. Most companies have a preferred style for these, which writers can find by looking at earlier reports in the files. The sample report on the following pages uses the style recommended by the Modern Language Association of America in the *MLA Handbook for Writers of Research Papers*, Third Edition. In this style, sources are cited briefly in parentheses (author and page number) within the text and are then listed alphabetically by author, with full publication data, at the end under the heading "Works Cited." Supplementary comments appear under the heading "Notes"; the reader is referred to these by superscript numbers within the text.

The following documented report was written for an executive who wished to determine whether his company should adopt alternative work schedules. The report presents the findings of a preliminary study. The source material for the first three citations on page 3 of the report is presented below so that you can see how the writer handled both paraphrasing and direct quotations. Study the report to see where the headings are placed and how they are capitalized, how the pages are numbered and where the numbers appear on the typed pages.

SAMPLE SOURCE MATERIAL

(Toffler 246)

> Once we understand this, it comes as no surprise that one of the fastest-spreading innovations in industry during the 1970's was "flextime"—an arrangement that permits workers, within predetermined limits, to choose their own working hours. Instead of requiring everyone to arrive at the factory gate or the office at the same time, or even at pre-fixed staggered times, the company operating on flextime typically sets certain core hours when everyone is expected to show up, and specifies other hours as flexible. Each employee may choose which of the flexible hours he or she wishes to spend working. —ALVIN TOFFLER, *The Third Wave*

(Wolman 8)

> A typical flextime arrangement allows employees to put in their eight hours anytime within, for example, a 12-hour period, providing they work a mandatory "core period" that provides midday stability.
> —JONATHAN WOLMAN,"Work Place 2000"

(Toffler 246)

> This means that a "day person"—a person whose biological rhythms routinely awaken him or her early in the morning—can choose to arrive at work at, say, 8:00 A.M., while a "night person," whose metabolism is different, can choose to start working at 10:00 or 10:30 A.M. It means that an employee can take time off for household chores, or to shop, or to take a child to the doctor. Groups of workers who wish to go bowling together early in the morning or late in the afternoon can jointly set their schedules to make it possible. —ALVIN TOFFLER, *The Third Wave*

ALTA ENTERPRISES' WORK SCHEDULE:

UPDATING OUR POLICIES

Prepared for
Harold W. Barnes
Development Officer
Alta Enterprises

Prepared by
F. Frederick Skittie
Senior Analyst

May 26, 1990

ALTA ENTERPRISES
1124 48th Avenue
Boulder, CO 33675
(303) 262-3098

May 26, 1990

Mr. Harold W. Barnes
Development Officer
Alta Enterprises
6127 N. Drumheller
Spokane, WA 99205

Dear Mr. Barnes:

Here is the introductory study, which you authorized on January 20, 1990, examining alternatives to the traditional 40-hour workweek.

As you will see in this report, Alta Enterprises has several options available in scheduling its employees' working week. In the next phase of our study, we will probably want to contact other companies in our area who already use the options described here: flextime, part-time, shared time, and nighttime shift scheduling.

I believe you will find that this report answers your department's initial questions concerning employee scheduling. If you have any further questions, please call me at (303) 262-3098.

Sincerely yours,

F. Fredrick Skittie

F. Frederick Skittie
Senior Analyst
Personnel Department

FFS/mb
Enclosures

ii

ABSTRACT

Alta Enterprises currently structures its working week on the standard 40-hour plan.

Other options exist: flextime, part-time, shared time, and nighttime. Adopting one or

more or these alternatives would give both our company and our employees greater

flexibility. Offering employees a choice of schedules would improve morale and

increase efficiency and productivity.

TABLE OF CONTENTS

iv

ALTA ENTERPRISES' WORK SCHEDULE:

UPDATING OUR POLICIES

I. Introduction

Authorization and Purpose

This report was authorized on January 20, 1990, by Harold W. Barnes, Development Officer for Alta Enterprises, as a preliminary study of the scheduling alternatives to the traditional 40-hour work week currently used at Alta.

The Problem with the 40-Hour Work Week

Not everyone finds the traditional "eight-to-five," five-day work week convenient. In response to the requests of some of our production departments to find ways to meet our employees' needs more satisfactorily, we have begun investigating alternative scheduling plans currently used by some U.S. companies.

Source of Data

Information for this report was drawn from books and periodicals.

Scope and Limitations

This report represents a preliminary study of innovative work schedules. Because this study is preliminary, the descriptions of each option are brief. In gathering material for this initial phase of our study, we limited our sources to published studies; no interviews were conducted.

Plan of Presentation

After reviewing Alta Enterprises' current policies, this report presents brief descriptions of each of the following scheduling options: flextime, part-time, shared time, and nighttime. Based on the analysis of Alta Enterprises' needs, the report then

makes recommendations regarding the steps we should take to complete our study

and improve working conditions for our employees.

II.   Alta Enterprises' Current Scheduling Policies

Like most companies its size, Alta Enterprises schedules a traditional 40-hour

work week, with the working day beginning at 8 a.m. and ending at 5 p.m. Monday

through Friday. Until recently, we had given no thought to alternatives; however,

more and more people have expressed a need for greater flexibility in their working

schedules. We employ many single parents, people who attend the local university

part-time, and others who work in areas of our company that routinely conduct tests

that run much longer than the regular 8-hour work day.

It has become increasingly clear to us that our current scheduling policy ignores

the needs of our employees. Because dissatisfied employees are less productive, and

also because this type of dissatisfaction tends to contribute to a high employee turnover

rate, we believe that it is necessary to re-evaluate the ways in which we utilize our

time.

III.   Flextime

Alvin Toffler, in his best-seller about life in the 1980s, The Third Wave, describes

flextime as ''an arrangement that permits workers, within predetermined limits, to

choose their own working hours.'' Although there may be a set number of core hours

when all employees are expected to work—for example, from 10:00 until 2:00—the re-

maining three or four hours of the workday may be completed whenever the employee chooses (Toffler 246). The "core period"—from 10:00 to 2:00—insures a stable midday

staff (Wolman 8), while the flexible schedule for the rest of the day gives employees

the freedom to plan their days to accommodate their own and their families' needs.[1]

Even more important, perhaps, workers can schedule their jobs around their biologi-

cal rhythms; people who awaken early can report to work by 8:00 while those who stay

up late and so awaken late can start working at 10:00 (Toffler 246). One final advan-

tage of flextime is the improvement in traffic patterns resulting from different starting

and finishing times for workers (Harris 24).

Flextime, which was introduced in West Germany in 1965 as a way to make the

job market more appealing to women with small children, was so successful that

within two years all 12,000 employees of a German aircraft company experimenting

with it were using flextime schedules. Flextime spread rapidly throughout other Eu-

ropean nations as well as in Great Britain. Then during the 1970s multinational firms,

like Nestlé and Lufthansa, exported flextime to the United States. Just a year after

its introduction in this country 13 percent of all United States companies were making

some use of flextime scheduling (Toffler 246–47).

Surveys, like one conducted by Psychology Today in 1978, suggest that the Ameri-

can worker strongly approves of flextime; fully 78 percent of those questioned by

Psychology Today wanted to have some say in the time they started and finished their

workday (Renwick, Lawler, et al. 54). Employers, while acknowledging some prob-

lems with individualized work schedules, seem equally satisfied with the system; as

proof, only two percent of the companies that have tried flextime have returned to

conventional schedules (Toffler 247). Based, then, on present trends, flextime seems

certain to replace the rigid work schedules that people have followed since the outset of the Industrial Revolution. Looking ahead to the workplace in the year 2001, William

Abbott, editor of the World Future Society's newsletter, Careers Tomorrow, says quite

confidently, "Workers will schedule their own hours under flextime" (Abbott 25).

IV.   Part-time

Just as remarkable a variation from rigid work schedules as flextime is the part-

time movement that has swept the country during the past twenty years. In 1977 the

economist Eli Ginzburg pointed out that 30 percent of all the work in this country was

being done by part-time workers (qtd. in Abbott 25). Alvin Toffler summarizes the

increase in the number of part-time workers in this way: "In all, there is now one part-

time worker for every five full-timers in the United States, and the part-time work

force has been growing twice as fast as the full-time force since 1954." Indeed part-

time employment has proved so popular with workers that researchers at Georgetown

University have predicted almost all jobs in the future will be performed by part-time

workers (Toffler 248).

Part-time work has flourished during the last twenty years for a number of rea-

sons. Perhaps most important has been the growing number of working mothers in

the job force who need to increase their family's income but who do not want to be

separated from their children for the entire day. Part-time work also appeals to the

elderly, who have retired from full-time work, and to students and the handicapped,

who often cannot work a full eight-hour day (Wolman 1). In addition, there are many

people today who simply choose part-time work because it gives them the free time they

need to explore other goals—like a hobby, a sport, art, or education. "We are in the

midst of a Value Revolution," according to William Abbott. "For many people, the acquisition of material symbols no longer is the primary goal in life'' (Abbott 29). Such

people will settle for the decrease in pay that comes with part-time work to satisfy their

other ambitions (Guyon 1).

Part-time work has become popular with employers because of the high incidence

of absenteeism among workers. For example, in automobile plants, where a high per-

centage of workers invariably have an ailment dubbed ''the Friday flu,'' employers have

resorted to hiring part-time workers to fill in. A benefit offered by many companies

today—the sabbatical—also causes employers to seek part-timers for the absent work-

ers' positions. Steelworkers today have a thirteen-week sabbatical every seven years

as part of their contract; the Rolm Corporation has gone a step further and permits

employees with six years of service to periodically take time off with pay. Part-time

workers are also needed to fill the spaces left by vacationing employees. The United

Auto Workers claims that each day there are 2,368 Ford workers on a personal holiday

(Wolman 1, 8). In a variety of situations, then, the part-time worker provides security

for large companies so that they can continue to function.[2] As more and more bene-

fits—such as longer vacations, sabbaticals, and educational leaves—are provided, the

need for part-time workers increases.

V.   Shared Time

One type of part-time work gaining popularity today is referred to as job sharing.

In job sharing a full-time position is simply ''split in two'' (Wolman 1). With a shared-

time arrangement, the job may be split into a four- or five-hour shift for each worker,

or it may be divided into full-time work for each for a certain period of time—for example, a six-month work period followed by a six-month free period for each worker (Rich 5).

Job sharing or shared-time work has obvious benefits for both employers and employees. Employers usually get more than an eight-hour day out of each shared job without paying overtime (Wolman 1). Also, with the increasing automation of assembly lines, companies can avoid massive lay-offs by using job sharing (Rich 5). Employees benefit, too, from shared jobs. Working as a team, many are able to have permanent employment and still continue their education. Other people who want the security of a full-time position but who are unwilling to work a full seven- or eight-hour day find job sharing the perfect solution to their problem. Women, in particular, have opted for job sharing, especially those women who need less than a full-time wage (Rich 4–5).

Job sharing is particularly popular in California, where various types of labor ranging from clerical and factory work to teaching are being set up as shared jobs. One of the promoters of job sharing, Barry Olmsted, sums up the rationale for this kind of work schedule: "We want to face reality: most jobs are set up on a 40-hour-a-week basis. Job sharing is an effort to plug part-timers into that framework" (qtd. in Wolman 1).

VI. Nighttime

Perhaps the most noticeable proof that our country is moving away from the eight- or nine-to-five schedule is the increasing number of people one sees heading for work at odd hours of the evening or night. Alvin Toffler comments that "in the technological nations the number of night workers now runs between 15 and 25 percent of all employees." Manufacturing firms, of course, have long operated 24 hours, using three shifts. But today not only manufacturing but also service- and computer-based companies are employing nighttime workers (Toffler 248).

The advantages of nighttime work for the person who likes to sleep most of the day are obvious. Night shifts also fit the needs of men and women who must take turns caring for their children; one parent is always at home, eliminating the need for sitters or day-care centers.

VII. Conclusions and Recommendations

From the information gathered so far, it is clear that Alta Enterprises has at least four new options from which to choose if it wishes to restructure its current work schedule pattern. Furthermore, based on the demands of our workers, it would seem that flextime offers both management and workers the greatest possibility for increasing morale and production.

For this reason we recommend that Alta Enterprises initiate an in-depth study of flextime, including a review of available published data and consultation with companies similar in size to Alta in order to learn how effective flextime scheduling has been. If, after completing this second stage of our study, flextime continues to look as though it would be an improvement for Alta Enterprises, we would recommend that such a revised scheduling plan be put into effect as soon as possible.

Notes

[1] A variation on this method of scheduling is nighttime, discussed in Section VI.

[2] In many instances the part-time employees also provide companies with a pool from which to fill full-time vacancies when they occur.

Works Cited

Abbott, William. "Work in the Year 2001." The Futurist Feb. 1977: 25–30.

Guyon, Janet. "The American Workplace." The Wall Street Journal 29 Apr. 1981: 1.

Harris, Lillian Craig. "Work and Leisure: Putting It All Together." Manpower Jan.

    1974: 22–26.

Renwick, Patricia A., Edward E. Lawler, and the Psychology Today Staff. "What You

    Really Want from Your Job." Psychology Today May 1978: 53–65.

Rich, Les. "Job-Sharing: Another Way to Work." Worklife May 1978: 4–7.

Toffler, Alvin. The Third Wave. New York: Bantam, 1980.

Wolman, Jonathan. "Work Place 2000," part 2 of "Working in the Year 2000."

    Atlanta Journal-Atlanta Constitution. 20 Aug. 1978, sec. C: 1,8.

The Documented Report   Exercise 35-4

NAME _____

DIRECTIONS   Following the pattern illustrated in "Atla Enterprises' Work Schedule: Updating Our Policies," prepare a documented report on one of the topics listed below. Use the card catalog and the *Readers' Guide to Periodical Literature* or the *Social Sciences Index* at your library to locate information about your topic. Try to use at least five sources in preparing your report. Before you begin writing, identify your reading audience (the person who requested the report) and define the problem to be solved. Remember that the more you know about your intended reader, the better able you will be to communicate clearly and effectively.

SUGGESTED TOPICS

1. Why a person should drop out of college and gain practical work experience.
2. What is wrong with the work ethic?
3. Using the microprocessor in _____ (your field)
4. What to do with your time if you retire early
5. Some problems with flextime and some solutions
6. Identifying and helping the workaholic
7. What types of internships are available in _____ (your major)?

AUDIENCE

STATEMENT OF PROBLEM

APPENDIX

Parts of speech	Uses in the sentence	Examples
1. **Verbs**	Indicators of action or state of being (often link subjects and complements)	Tom *hit* the curve. Mary *was* tired. He *is* a senator.
2. **Nouns**	Subjects, objects, complements	*Kay* gave *Ron* the *book* of *receipts*. *Jane* is a *student*.
3. **Pronouns**	Substitutes for nouns	*He* will return *it* to *her* later.
4. **Adjectives**	Modifiers of nouns and pronouns	*The long* memo is *the best*.
5. **Adverbs**	Modifiers of verbs, adjectives, adverbs, or whole clauses	sang *loudly* A *very* sad song *entirely too* fast *Indeed*, we will.
6. **Prepositions**	Words used before nouns and pronouns to relate them to other words in the sentence	*to* the lake *in* a hurry *with* no thought *beside* her
7. **Conjunctions**	Words that link words, phrases, or clauses; may be either coordinating or subordinating	win *or* lose in the morning *and* at night We won today, *but* we lost last week. Come *as* you are.
8. **Interjections**	Expressions of emotion (unrelated grammatically to the rest of the sentence)	*Woe* is me! *Ouch!* *Imagine!*

Common auxiliaries (helping verbs)

am	could	have	should
am (is, are, *etc.*)	did	have to	used to
going to OR	do	is	was
about to	does	may	were
are	had	might	will
be	had to	must	would
been	has	ought to	
can	has to	shall	

Forms of the verb to be

am	have been	were
are	is	will OR shall be
had been	was	will OR shall have been
has been		

Common indefinite pronouns—those usually considered singular

another	each	everything	nothing
anybody	either	neither	one
anyone	everybody	nobody	somebody
anything	everyone	no one	something

—those considered singular or plural

all	more	none
any	most	some

Relative pronouns

that	which	whoever	whomever
what	who	whom	whose

Common prepositions

across	between	in regard to	through
after	by	like	to
as	for	near	under
at	from	of	until
because of	in	on	up
before	in front of	over	with
beside			

Subordinating conjunction (OR *subordinators*)

after	because	so that	when
although	before	that	whenever
as	if	though	where
as if	in order that	unless	wherever
as though	since	until	while

Coordinating conjunctions (OR *coordinators*)

and	nor	yet
but	or	
for	so	

Conjunctive adverbs

accordingly	henceforth	otherwise
also	however	still
anyhow	indeed	then
besides	instead	therefore
consequently	likewise	thus
first, second, third, *etc.*	meanwhile	
furthermore	moreover	
hence	nevertheless	

Common transitional phrases

as a result	in addition	on the other hand
at the same time	in fact	that is
for example	in other words	
for instance	on the contrary	

Principal parts of some troublesome verbs

PRESENT	PAST	PAST PARTICIPLE
begin	began	begun
blow	blew	blown
break	broke	broken
burst	burst	burst
choose	chose	chosen
come	came	come
do	did	done
draw	drew	drawn
drink	drank	drunk
drive	drove	driven
eat	ate	eaten
fly	flew	flown
freeze	froze	frozen
give	gave	given
grow	grew	grown
know	knew	known
lay	laid	laid
lie	lay	lain
raise	raised	raised
ring	rang	rung
rise	rose	risen
run	ran	run
see	saw	seen
set	set	set
sit	sat	sat
speak	spoke	spoken
steal	stole	stolen
swim	swam	swum
take	took	taken
wear	wore	worn
write	wrote	written

Case of pronouns

SUBJECTIVE	OBJECTIVE	POSSESSIVE
I	me	my, mine
you	you	your, yours
he, she, it	him, her, it	his, her, hers, its
we	us	our, ours
they	them	their, theirs
who or whoever	whom or whomever	whose

INDIVIDUAL SPELLING LIST

In this list write every word that you misspell—in spelling tests, in themes, or in any other written work.

WORD (CORRECTLY SPELLED)	WORD (SPELLED BY SYLLABLES) WITH TROUBLE SPOT CIRCLED	REASON FOR ERROR*

*See pages 233–53 for a discussion of the chief reasons for misspelling. Indicate the reason for your misspelling by writing a, b, c, d, e, f, g, or h in this column.

a = Mispronunciation
b = Confusion of words similar in sound and/or spelling
c = Error in adding prefix
d = Error in adding suffix

e = Confusion of *ei* and *ie*
f = Error in forming the plural
g = Error in using hyphens
h = Any other reason for misspelling

Individual Spelling List (cont.)

WORD (CORRECTLY SPELLED)	WORD (SPELLED BY SYLLABLES) WITH TROUBLE SPOT CIRCLED	REASON FOR ERROR

Individual Spelling List (cont.)

WORD (CORRECTLY SPELLED)	WORD (SPELLED BY SYLLABLES) WITH TROUBLE SPOT CIRCLED	REASON FOR ERROR

A 9
B 0
C 1
D 2
E 3
F 4
G 5
H 6
I 7
J 8